"An intimate window into the quirky world of table tennis, full of poignant insights reaching well beyond the sporting world."
—Will Shortz, New York Times Crossword Puzzle Editor

"An engrossing read, full of humor, about the world of table tennis and the love between a father and son. I give it five stars."
—Danny Seemiller, 5-time US National Men's Table Tennis Champion and Olympic Table Tennis Coach

"This often humorous yet always perceptive account of US table tennis brings to life the culture, communities, and competition of an Olympic sport better known to most Americans as "ping pong." Through the author's personal journey—first as a competitive player himself, and then as the parent-coach of his youngest son—the reader is transported into a world replete with camaraderie, competition, and drama relatable to any sports parent who has cheered a child's victory or consoled a defeat. Throughout this journey US table tennis transforms from an essentially egalitarian enterprise into an increasingly elite experience as a beloved son grows up and departs from the family nest. It is a sports ethnography rich in history and human insight that will engage table tennis enthusiasts and sports fans alike. It is also a love story of father and son that speaks eloquently to parents everywhere."
—Candace Alcorta, University of Connecticut

"*The Ping Pong Player and the Professor* is a captivating and heartwarming memoir that chronicles the personal story of an accomplished anthropology professor raising his gifted table tennis-playing son, and the unexpected ways in which both parent and child experience personal growth along the way. Written from the perspective of a loving father, the book explores the challenges and rewards of parenting, the pursuit of excellence, and the transformative power of competitive sport to foster human connections. Written in an engaging and accessible style, Professor Sosis's memoir also provides readers with a fascinating glimpse into the diverse and dynamic table tennis communities in the US, showcasing their history and the colorful personalities that make them so captivating. *The Ping Pong Player and the Professor* prompts readers to contemplate the significance of family, sports, community, and personal development. I found the book thoroughly enjoyable and strongly recommend it to parents, sports aficionados, or anyone interested in the ways in which meaning emerges through the interplay of tradition, improvisation, and loving relationships."
—Joseph Bulbulia, University of Victoria, Wellington

"With the objectivity of an anthropologist and the passionate engagement of a father, Professor Sosis guides us on a multifaceted journey through parenthood, table tennis, and Jewish life and practice with humor, contagious curiosity, deep insight, and broad knowledge. This book is a gift to both head and heart, especially for anyone who struggles with life across multiple worlds."
—Ariel Burger, The Witness Institute

"Richard Sosis knows anthropology, he knows table tennis (ping pong), and he is a father. In this book he weaves these realities together in an intricate, engaging, and thoughtful narrative about a journey into the world of competitive table tennis in the USA. Taking us on an intellectual, emotional, and parental ride into a sport many of us did not know existed, Sosis weaves identities of scholar, father, coach, and genuinely fascinated participant-observer into a seamless whole. Rarely, as his children warn, does Sosis fall into "Professor Daddy lecture" mode in this book. Rather, the reader is invited into the family life, the sports ethnography, and the anthropological analyses via a distinctive mode of care and compassion for all that is being experienced and analyzed. This is a rich and nuanced anthropology of USA table tennis, a personal and care-full story of family, and a damn good read."
—Agustin Fuentes, Princeton University

"A truly remarkable book chock-full of insight, laughter, and revelation—both personal and professional. Richard Sosis is not only entertaining company with an insatiable curiosity and inquiring mind, but I have come to realize that he is one of the geniuses of our generation, who has already gifted the world a veritable library of important and groundbreaking research on the evolution and behavior of ritual, signaling, and religion. In this book, we get an insight into the world behind his work—his life and loves, his triumphs and disasters—and see how his oeuvre is all the more amazing given the improbable fact that he did it while not only raising four kids, but also playing thousands of hours of table tennis! And what a story that sport makes for his life and work. I must admit I never thought ping pong could be so interesting, but Professor Sosis has enlightened me once again. I would happily read about anything through the eyes and words of this master observer and storyteller, but this book has somehow crowned it all."
—Dominic Johnson, University of Oxford

"Every sport deserves a loving literary homage—offered by a devotee acclaiming the virtues of a beloved game. Think Plimpton's *Paper Lion* or Hornby's *Fever Pitch*. Among the best tributes are those told through a father-son relationship—Kinsella's *Shoeless Joe* for instance. Now table tennis has its own amorous treatment thanks to anthropologist Richard Sosis, who weaves together the absorbing history of table tennis with the story of the bond it forged between the professor/author and his champion son. With the eye of an anthropologist, Sosis unpacks the "sports community" surrounding table tennis—the grips, the equipment, the summer camps, tournaments, and eccentric table tennis centers. Then through the eyes of a father, we watch his talented son rise through the ping pong ranks almost to the Olympics. It might be "a strange marginal sport," as Sosis jokingly suggests, but it well deserves this charming deep dive."
—Edmund F. Wehrle, Eastern Illinois Univesrity

"The Tao of Table Tennis as related by a very wise anthropologist and very loving father."
—Adam Seligman, Boston University

"The structures of love from kashrut to ping pong—fathers and sons, games and their players, religion and their adherents—a warm and wonky thick description of the game and those it brings together. A cult classic in the making."
—Eugene F. Rogers, Jr., University of North Carolina, Greensboro

"As a mom of two table tennis players, *The Ping Pong Player and the Professor* resonated deeply with me. Professor Sosis's unwavering love for the sport, coupled with his anthropological expertise and deep knowledge of table tennis history, has culminated in a truly captivating and delightful book. I have had the pleasure of watching the Sosis duo in action, as both a father and son, as well as coach and player. Their bond is exceptionally strong and shines through brilliantly in the book. Professor Sosis is a witty and gifted storyteller, and his candid portrayal of his journey with Eliel offers readers an intimate view into the colorful life of the table tennis community. *The Ping Pong Player and the Professor* deftly shines a light on table tennis's remarkable elite athletes as they navigate and compete in one of the more underrated sports in the US."
—Sangita Santhanam, ping pong parent of the Naresh brothers

"The Ping Pong Player and the Professor is a sheer delight. An inspiring yet all-too-rare intertwining of learned analysis and love—a parent's love of a child and a sport they both share. Professor Sosis explores the way sport is far more than a mere pastime, and contributes meaning by provoking personal growth and fostering social connection. And he transparently shares the joys and challenges of a parent seeking to support his child's passion for excellence on a national stage. In so doing he invites readers to appreciate the way anthropology helps us understand how others seek to understand. And earnest though this focus is, literally every page is laden with subtle irony, insightful wit, and self-effacing humor. It cherishes learning without pretentiously brandishing intellect; it reflects the desire and capacity to sympathetically enter into the personal experience of others and their collective worlds; it honors lifelong professional commitment while also viewing "mere sport" as not mere at all, but central to our meaning. The book's sympathetic insights stand to reduce the chasms that divide us, and expand the absorptions that fulfill us."

—Jeffrey Schloss, Westmont College

"In The Ping Pong Player and the Professor, Richard Sosis weaves together the passion and expertise of a high-level player, the keen insights of a professional anthropologist, and the fierce love of a father ready to sacrifice and (quite literally) sweat to support the athletic career of his talented son in an often underestimated sport: the world of table tennis. With wit and no small measure of humor, we meet a formidable father-son duo who take on the table tennis world, from the local level to the national, all without losing their rootedness in the world of Jewish culture and religious observance. This marvelous book defies genres. It is a brilliant anthropological analysis of sport, a rousing athletic career retrospective, a poignant ode to fatherhood, and a wonderful tale full of humor, drama, suspense, even deep questions of community, sanctity, and the human pursuit of meaning."

—Sarah Willen, University of Connecticut

"Richard Sosis—anthropology professor and "ping pong pop"—has written a love story...love for four children in a story focused on one, love as a coach and player with ping pong lineage, love for details that carry meaning. In this tale of table tennis and tradition, parenting and play, Sosis invites readers into culture and community. His good humor and humility help us, too, pursue dreams with determination and the wisdom to discern what matters."

—Charlotte Witvliet, Hope College

THE PING PONG PLAYER AND THE PROFESSOR

The Ping Pong Player and the Professor

An Anthropologist Explores Fatherhood and Meaning in an Extraordinary Sport

Richard Sosis

Wildhouse Publications

Copyright © 2023 Richard Sosis

Design by Melody Stanford Martin

Published by Wildhouse Publications, an imprint of Wildhouse Publishing (wildhousepublishing.com). No part of this book may be reproduced in any manner without the written permission from the publisher, except in brief quotations embodied in critical articles or reviews. Contact info@wildhousepublishing.com.

Printed in the USA

All Rights Reserved

ISBN 978-1-7360750-8-1

For my other tzaddikim, who have tolerated, sometimes begrudgingly but more often appreciatively, the amount of time I've spent with the youngest in our pack. And for my parents, who showed me how to raise tzaddikim.

It is the people not like us who make us grow.

— Jonathan Sacks

Contents

Preface iii

Prologue 1

Chapter 1. Escape from the Basement 7

Chapter 2. To Tennis or Not to Tennis … 17

Chapter 3. Almost a Brief History of Whiff-Waff . . 27

Chapter 4. For the Love of the Sport 39

Chapter 5. A Guide for the Perplexed:
　　　　　Serves, Sounds, and Status 53

Chapter 6. The Letter 67

Chapter 7. All That Is Gold Does Not Glitter 75

Chapter 8. Where Everybody Knows Your Name . . 87

Chapter 9. The Pilgrimage 105

Chapter 10. Identity 125

Chapter 11. Ping Pong Popping 139

Chapter 12. Invisible Things 153

Chapter 13. Growing Pains 175

Chapter 14. Olympic Dreams 183

Chapter 15. On Timeouts and Empty Nests 197

Epilogue 207

Appendix A. What an Anxious Ping Pong Pop
　　　　　Keeps in His Table Tennis Bag 213

Appendix B. How an Anxious Ping Pong Pop
　　　　　Affixes Table Tennis Rubber 227

Acknowledgments 237

Notes 241

Preface

"Could you please not use your hands when taking the green beans?" I ask, as calmly and politely as I am able, although my frustration at having to endlessly repeat such requests is surely evident. My children, I fear, hear my request as just another optional appeal. My eldest has told me that I may look scary—bearded and comfortably over six feet tall—but the moment I open my mouth it is obvious that I'm a pushover. Apparently, my voice lacks authority.

Authoritative or not, I can't leave this breach of dining etiquette alone. I point out that the dish of sautéed green beans, a favorite among our family of vegetarians, has a perfectly functional serving fork that should be used.

"Yes, but Eliel was using it," Naftali quickly retorts without looking up.

"Have we ever let you starve?" I ask rhetorically, or so I assume.

Naftali doesn't hesitate. "Who said anything about starving? I just want my fair share before they all disappear." Half a green bean is sticking out of his grinning mouth. Thank goodness he is so cute.

"Should we count the green beans out," I offer, "like the way we used to share a pack of M&M's when you were all little?"

"Brilliant idea Daddy," Rivka, the one who thinks I'm a pushover, adds in a tone that conveys just the right level of sarcasm to elicit smiles rather than stern stares. But the siblings do indeed begin to count the green beans they've consumed, a little too precisely for comfort.

I can see we are at risk of heading down the rabbit hole that only parents know how to dig, in spite of ourselves. I often find myself at the bottom of that hole, with my ego scathed and bruised, whereas my four teenagers always seem to know how to climb out unaffected. Attempting to distract them from obsessive counting, and the inevitable conclusion that the green bean distribution was unequal, I tactfully divert the conversation to safer territory.

"Eliel, how was school today?" Eliel, who is in eighth grade, hasn't yet been possessed by the snarkiness demon that inevitably invades and transforms angelic children during their teen years. If I wish to avoid digging another hole, I know it is prudent to start this ritualized inquiry about their school day with the youngest in our pack. I speak from experience, possibly too much experience.

"There was an argument in Hebrew class today," Eliel offers without the usual coaxing.

"A fight?" Aviva asks excitedly.

"No fight. Just an argument over sports."

"Oh no," I interrupt. "Not a Yankees-Red Sox argument I hope," knowing that living outside of Boston our family's sympathies in this rivalry are in the minority.

"No. In Hebrew class we are doing a unit on sports and Morah Katzenbaum asked how we would define sports."

"Funny she should ask that," I interrupt again. "In my *Anthropology of Sport* course I ask the same question on the first ..."

This time it is my turn to be interrupted. "Here we go," Naftali mischievously smiles. "Prepare for a Professor Daddy lecture."

Everyone laughs, although mine is a bit forced. Long gone are the days when my kids at least feigned interest in my anthropological wisdom. Parents and professors need thick skins to endure their lives of relentless critique. I could still use a few more layers.

Eliel continues. "In class Joshua said that you know something is a sport because you get exercise while doing it. Morah Katzenbaum asked him for examples and Joshua said that soccer and basketball were sports. Ping pong—he didn't know the Hebrew word for it—was not."

"Did you correct Joshua?" I ask, knowing that Joshua had hit on a topic closer to home than I had anticipated.

"Of course," Eliel replies calmly, although given Eliel's easygoing and conciliatory nature, it certainly was not obvious to me that he would correct Joshua's misperception. "That's how the argument began. Joshua insisted that sports require movement and since you don't have to move to play ping pong, or so he said, it's not a sport. I told him there was plenty of moving in ping pong and it was definitely a sport. Everyone in class agreed with me."

As the youngest in our family, Eliel doesn't win too many arguments at home, so I was glad to hear that he got the better of this one. And I was particularly delighted that he stood up for *his* sport.

Despite Joshua's ignorance about the physical aspects of playing what he referred to as ping pong, his intuition about how to define sport was not far off from the definition of sport I offer my college students. Sports are organized competitions, although as I'll discuss later, anthropological investigations into sport show that our understanding of competition as having winners and losers is hardly universal. Sports differ from other types of organized competitions, such as games, because in sports the movements of competitors impact the outcome of the competition. This proviso—the manner and impact of movement—helps distinguish games, such as chess and Go Fish, from sports, such as hockey, gymnastics, and archery. Chess and Go Fish require players to move pieces and cards respectively, but the manner in which these movements are performed does not affect who wins or loses. As I tell my students, if someone else could perform the required movements without impacting the competition, such as moving your rook or queen, you are probably looking at a game rather than a sport. There are of course activities that blur and challenge these borders, ranging from card games like Spit to human warfare. But as I'll note throughout this book, and as anthropologists have long appreciated, human activities don't fit neatly into boxes. Life is messy. Wonderfully messy, in my opinion. Yes, I've slipped into Professor Daddy lecturing mode, an experience my teenage children were, understandably, trying to avoid. In this book I am both Daddy and Professor, but as I'll explain shortly, much more the former than the latter.

Double Identities

It would be another year or two before Eliel's classmates and teachers would become fully acquainted with ping pong the sport, that is, table tennis. But by the time Eliel entered high school, many students, teachers, and even administrators actively followed his exploits in this previously unfamiliar world. When Eliel was away at tournaments, his teachers often permitted his classmates to check the tournament results online during class to see how Eliel was faring. And during important competitions, teachers occasionally canceled class so everyone could watch Eliel compete on the tournament live-feed online.

Table tennis has a double identity. On the one hand, it is an Olympic sport and one of the most popular sports in the world, generally ranking within the top ten on most measures of popularity, and within the top five in number of active players worldwide. Yet, competitive table tennis is virtually unknown in mainstream America and the intense physical demands of the sport are not widely appreciated, as Joshua made all too clear. Indeed, in the United States, table tennis is largely seen as a basement recreation or party game, best enjoyed if accompanied by beer.

Often its double identity is distinguished by using different names to categorize the activity: table tennis for the competitive sport, ping pong for the basement game. While many competitive table tennis players in the US will correct newcomers, "This is table tennis, not ping pong," in fact, ping pong is the name of the sport in China, and by all measures the Chinese are the kings and queens of table tennis the sport. But if we accept this distinction, then this book is about table tennis, that is, the sport, not the basement game.

In this book I have a double identity as well. On the one hand, I am an anthropologist, and part of what I do in this book is look at table tennis through an anthropological lens. On the other hand, I am a participant in the world of table tennis. Not only am I a former competitive player during my teen years, but I am the equivalent of a soccer mom, or what you might call a "ping pong pop." That is, one of my children, Eliel, is a competitive player and I spend too many of my waking hours coordinating his table tennis activities.

Indeed, my double identity has delayed this book for years. As an academic I often juggle multiple projects simultaneously, but I was having trouble working on two books at the same time. One of the books I wanted to write was an ethnography of a table tennis community. Table tennis communities present so many interesting anthropological questions: When players from around the world come together to play, as they do in table tennis clubs throughout the US, how do they create a new table tennis culture together? How are the norms and discourse of these communities established? How do the norms of these communities become internalized? How do new players integrate into these communities? How do these table tennis communities foster personal meaning and identities? What are the stories table tennis players tell each other?

The other book I wanted to write concerned my experiences as a ping pong pop. Much of my life over the past few years has been consumed by my son's training and tournaments. Many mothers and fathers have similar experiences as they dedicate their time to their children's activities. But table tennis in this country remains somewhat hidden, so I wanted to share my experiences, partially to introduce this hidden world to others.

The Talmud relates that a person who regularly gives charity (*tzedakah*) merits having wise children. I doubt I've been charitable enough to lend support to such a claim, but my children are certainly more grounded and levelheaded than I am, so I often consult with them for advice. One afternoon I shared my dilemma, my inability to effectively work on two books simultaneously, with my teenage daughter, Rivka. I explained the premise of both books and asked her for advice on which one I should pursue first. She sagely responded that I'd misunderstood the situation and asked the wrong question. It is not a problem to work on two writing projects at once; rather, in her opinion, I was stalling because I didn't actually have two writing projects to work on. She has read and enjoyed a number of ethnographies—one of the underappreciated perks of being the daughter of an anthropologist—and she said an ethnography that fails to include my place in the sport, as player, coach, and dad, would be incomplete and unsatisfactory. Rivka argued that my views and experiences as a ping pong pop were interesting because I often viewed the table tennis community through an anthropological lens. Due to my professional life, I can't help but see it any other way. Likewise, turning my anthropological vision on the table tennis community is surely influenced by my position in the community. I am not simply an "objective observer," as anthropologists once envisioned themselves. I'm a member of the community and my place in the community is impacted by my various roles and identities in life. My daughter concluded, "You only have one book to write so there is no reason for further delay." Sage advice indeed.

PREFACE

What is Anthropology?

When I leave the cozy confines of academia there is one question in social situations that terrifies me more than any other: What do you do for a living? I usually respond "I'm an anthropology professor" or something similar. With the exception of the woman who exclaimed, "Oh how exciting to study dogs!"—which left me in dumbfounded silence—over the years I've found that my occupation typically elicits one of two responses. The first and most feared response is a puzzled expression accompanied by complete conversation-ending silence; maybe they are contemplating a dog-related comment, but wisely refrain. The second, less painful, response is: "Really? That was my favorite class in college!" I of course share that it was my favorite class too. But invariably, and stupidly, I must ask why if it was their favorite class they didn't pursue it further, like yours truly. Predictably, they tell me they wanted to earn a living, and then they catch themselves, realizing their faux pas, and the conversation fades into uncomfortable silence. Whoever said that all paths lead to the same destination was evidently on to something.

Since I plan to approach the world of table tennis as an anthropologist, at least partially, it is worth saying a few words about anthropology, as it is a field that is either unknown or misunderstood by many. Although the term *anthropology* has been in use for hundreds of years, anthropology as an academic discipline is relatively new, gaining traction with the development of university departments in the late nineteenth century. In the US, anthropology embraces a holistic four-field approach that was advanced by Franz Boas, who served as the chair of Clark University's anthropology department when it became the first US program to award a PhD in anthropology. The four fields are typically referred to as archaeology and cultural, biological, and linguistic anthropology.

ix

Clifford Geertz, one of anthropology's most influential scholars, describes anthropology as:

> perhaps the last of the great nineteenth-century conglomerate disciplines still for the most part organizationally intact. Long after natural history, moral philosophy, philology, and political economy have dissolved into their specialized successors, it has remained a diffuse assemblage of ethnology, human biology, comparative linguistics, and prehistory, held together mainly by the vested interests, sunk costs, and administrative habits of academia, and by a romantic image of comprehensive scholarship.

After thirty years of a life in anthropology, I am still infected by that romantic image. In my research career I have dabbled in other academic disciplines across the social sciences, humanities, and natural sciences, and although it is hardly an objective position, I remain continually impressed and compelled by anthropology's vision. I often joke that I study humans for a living because I don't understand them; particularly baffling to me is that on the whole humans ignore anthropological scholarship. Anthropology, by all measures, is a muted child in public discourse, overshadowed by psychology, economics, and the health sciences.

Anthropology distinguishes itself from the other social sciences as the study of humanity across time and space; its focus on all human cultures, wherever and whenever they exist, is unique in the academy. Anthropology has also carved out its intellectual niche by studying humans with a particular set of theories and methodologies.

Theory and method in anthropology are often intertwined, as anthropological theories of the human condition frequently emerge from the discipline's primary research method, broadly referred to as ethnography. Participant observation is at the core of ethnographic research, and it entails living—that is, eating, sleeping, conversing, making friends, making enemies, celebrating, mourning, and pursuing every other imaginable human activity—with the people the ethnographer is studying. Apprenticeship as a mode of ethnography has been a particularly important avenue for studying embodied activities, including sport. Apprenticeship allows the ethnographer to encounter the socialization process just as novices themselves experience the process and thus is a valued ethnographic method for exploring issues concerning cultural learning and integration. Indeed, anthropologists have become increasingly skeptical of non-participatory ethnography in which the ethnographer observes, but in striving for alleged non-interference and objectivity, does not learn how to partake in the activity under investigation. Nowadays, if the locals engage in peyote rituals, things get very interesting for the ethnographer.

This proactive participation is in contrast to earlier generations of anthropologists who collectively saw themselves as pursuing an objective science. That started to change around the 1950s and '60s, when cultural anthropologists began to appreciate their role in the ethnographic experience. Ethnographers recognized that they were not performing detached experiments on amoebae or mice; they were living with the people they were studying, influencing and being influenced by them.

Since that time anthropology has largely been divided between those who see themselves as pursuing a science of the human condition and those who see anthropology as an interpretive practice, many of whom argue that as humans, a science of the human condition is objectively impossible. I've spent much of my career straddling these two worlds because I see merit in both positions. Another double identity.

As anthropologists began to appreciate their role in the ethnographic process, one corrective was for them to be up front about their own backgrounds. The aim was to alert readers about potential biases in the forthcoming account. For example, in one of my favorite ethnographies,

Barbara Myerhoff explains that she was interested in studying elderly Jews at a Jewish Center in California because this is who she will become, an elderly Jewish lady (tragically, it was not to be; she passed away from lung cancer before she was fifty). Or Loic Wacquant, in his classic ethnography of an inner-city Chicago boxing gym, explains how as a Frenchman he was able to conduct fieldwork in this all-Black gym without racial tension because although he is White, as a Frenchman he was outside the Black-White tensions that pervade American life. Having been trained on the scientific side of the aisle, I've always been a bit skeptical of these autobiographical notes in ethnography. But I do see the point, and as my daughter has insisted, my own background in table tennis undeniably informs how I perceive and understand the table tennis community.

This book cannot be characterized as an ethnography—it is not a research study—but it does bear several similarities with ethnographic monographs, especially contemporary ones. For instance, anthropologists make a living out of studying and writing ethnographies about marginalized peoples in marginal places. While table tennis is one of the most popular sports in the world—hardly marginal—table tennis communities in the US are commonly hidden away in indistinct buildings and the sport itself is marginalized, generally not even recognized as a sport in this country. Also, anthropologists appreciate that history plays a critical role in shaping cultures, so like most ethnographies I will include the requisite historical chapter to provide some background on the origins and development of table tennis. Moreover, in addition to autobiographical material aimed at revealing their biases, anthropologists since the latter half of the twentieth century nearly always intersperse personal narratives with cultural descriptions to present their ethnographic material, as I do in the pages that follow. Autobiography, as anthropologist Ruth Behar has put it, can be viewed as "the handmaiden of ethnography."

One last point on this book's relation to ethnography. In the public imagination, anthropology is exotic and possibly even mysterious. But ethnographic writing, the gateway into the exotic worlds that anthropologists study, frankly, is often mind-numbing. Or let me rephrase that. Ethnographic writing is like olives: it's an acquired taste. I love reading ethnographies (and eating olives), but reading ethnographic work requires a different mindset than reading most other books. Why? It's the details. The insufferable, excruciating, hair-pulling, exhaustive descriptions of everything from basket-weaving styles to tuber-harvesting strategies. Anthropologists are obsessed with documenting details. The rest of humanity evidently prefers texting and Twitter.

It is through the details that we as anthropologists are able to interpret a culture, recognizing that cultural behaviors contain many layers of meaning. The details, or "thick description" as Geertz put it, allow us to distinguish between an eye twitch and a wink, or even a parody of a wink. At times in the pages that follow I will offer a thick description of the American table tennis world. In other words, I'll describe minor and often mundane facets of life in this community that would likely go unmentioned and even unnoticed in other accounts of table tennis in America. Optimistically, these details will bring you into an unknown world, as well as permit me to make some meaningful interpretations of the lives that inhabit this world. And perhaps, if I'm lucky, these details will even reveal symbolic truths about meanings of the human condition. Those who are wiser than I am, however, have warned me that "readers are at risk of getting lost in the table tennis weeds." Yet, I'm hoping that I can offer a shift in perspective and that in your stroll through the meadow of this book, so to speak, the weeds will be experienced as wildflowers. I'm inclined to describe each wildflower, because, as an anthropologist I'm a firm believer that when entering another world there is value in such attention. I've heard it said that beauty, truth, the devil, angels, and even God is in the details. For me, the anthropological message is that *understanding* is in the details.

A Third Identity

Like everyone, I have many identities and roles, including son, brother, Trekkie, jazz-enthusiast, guitar-picking folkie, and wannabe hobbit. Aside from being a father and a paddle-wielding anthropologist, though, my most important identity in this book is that my family is Jewish, and we are so-called "observant" Jews. That requires a little "unpacking" as anthropologists are wont to say. We are not observant in the anthropological sense of being "watchers" (although we do that as well, typically on Shabbat, when birds at our two birdfeeders, rather than humans, are our object of interest). We observe Jewish law (*halacha*), or at least we try to.

I need to place great emphasis on that last phrase. Jewish observance for us is not black and white, nor is it grey. A blurry kaleidoscope might be the most apt image. There are some *halachot* that are non-negotiable, but most of those are probably the same laws we all live by, such as avoiding killing, stealing, and deli sandwiches on white bread with mayo. Other Jewish laws are under somewhat regular negotiation, and the line we are trying not to cross often moves in ways that it doesn't for most so-called observant Jews. Nor do all those in our family pack—there are six of us—draw these lines in the same places. I marvel at families who are all on the same page and clearly follow *halacha* according to the interpretation of this or that erudite rabbi. Like most anthropologists, I have a genuine problem with authority—my father told me repeatedly throughout childhood: "you'd better find a job where you are your own boss"—which means my Jewish life gets a little messy and inconsistent. One manifestation of my anti-authoritarianism is that I have an incurable allergy for adjectival Judaism, whether it is Reform,

Reconstructionist, Progressive, Liberal, Conservative, Orthodox, or Conservadox Judaism. I have trouble hearing anyone who tells me *this* is the correct way. I'm thrilled that there are so many flavors of Judaism (and there are countless more than I've listed), but to put it simply, I'm just Jewish and have spent most of my life trying to figure out what that means. I know it means I'm connected with a people who have a long and remarkable history. They are a geographically and intellectually meandering people—the Wandering Jew—who have introduced the world to many fascinating and revolutionary ideas throughout their journeys. They are also a people with curious affinities for chess, economics, Chinese food, complaining and arguing, anthropology, and table tennis.

The last item on this list deserves a comment, if for no other reason than that I recently mentioned to a Jewish friend that one day I would like to write a book on the history of Jewish table tennis players, which literally sent him to the floor, laughing uncontrollably. When I am able, I get great satisfaction in making my friends laugh, but in this case, I was being serious. As will be evident throughout this book, Jews have played an outsized role in table tennis, especially in the first half of the twentieth century. Prior to World War II, Jews dominated the sport, much like the Chinese do today. For example, of the ten Men's Singles World Championships from 1930 until 1939, when world sporting competitions were curtailed because of the war, Jews captured eight of these championships and 1933 was the only year in which there was *not* a Jewish runner-up. One of those champions, Richard Bergman, was able to win two more singles World Championships after the war (1948 and 1950), but Asia would take the domination baton from Jewish men shortly thereafter. The reign of Jewish women lasted slightly longer. Anna Sipos and Ruth Aarons, from Hungary and the United States respectively, each won two singles World Championships in the 1930s. But the most successful women's player of all time is Romania's

Angelica Rozeanu, née Adelstein. She captured the Women's Singles World Championship for an unprecedented six consecutive years (1950–1955), despite unrelenting anti-Semitism from Romanian authorities that limited her training and travel, and the disruption of her career because of the war. Beginning in 1936, she was the Romanian national champion for more than twenty years until her eventual immigration to Israel in the late 1950s.

Jews similarly dominated the US table tennis scene in the first half of the twentieth century, a history that for some reason has not been told. In probably the most comprehensive historical treatment of American Jews and sport in the early twentieth century, *Ellis Island to Ebbets Field: Sport and the American Jewish Experience*, Peter Levine discusses everything from Jewish bullfighters to Jewish weightlifters, but table tennis players are not mentioned even once. Yet Dick Miles won an unmatched ten US Opens, which served to crown a national champion until official national championships were introduced in the 1970s. Miles's record is particularly impressive because US Opens are more competitive than US National Championships since foreign players can compete in them. Other Jewish Men's US Open Champions include Marty Reisman, Erwin Klein, Sol Schiff, and Abe Berenbaum. Jewish Women's US Open Champions include the aforementioned Ruth Aarons and Leah Thall-Neuberger, a nine-time US Open Singles Champion, which like Miles's record is also unsurpassed. Maybe I'll write that book someday after all.

Early in Eliel's table tennis adventures it became evident that he needed to explain his Jewish observance to the diverse people he was meeting, especially his newfound friends from China who were baffled that he was uninterested in sharing their pork lo mein. Jews are a tiny people. As Milton Himmelfarb memorably put it, Jews are a statistical error in the Chinese census. In the US, Jews have attained notable success, and thus visibility, beyond what our demographic numbers would suggest. Most Americans have had some exposure to Judaism, if not in person, at least via television, movies, and social media. Understandably though, most Asians have little knowledge of Judaism or the Jewish people. How was Eliel to explain our funny practices—keeping kosher, sabbath rest, Chinese food on Christmas eve—to the uninitiated?

Thankfully, Eliel is not the first who has needed to "unpack" Jewish observance for others. I don't think we can do any better than bowling great Walter Sobchak, who describes Judaism as "three thousand years of beautiful tradition from Moses to Sandy Koufax." He explains what it means to observe the Jewish sabbath, that is, be *shomer Shabbos*, to his friend Donny in *The Big Lebowski*. His explanation is as lucid, or at least as forceful, as any rabbinic explanation I've ever encountered. However, I should preface Walter's dialogue with Donny by noting that among its many charms, *The Big Lebowski* is currently ranked twenty-third in the history of American cinema for its use of the f-word, and at the time of its release in 1998, it was in the top five.

> WALTER: I told those f***s down at the league office a thousand times that I don't roll on Shabbos!
>
> DONNY: How come you don't roll on Saturday Walter?
>
> WALTER: I'm shomer Shabbos.
>
> DONNY: What's that Walter?
>
> WALTER: Saturday, Donny, is Shabbos, the Jewish day of rest. That means that I don't work, I don't drive a car, I don't f***ing ride in a car, I don't handle money, I don't turn on the oven, and I sure as s**t don't f***ing roll!

Move over Rabbi Hillel. Next time I need to explain Judaism while standing on one foot, I'll just direct the inquirer to *The Big Lebowski*. Yet Walter never reveals exactly why he observes Shabbos. I once asked this question to an observant friend in graduate school (that is, why he observes, not Walter). He replied, "Because it makes me feel human." That seems right to me. I enjoy Jewish life because it affords opportunities to sing, dance, tell stories, recite poetry, hang out with family, share food, and celebrate. Unless you and your family are on tour with the Grateful Dead, these are all things that we just don't do enough of in the modern world, but they are all things that make us human.

And I can add one more to the list: sport also makes me feel human.

Finishing the Warm-ups

So, to wrap up this Preface, I should be clear about what lies in the pages ahead. If this book is not an anthropological ethnography, what is it? It is probably best characterized as a love story. Gushiness is kept at a minimum, although I make no promises about sappiness. I am a daddy after all, and as I mentioned, in this book I am more daddy than anthropologist. The book relates the love of an introverted father for his introverted son, who share a common bond over a nine-foot-by-five-foot table. Along the way it also recounts stories about sport, religion, and ethnicity in America.

All my children are avid readers. But my youngest daughter, Aviva, realized early on in life that she didn't have the patience to read an entire book to find out how it ends ("Daddy, will Frodo save Middle-earth?"). Thankfully, kids are resourceful. Her solution? When she picks up a book, she reads the last chapter first. She claims that this way she can read at a leisurely pace; she does not feel compelled to speed through the book to find out how it ends. I never told her that Harry Burns, of *When Harry Met Sally*, also reads book endings first, but he rationalizes this eccentricity with a little less optimism about life than Aviva: "That way, in case I die before I finish, I know how it ends." I'm counting on your survival to the end of this book, so, in Aviva's rather than Harry's honor—and that nobody mistakes this book for a thriller or page-turner—I will relieve you of any suspense or tension that might build up as the story unfolds. It is just not that type of book. And if such information will ruin the book for you, feel free to skip the next paragraph.

Spoiler alert: Eliel does not win a national championship of any kind, nor does he capture a spot on the US Olympic team. There are no murders nor crimes of any sort. No diagnoses of depression, divorce, drug addiction, nor doomsday devices that destroy the planet. The book ends with a son who continues to grow into a kind and responsible adult, and a father who is still coming to terms with the fact that his children, the most important accomplishment in his life, are no longer at home.

Our society, during the years in which I wrote this book, has been repeatedly described as contentious, combative, and hopelessly divided, culturally and politically. This book is not intended to be political. As those who know me can attest, I'm quite averse to politics, as hard as that is in times such as these. I prefer real sports. That is, politics strikes me as a despoiled team sport. I know this is not a novel assessment, but I have been surprised to learn how many others share this view. How one political team can always be correct and the other team always be wrong utterly escapes me. At least in real sports, fans are not pretending to be objective. My anthropology colleagues tell me that everything is political—we must always consider issues of power, they contend—so it is pointless for me to try and avoid it. In some ways they are correct; we can always understand social phenomena in terms of power dynamics.

This book, however, will not deal directly with issues of politics and power, or at least I will have little to say about these issues. Yet, it is in some ways motivated by a desire to heal the deep divide in this country. One of my favorite lines in the entire anthropological literature is the opening sentence of Gregory Bateson's *Naven*, a classic ethnography about ritual transvestitism among the Iatmul of Papua New Guinea. He writes:

> If it were possible adequately to present the whole of a culture, stressing every aspect exactly as it is stressed in the culture itself, no single detail would appear bizarre or strange or arbitrary to the reader, but rather the details would all appear natural and reasonable as they do to the natives who have lived all their lives within the culture.

Undeniably, it would be a tall order to present the whole of any culture, and I cannot hope to comprehensively present even a small corner of America's table tennis world within these pages. However, I do hope to describe enough of it so that this hidden sporting community does not "appear bizarre or strange or arbitrary to the reader." If we, as a society, were able to achieve such an understanding and appreciation of the communities on the other side of whatever divide we imagine separates us, I believe the world would be a better place. Indeed, anthropology's central dictum "understanding before judgment" seems to me like the best path out of our current social morass. It is not an overnight solution, but it is a simple approach to life that can move us closer to reconciliation. This book, in its own way, is one small step in that direction.

Prologue

The fourth game is over and Eliel has tied the match at 2–2. After writing down the game score on the match sheet he hurries over to me. I offer Gatorade and water. He grabs the water and takes a small drink.

"Nice game," I say as casually as possible, although after another close game I feel emotionally exhausted. "I like the way you're playing. Remember, if you serve wide to his forehand you should be able to pin him on his backhand side on the next shot. When you have the opportunity, take it down the line."

Eliel never looks at me. His face is expressionless but serious. I continue to offer advice, although I have no idea if he hears me. I lean closer to him as I speak and he moves back, repositioning himself to keep the same distance between us. I know he is listening.

"Keep your feet moving and stay focused on every point. And don't worry about his antics."

Pointless advice. Eliel never seems to be bothered by what his opponents or their fans are doing. I get distracted enough for both of us.

"It's time!" his opponent growls. His antics have begun.

"Go do it!" I exclaim with some force, pumping my fist, trying to sound confident. Actually, I am confident, although admittedly nervous as well. Eliel is ranked higher than this player and Eliel beat him in three straight games last month. But it has been a long day and I notice that Eliel's legs are not moving like they were earlier.

Eliel calmly nods, looking at me for the first time, and returns to the table. He dries his sweaty hands on his towel, which is draped over a ball barrier separating his court from the neighboring court. He picks up his paddle and the ball and takes a few short hops to get himself moving again. His opponent, a physically imposing man in his mid-twenties, also takes a few hops before settling in to return Eliel's serve.

Eliel straddles the corner of the table, with his left leg on the left side, while his right leg is bent low running parallel to the end of the table. His body is leaning forward so that his right knee advances beyond his foot. The ball rests on his open palm, which is motionless and held at table height. As usual, he holds this position for several seconds, concentrating on how he wants the point to unfold. It is a position that would send me crashing to the floor, but he is nimble and this is how he begins all his forehand serves. He tosses the ball about a foot in the air and on its descent he rotates forward, quickly striking the ball for a fast deep serve. The final game begins.

Eliel loses his first two service points, missing an attack and an opening flip. He then prepares to receive the serve. He crouches low, with his eyes slightly above the level of the net, intently tracking the racket motion of his opponent, who delivers a pendulum serve to the middle of the table. Eliel's return pops up a little and is fittingly ripped crosscourt for a winner and celebratory scream from his opponent. Down 3-0, Eliel finally wins a point when his opponent sends a forehand loop long. Eliel loses two of the next three points, quickly digging himself into a hole.

With his opponent leading 5-2 they switch sides, as is the rule when one player reaches five points in the final possible game of a match. They take the opportunity to move their towels to their new side, dry their hands, and think. The players pace slowly and prepare themselves for the final battle. My confidence is slipping away with each elevated heartbeat. I glance around and notice that the other matches at the tournament have already been completed; everyone who remains is watching this match.

PROLOGUE

Eliel's opponent prepares to serve, holding his position an excruciatingly long time before beginning his service motion. Eliel flips the serve cross-court with his backhand, and they exchange several fast-paced backhands. But Eliel's shots are becoming too predictable, and his opponent anticipates a shot to his backhand, positions himself to take it with his powerful forehand, and smashes it down the line for a winner. His opponent screams, jubilantly raising his fist. Eliel is down 6–2 and I begin to think about what words of comfort I will offer after the match.

Eliel wins his next two service points to close the gap to 6–4. It looks as though he has begun his comeback, but he drops the next point, misreading a heavy underspin serve and pushing the ball into the net. He successfully returns the next serve and the players push each other off the table with powerfully spinny forehand loops. Eliel is at a disadvantage in such a rally as he does not have the strength of his opponent, but after being pushed about ten feet back he charges the table and counters the ball right off the bounce, sending it down the line for a winner. Cheers from those watching and even Eliel exclaims "Yes! Let's go!", which is as emotional as he gets. Coaches and other players tell him that he should be more vocal during matches; intimidation wins points.

It is now 7–5. Eliel serves with his backhand and I recognize he is in comeback mode: when trailing he always relies on his backhand serve. But his opponent has seen this serve one too many times and positions his paddle as though he will return short to Eliel's forehand, then at the last second he bends his wrist and surprises Eliel with a deep push to his backhand. Eliel is off-balance and misses the shot. More celebratory shouting. Down 8–5, every point is vital. Eliel doesn't deviate from his backhand serve. He has seen too many close matches slip away after missing his more challenging forehand serves on critical points. Eliel serves short and his opponent follows through on what he had only faked last point: short to the forehand. But Eliel is ready and drives the ball right back at his opponent before he has time to recover from his own shot.

Eliel is a clutch player. He seems to play his best when the match is on the line and I've seen him come back from much greater deficits. Indeed, earlier in the day I watched him pull out a match against a higher-ranked player in which he was down 7–3 in the fifth game. Other players describe him as cool as ice and parents have confided that they wish their sons had Eliel's composure. What he lacks in physical strength he makes up for in mental toughness. I was nervous but I forced myself to have positive thoughts; Eliel had won four out of the last six points so he had the momentum.

At 8–6, Eliel's opponent decides to use his backhand serve, which he had only tried for a few points in the match thus far. He holds his service position interminably long, as is his wont, and serves a short side-topspin ball to Eliel's forehand. Eliel doesn't read the amount of topspin and the return is too high. His opponent unleashes a blazing forehand right into Eliel's body. Eliel stumbles backward from the force of the shot, but he gets his paddle on the ball and returns it. The return is weak, however, and the next shot is blown past Eliel for a clean winner. More shouting and fist pumping.

Nine–six is uncomfortable territory. Not only is there no room for error, but a lucky edge or net ball would give his opponent match point. His opponent sets up for his usual pendulum serve, but after a few moments he steps out of his position, pacing and talking to himself to finish the job. Eliel moves out of his service return position and wipes his sweaty palm on the side of the table by the net. His opponent returns to his service position, takes a deep breath, and delivers a side-under pendulum serve. Eliel flips it to his backhand. They exchange several backhands and then his opponent quickly gets his forehand into play, driving the ball to Eliel's forehand. Eliel blocks it cross-court and his opponent rips another loop to Eliel's forehand. Eliel counters toward the middle of the table and his opponent loops it to Eliel's backhand. Eliel punches the ball down the line for a winner. I shout with joy, but others who are watching drown me out with their cheers.

Eliel is serving, down 9-7. He keeps it simple with a backhand serve. His opponent pushes, Eliel loops, and they begin a looping exchange. His opponent drives the ball to the middle of the table. Eliel doesn't have time to set his feet so he leans to the side, taking the ball with his forehand, hitting to his opponent's backhand. His opponent, who has fantastic footwork and fresh legs, as this was his only event for the day, takes the ball with his forehand and loops it down the line. Eliel anticipates this and beautifully counterloops the ball wide to his opponent's forehand. His opponent scrambles, running full force trying to reach the ball, but he is too late.

His opponent is shaken up and drops the next point easily. It is another miraculous comeback. If I could only get Eliel to always play with the same intensity as he plays with when he is down, he'd be a much better player. At 9-9 they each go to their towels and slowly prepare for the final points. His opponent settles himself after dropping the last three points, then, bouncing up and down several times, vocally urges himself to play strong. He finally steps to the table to serve. Eliel returns the serve and the next ball is hit to the middle of the table. Eliel shifts to his backhand side to open with his forehand, but he drives the ball long. His opponent roars.

As his opponent approaches the table to serve, ahead 10-9, he begins a quiet mantra of "one more point, one more point …" Otherwise the tournament hall is completely quiet and still. After the usual tactical delay, he serves and Eliel pushes the ball short to his forehand. After several pushes Eliel flips the ball to his opponent's middle but the flip is too weak. His opponent readies his powerful forehand. Eliel, realizing his mistake, takes a step back to prepare for the attack, but the shot is too powerful and it blows past him. His opponent drops his racket and with chest out, shoulders back, and arms by his side he lets out his loudest scream of the match. The audience claps in appreciation of a competitive match, and Eliel walks to his opponent's side of the table and shakes his hand, looking dejected. His tournament is over.

After the handshake, Eliel strides off the court without looking at me, as he always does when he loses a match he feels he should have won. I know better than to say anything. I wait a few moments before I approach him, by which time he is ready to explain to me—although I suspect he is really explaining to himself—why he lost. I continually marvel at his capacity for recovery after tough losses. Within minutes we are laughing about bad decisions and poor shots. And he is already thinking about what he can work on to improve for his next tournament.

CHAPTER 1

Escape from the Basement

There is a strange affinity between ping pong and basements; like baseball diamonds and Iowa cornfields, they simply go together. So any good ping pong story should begin in the cellar, and that is exactly where we'll start. If you wish to read that as a metaphor for the beleaguered status of the sport, be my guest. The tale that unfolds on the pages that follow is not so much about my life in the cellar, but rather how I left the basement, only to return to the basement when I became a father, eventually escaping the basement once again, this time with my youngest child. Although my own journey to the world of table tennis began in the underbelly of a house, so to speak, it was not my house or basement. It was my best friend Timmy's basement. Timmy lived in a large historically protected farm house on several acres of land that was unique in the otherwise homogenized 1970s suburban neighborhood in which we lived. The size and antiquity of Timmy's house made it frightening for a seven-year-old, but the basement had been remodeled and was completely modernized and familiar. In a brown-paneled room with thin carpet stood a ping pong table, and we spent hours in that room hitting, competing, and listening to *Frampton Comes Alive!* on his phonograph.

Timmy was competitive and so was I. At first, he had the advantage— it was his table and he could practice with his father and other friends. But after a short time it became evident that I had some natural skill at this game and I began to beat him regularly. I had already begun taking tennis lessons, so ping pong was not my first racket sport. And if hand-eye coordination has any genetic inheritance, it was I who had the unfair advantage. My maternal grandfather and my mother's twin brother were both exceptional tennis players, and my mother herself, although too humble to admit it, was also a good player. In any event, I loved playing tennis and ping pong—which is what it was for us—and for whatever reason, I was good at both.

For most of elementary school I was limited to playing ping pong in Timmy's basement. But in the summer before sixth grade my family moved to the other side of town into a larger suburban home. One of the neighborhood teenage boys babysat me and my younger sister and one evening he asked whether I wanted to play ping pong. I said yes, but we had no ping pong table to play on. My babysitter, who oddly enough was also named Timmy, said this was not a problem. He ran to his house to get paddles and a ball. Upon his return he cleared off the kitchen table, set up some kitchen items such as cups and the salt and pepper shakers to serve as a makeshift net, and we began to play. We played each time he babysat, eventually upgrading from the kitchen table to the dining room table. This was even better than the babysitter who let my sister and I eat our meals while sitting on top of the refrigerator.

At some point my parents stopped using Timmy as a babysitter, which at the time I assumed was because they had discovered that their expensive dining room table was being used for purposes other than as a place to eat meals when relatives visited. It was apparently not so, as our treachery was news to them when it was finally revealed in one of those conversations you have as an adult with your parents, coming clean about what your childhood was really like when their backs were turned. They were less amused than I thought they'd be; they definitely preferred the story about lunchtime on the fridge.

Apparently it was just a coincidence, but shortly after Timmy's babysitting tenure came to an end, my parents bought a ping pong table for our basement. To my delight, this table had one side that could fold up and be used as a backboard. I spent countless hours hitting to myself against that backboard. Some of my parents' friends fancied themselves good players, so they would come to the house to challenge me. At first the matches were competitive, but soon enough I surpassed them all.

MY TRANSITION FROM PLAYING the game of ping pong in the basement to competing in the sport of table tennis occurred when I was eleven years old. My father saw an advertisement in the newspaper for a two-day table tennis clinic in the neighboring town. He asked if I was interested in attending and I said sure. We signed up for the first day, assuming one day would be enough, but within minutes of my arrival I realized I had entered a world I would not be leaving soon.

The weekend clinic was held in the gym of a community college and organized by Dan Simon, a computer science professor. He greeted us when we arrived and although I was a very shy child, it was obvious that Dan was gentle and kindly, so I felt comfortable in this new environment. Dan had a daughter who played as well; she was a few years my senior and much better than me. Upon entering the gym, I was struck by two things. First, I had never seen so many tables together in one place. In my world, ping pong tables only existed in basements, yet here were twenty tables evenly spaced across the gymnasium floor. Second, this was serious: the gym was filled with adults. Dan's daughter was hitting with another teenage girl, but otherwise there was only one other child to be seen. This child was a Chinese-American boy, also eleven years old, named Howard. Howard and I would spend just about every minute of the next two days hitting and becoming fast friends. We would eventually compete in the finals of the Pennsylvania State

Championships for the next several years and pair up to claim many doubles titles together.

The coaches who led the clinic were Randy Seemiller and Perry Schwartzberg. They were young, athletic, and could play table tennis in ways I had never imagined possible. Before getting on the table, Randy and Perry led us in stretching exercises, and then, finally (I was eleven), we were assigned tables and hitting partners. Howard and I were the obvious hitting mates and Randy and Perry instructed us on how to hit the forehand stroke. One dividing line between basement players and competitive tournament players is the development of a strong forehand. Basement players often forgo the forehand entirely, covering the whole table with a backhand that alternates between a block and a punch. But elite players overwhelmingly rely on a powerful forehand, usually aiming to cover two-thirds to three-quarters of the table with their forehand. And it is not unusual for top players to "turn the corner" and hit a forehand from wide on the backhand side. This is one of the most powerful shots in table tennis because there is no table obstructing the body's full movement into the shot.

The basic forehand stroke, we were instructed, is essentially a salute, but after smacking my forehead with my paddle, I was informed that it was more like an abbreviated salute. For the record, I was a very literal kid. My father claims that when I was told to keep my eye on the ball while playing catch, I took the ball and held it on top of my closed eye. Also, for the record, I have no memory of this, but I am a firm believer that parents, having endured the challenges and insults of parenthood, have every right to tell embellished stories of their progeny.

Once we were able to perform the stroke with some competency, our task was to hit a hundred in a row. At first impossible, Howard and I worked for what must have been hours to achieve our goal. Our reward? Learning how to hit proper backhands!

Backhands are usually less powerful than forehands because the backswing is much shorter for a backhand. Unlike a tennis backhand, which is hit from the side of the body, a table tennis backhand is hit from in front a player's body. Table tennis is simply too fast and there is not enough time for players to rotate their bodies to the side to hit a tennis-like backhand. Rather, when hitting a backhand the feet are roughly parallel to the table. In order to generate power, players bend and lean forward to create space for a backswing in front of their stomach, which is where the stroke initiates. Backhand loops (loops are shots that lift and drive the ball, generating heavy topspin) often create backswing space by beginning the stroke between the legs. As it turns out, Eliel is one of those unusual players whose backhand is more powerful than his forehand. This is probably partially a result of receiving most of his training, as I'll describe in the next chapter, from a hobbit-wannabe grizzled anthropologist, rather than a proper professional coach.

Backhand and forehand strokes impart topspin on the ball, but Randy and Perry also taught us how to hit the two primary underspin strokes, which are distinguished by where they occur. A push, whether forehand or backhand, occurs over the table. It is a short stroke that requires considerable touch. Pushes that "leak" long will be attacked by strong players, so effective pushes are typically short, meaning they would, if unimpeded, bounce twice on the opponent's side of the table. In fact, the best pushes are known as half-long pushes, which means the second bounce is right at the edge of the table. It takes great control to execute a half-long push, but when successful an opponent will be unsure whether the ball will go long and can thus be attacked, or whether it will bounce a second time on the table. Good half-long pushes set players up for their own attack since half-long pushes are often returned weakly. Long pushes can be effective when used as a surprise tactic. Long pushes that are anticipated, however, are generally vaporized by top players.

The second underspin stroke is known as a chop and it occurs off the table. Chops are downward in motion and since the table is not in the way, the stroke is much longer and generates more spin than the push. Chopping is a specialty; it's a stroke most players don't fully incorporate into their game unless they are choppers. Choppers are defensive players and they feed on their opponents' mistakes. Playing a good chopper is mentally and physically exhausting—like taking a calculus exam while running a marathon—and requires great patience.

Over the course of the weekend we also learned how to loop, smash, lob, and block. Perry even showed us how to fish, a peculiar name for a style of playing that is a lot more active than the pastime from which its name is derived. Fishing consists of standing deep behind the table while hitting heavy topspin shots that are a cross between a loop and a lob. It is a style of play that was perfected by the Swedes in the 1980s and '90s, when they were among the best in the world, capturing three Men's World Team Championships and finishing second to the Chinese four times. They were led by the Roger Federer of table tennis, Jan-Ove Waldner, the smoothest player the world has ever seen. But the best fisher ever was his teammate, Mikael Appelgren. Appelgren's habit of standing far from the table and making seemingly impossible returns dazzled audiences and frustrated opponents throughout the eighties and nineties. Years after the clinic I had the honor of playing Appelgren at a US Open, but he never had to back up from the table while playing me. I was starstruck, and my only wish was the same wish I have every time I go to the dentist: let it be quick and painless. It was. He didn't even bother to take off his sweatpants. I'll never forget his unsolicited advice to me after our match: "You need more practice." Thanks Mikael, I hadn't noticed.

While Randy and Perry demonstrated the proper arm movements involved in each type of stroke, they also emphasized the importance of using one's feet and legs. Quite simply, players can have excellent strokes, but a perfect stroke is ineffective unless the player is in the appropriate place and position. Good footwork is vital for table tennis success, and, once players have mastered the basic strokes, those who wish to improve spend most of their training time on footwork drills. Japanese players are especially known for their strong footwork; apparently, when Japanese children are introduced to table tennis they are taught footwork movements long before they ever pick up a ball and paddle. I have no idea how they keep children interested without actually hitting a ball; I would have been thoroughly disappointed had Randy and Perry not allowed me to play all weekend. But the success of the Japanese players—only second to China—speaks for itself. Eliel has played some Japanese professionals and he was literally unable to force them to hit a backhand; their footwork was so good they could play the match entirely with their forehand. And these were not even Japan's top players.

All sports are challenging, and learning and training are essential for success. But table tennis seems to have a particularly steep learning curve, which is one of its utmost impediments to wider acceptance and popularity. As Steve Brunskill, head coach of Swerve Table Tennis Centre in England, notes about what he considers the world's hardest sport, "It has the smallest court, the smallest ball, the smallest bat, the quickest reaction times, the most spin ... and you have to learn to cope with different styles of opponent." Well put, coach. Recently, a friend asked to move the day we were scheduled to practice—yes Mikael, I was listening—because the weather was supposed to be nice, unusual for March in New England; he was hoping to play tennis with his wife. I hadn't known that his wife liked tennis so I asked whether she ever considered playing table tennis. His response, I thought, was informative.

He said she had indeed tried both tennis and table tennis and she found tennis to be more immediately rewarding. Even as a novice she was able to keep the tennis ball in play and get exercise while doing so. The early stages of learning table tennis, on the other hand, are frustrating and physically unrewarding. Spins are baffling and overwhelming, balls are flying everywhere, and more time is spent picking up missed shots than actually rallying. It is only after a player gains some mastery of the intense spins and speed of the game that a full physical workout even becomes possible. No wonder the drinking game is more popular than the sport.

STEEP LEARNING CURVE or not, I was smitten. Hitting the same stroke to the same place for hours on end, which is exactly what we did all weekend at the clinic, might sound like drudgery. Yet I thought I was in heaven. I loved to play this game, and just being at the table, hitting the ball, was a joy, even if it would appear to most to be monotonous. I watch kids nowadays taking lessons, hitting the same shot over and over again with a coach, and wonder if they have the same thrill and excitement I had that weekend.

After two straight days of nonstop playing, I wanted more. Dan, the kindly computer science professor, informed my dad and I that he ran a club that met two nights a week. The club had four tables they set up in a dance studio on the same college campus. I was welcome to visit the club any day it was open, and I did indeed visit it. My parents regularly drove me the forty-five minutes each way so that I could compete with real table tennis players, all of whom were much better than me.

Each night the club was open, ten-to-fifteen players, mostly men, would gather to play matches against each other. Although I was a beginner in their eyes, everyone was incredibly generous with their time and knowledge. And when I improved, these selfless table tennis players served as coaches, guardians, and chaperones as they took me to tournaments across the country. I wish I knew where they are now so I could thank them for their kindness.

It is clubs like these that are the heart and soul of the US table tennis community. Despite the fierce competition at the table, these clubs create community, bringing people together who share a passion for table tennis. Like in all human communities, there are good friends, grudging friends, and those who refuse to speak to each other because of some past grievance. At Dan's community college club, some of the guys would meet at a pub after playing, and my impression was that everyone was welcome—except of course the eleven-year-old. At the time I didn't quite recognize it, but this club was surprisingly made up, almost exclusively, of White, US-born, middle-class players. The only exception I can recall was a Turkish graduate student who was often my doubles partner at local tournaments. It is safe to say there is no club that looks like this today. Table tennis clubs in this country are more likely to resemble the halls of the United Nations. The primary club where my son and I play has members from China, Korea, India, Sri Lanka, Dominica, Brazil, Russia, Iran, Israel, France, Belgium, and at least a dozen other countries. Nonetheless, while America's table tennis clubs have changed drastically over the past forty years in terms of their size, organization, and clientele, they remain the center of table tennis activity in this country.

Over the next several years I won many Pennsylvania State Championships for my respective age categories, participated in several Olympic training camps, played on the US Junior Team on various occasions, and was ranked in the top ten Juniors (players under eighteen years old) in the country for much of high school. Within my first year of college I was ranked in the top one hundred players in the country. That all sounds good, and possibly impressive, but the truth is I was never very good. The State Championships were not very competitive. I was never close to being an Olympian; the gap between my skills and this country's eventual Olympians' skills was vast. Participation on the US Junior Team in those days was informal and quite unlike today. I would simply receive a phone call from a coach asking if I was interested in playing in an upcoming event if the better players were unavailable. I can't recall ever winning a match while representing the US. And while my rankings were high, the truth is that the level of play in the US at this time was extremely weak. We had a few excellent players at the top—two who in fact broke into the top twenty-five in the world—but the gulf between the top players and everyone else was wider than the Atlantic.

That is my story, briefly, but the story I really want to tell is about Eliel, my youngest child. Like his old man, he has been a top-ten Junior throughout his teen years and a member of the US Junior Team, surviving much more rigorous and stressful trials to make the team than I ever had to endure. Unlike his father, however, Eliel's achievements are not limited to the Junior ranks. He is a Men's State Champion and member of the US Team that competed at the World University Games, and recently he reached the round of sixteen (in other words, the final sixteen players) in the Men's Open Singles at the US National Championships. He is a much better player than I ever was.

But that wasn't always the case.

CHAPTER 2

To Tennis or Not to Tennis ...

My father has always loved hobbies, or more precisely, new hobbies. Hobbies hold his interest for about the lifespan of a tube of toothpaste, but when one attracts his interest, his initial passion is irrepressible, often resulting in a flurry of purchases and revised weekend plans to accommodate his new obsession. The basement ping pong table, on which I had spent countless childhood hours, was a casualty of one such fleeting interest. When I left my parents' home for college, the ping pong table was quickly replaced by a pool table. Why the ping pong table remained folded up in a corner and was not discarded, donated, or resold like other items of my childhood remains a mystery. There was no possibility of ever using it in my parents' basement; without a sledgehammer, pool tables can't be folded up like ping pong tables, so there was simply no space. Maybe my father realized his newfound enthusiasm for billiards would be a passing phase, soon joining model airplanes, kite flying, pen collecting, calligraphy, photography, collecting chessmen (not Kasparov and company, but rather the pieces they play with), and so forth in his ever-expanding hobby graveyard. Whatever the reason, it remained in the basement for more than a decade until I had a house and a burgeoning family of my own.

Although we had no room to set it up either, my parents were finally threatening to send the table to the hereafter, so I took it. All four of our kids were still in their single digits, and like most young couples, we moved quite frequently in those days. The ping pong table, much to my wife's dismay, moved with us. Somehow the table even followed us to Israel, which in hindsight is puzzling since none of my kids had shown any interest in playing and Eliel was still in diapers when we moved there. By the time we moved back to the US, several years later, the table had no legs. It was just two four-and-a-half-by-five-feet pieces of slightly warped green wood with chipped corners. But it came with us like a faithful pet, and after a few years I decided to purchase four foldable sawhorses, hoping they could serve as legs for the table. It was not the best idea I ever had—the table rested quite precariously on the sawhorses—but it was not the worst idea I ever had either. There are many examples in the pages that follow that might warrant the latter distinction.

I set up the table in our basement and it was a tight squeeze. Incidentally, when Eliel eventually became a serious table tennis player, I set up a tournament-level table—gifted to us by a thoughtful friend—in what most families would use as a dining room since it offered the largest space in our house. Yes, life comes full circle and I get the irony, although it seems to have been lost on my parents, who undoubtedly wish my home was arranged like the home of normal grownups.

Back in our basement, it was a tight squeeze indeed. There were about two feet at each end of the table, just enough to stand upright but not enough to fully swing, and there was a similar amount of space on the sides of the table. But nobody in the house—at that point—was training for the Olympics, so it was sufficient. Indeed, moving wasn't necessary or even possible, since I often played on my knees, a habit I had picked up as a teenager to make matches more competitive with my friends. Each of my kids went through brief phases of mild interest; it was something to do with Daddy when it was too cold or rainy to play soccer or whiffle ball. None of my kids, with the eventual exception of Eliel, showed any athletic promise. I cruelly spent hours tossing an inflatable ball to my eldest son, Naftali, watching it bounce off his forehead as he stood motionless with his arms outstretched, still waiting for me to throw the ball. The passing years have not clarified what possessed me to do this; possibly, my children are correct and I am really Sauron reincarnated. It was no surprise that Naftali, like my wife, was sporting glasses in first grade. And for the record, my cruelty has been repaid many times over by the thousands of table tennis balls that Eliel has smashed off my forehead and other parts of my body as I, too slow to react, stood motionless waiting for his shot. It's the best evidence of a karmic force in the universe that I'm aware of.

Author Michael Chabon, who, like me, is personally all too familiar with the challenges of raising four children, observes:

> By the time a fourth child comes along, the siblings have usually managed among them to stake out a wide swath of traits, talents, crotchets, flaws, phobias, and strengths. Finding one's difference can often be a fourth child's particular burden and challenge.

This was never a problem for Eliel. Because of his athleticism, he naturally gravitated toward sports, unlike his siblings. Indeed, when I recently took Naftali sneaker shopping, the salesman, in order to guide Naftali toward the most appropriate footwear, asked what he needed the sneakers for. Naftali responded concisely and accurately: "Reading." Eliel and I, however, spent hours shooting hoops, throwing a football, and eventually playing tennis. He seemed to be my only child who had inherited my maternal family's hand-eye coordination, and it was readily apparent he was a naturally gifted tennis player. Our town has more than a dozen free tennis courts and we regularly took advantage of them. When he was nine I signed him up for a tennis camp and within a few weeks the instructors had moved him up several age categories so he could play with kids at his level.

Tennis camp ended the same way soccer camp had ended the previous summer: with a broken arm. Breaking arms is an unfortunate habit if you like racket sports. Eliel seemed to arrive at this same nugget of wisdom and decided teeth were better than arms to break. Actually, there was no need for the plural in that last sentence; within the span of three years, following his arm-breaking episodes, Eliel broke the same tooth four times. Rather than catching his falls with his arms, thus breaking them, he decided to brace his falls with his face, breaking the same incisor with each tumble. We still have a dent in the wood floor of our living room, where Eliel planted his tooth one evening after tripping over his sister Aviva. Whether or not Aviva's leg was intentionally or fortuitously extended remains a point of controversy in family lore. Since the extended legs of Aviva's two older siblings—and here, there is no controversy about intentionality—delayed her toddler transition from quadruped to biped for nearly a year, a little reinforcement of her ranking above Eliel in the sibling hierarchy doesn't seem unreasonable.

OVER THE 2012–2013 WINTER I found myself playing table tennis with Eliel most evenings and the same skills he was showing on the tennis court were evident at the table as well. It was equally obvious that he enjoyed playing and he *loved* competing. I would devise various games that would handicap me in certain ways to make the matches competitive. These included giving him a nine-point lead in an eleven-point game, limiting my shots to one area of the table, or his favorite, playing left-handed on my knees. Although I write and eat with my left hand, I throw a ball and play racket sports with my right hand. Initially, I would give him a five-point lead in these left-handed-on-your-knees matches, but over the course of the winter my handicap shrunk until we both started at zero.

In all our competitions, one thing I never did was let him win. I have no idea what parenting advice books say on this matter. Lord knows, as my children will attest, I would have benefited from reading a few of them. Frankly, I've always been dumbfounded, and grateful, that I live in a world where I was allowed to reproduce without passing an exam, but I think I was too busy raising kids to read about what I was doing wrong. A little bit of study, something I've been doing all my life (I'm still in college, so to speak), would surely have been natural and prudent. I think most parents, whether or not they've read the advice books, are inclined to let their children beat them, at least on occasion, to boost their morale or simply avoid the hysterical meltdown that often accompanies a child's defeat. I certainly followed that instinct in everything from badminton to Monopoly, at least some of the time. But for some reason table tennis was different. I never let Eliel win.

This was either the smartest or dumbest thing I ever did. If Eliel were reading this he would point out that this is an utterly illogical statement, although he would acknowledge that this is what he expects from me. Or in his own words, "It's a typical Daddy statement." Despite its failure to conform to Spockian principles, the point I wanted to convey is that the merit of my never-let-him-win posture is a matter of perspective. It turns out that what motivated Eliel in his early years of playing was his burning desire to beat me. Indeed, as his playing-level rose, one of the top players in New England commented to me that once he did finally beat me—and that was inevitable—it would be interesting to see if he is still motivated to improve. In other words, my stubborn refusal to let him win at least partially fueled his passion for the game.

So, smart or dumb? Well, on one hand, indefensibly dumb. If you have a child who loves racket sports and excels at both tennis and table tennis, which direction should you nudge him? That is a no-brainer: the profits in professional tennis exceed those in table tennis by such a wide margin that the comparison is laughable, like comparing the salaries of our country's top male lacrosse and basketball players. Even for those players who never win a professional tennis tournament, the hourly fee for tennis instructors is considerably higher than for table tennis instructors, not to mention tennis boasts a much broader and more vibrant employment market. In other words, the logic of economics suggests that nudging your child toward table tennis if tennis is an option is not just irrational, it's inexcusably idiotic.

Perhaps it is excusable if you live in China, or if you are somehow oblivious to the economic realities of the two sports (but then it would be fair to question what universe you are living in), or you are so fabulously wealthy that future earnings are of no concern, but I couldn't claim any of these excuses. As I saw Eliel's interest in table tennis grow, and his interest in tennis slowly wane, I expressed my concern—future wage earnings—to my wife. But as we talked, the other economic factor stared us directly in the face and it didn't look as good as the Rolex on Federer's wrist: we simply did not have the financial means to create a tennis star. With outdoor public courts and a father who spent many summers as a camp tennis counselor, learning to play tennis was initially cheap. But competitive tennis is expensive, especially in a place like New England where it is necessary to pay the fees for indoor court time for at least half the year. If he wanted to continue playing tennis we would of course support him financially in whatever way we could, but club membership and private lessons were not a possibility.

In the end, I did not have to decide which direction to nudge him. He made the choice himself, as it should be. And I didn't need to read a parenting book to figure that one out. In fact, it was a little anthropological insight that suggested the right course of action. Or more specifically, it was Balinese cockfights. When in college, if you are a biology major you will master the theory of natural selection; if you are a premed student you will suffer through organic chemistry; statistics majors have to wrap their heads around Bayes' theorem; history majors will analyze revolutions, from American to French; and if you are an anthropology major you will learn everything you ever wanted to know, and more, about Balinese cockfighting. Maybe it is not so baffling why anthropology, as I noted earlier, "is a muted child in public discourse."

One of our anthropological companions whom you met in the Preface, Clifford Geertz, used Balinese cockfights to explore philosopher Jeremy Bentham's concept of "deep play," which refers to play that from a utilitarian viewpoint is irrational. In other words, it makes no economic sense. For Bentham, such play should be considered immoral; for the anthropologist, such play should be considered human. As Geertz argued with regard to Balinese cockfights, men are not passionately raising, training, and fighting their cocks for monetary reasons; cockfighting is about "esteem, honor, dignity, respect, [and] ... status." Likewise, as the coming years would confirm, youth training in table tennis is indeed financially irrational, but that is beside the point. Table tennis, I would learn through Eliel, is about friendships, commitment, and growth, matters that we might say are beyond monetary concerns.

Before leaving our detour into Balinese cockfights, I must address the question that every undergraduate who sits in an introductory anthropology course wants to ask but doesn't, at least not in front of their classmates. Yes, as Geertz writes, "[t]he double entendre ... is deliberate. It works in exactly the same way in Balinese as it does in English, even to producing the same tired jokes, strained puns, and uninventive obscenities."

For a while Eliel played both tennis and table tennis. But ultimately, table tennis won out until at some point he stopped playing tennis altogether. The risk of injury was not worth it; he saw too many other young table tennis players end their careers prematurely due to injury. And his time was limited: time on the tennis court was time away from the table tennis table.

I of course do not know the precise role my refusal to let him win played in his choice, but competing with me could not quite fuel his interest in tennis as it did in table tennis. There is no way I could play tennis on my knees, or left-handed, which meant that other than limiting the amount of the court I could use, I had to play right-handed and take it easy on him. Kids know when you are trying and when you are not, and kids like Eliel want real competition. I am grateful for his choice, as he has reminded me how much I enjoy table tennis, but I do often wonder what would have happened if we had the financial resources to fully invest in developing his tennis talents. After not picking up a tennis racket for at least four years, Eliel hit with one of his friends, the top player on their high school tennis team. I asked Eliel about how he played and he responded candidly, with no boasting in his voice, that after not playing for so long he thinks he would have trouble serving, but he felt he would still beat his friend.

Eliel and I have had many conversations that compare tennis and table tennis, and we are of course not the only ones who have crossed over, so to speak, into the table tennis world. And many less competitive table tennis players maintain strong allegiances to both sports. Anthropologists rarely take social conversations—what they refer to as discourse—at face value, and conversations at table tennis clubs comparing the merits of tennis and table tennis could be understood as much-needed rationalizations for why we are playing the lesser sport in terms of visibility, international fame, and wealth. Many who regularly play both sports contend that table tennis offers them a better workout. This will be difficult for many non-table tennis players to accept, but having played both sports competitively, I think such claims are not unreasonable. They both demand physical exertion: one demanding short, intense frequent bursts of movement around a nine-by-five-foot table, the other demanding less frequent but longer bursts of movement across a seventy-eight-by-twenty-seven-foot court. For professionals, the off-table and off-court training are likely similar, including running, weight training, core exercises, and so forth. But my experience is that table tennis training at the table can be a better workout than tennis training on the court. Multi-ball training, used in both tennis and table tennis, can be physically devastating in table tennis. On the other hand, a five-set tennis match requires much greater physical exertion and stamina than a seven-game table tennis match.

Most comparisons, however, are not concerned with the physical aspects of the sports. Some, in seeming contradiction to the "better workout" argument, praise table tennis as a lifelong sport. Indeed, I've watched matches at our local club where the age difference between competitors was eighty years. It is hard to imagine that kind of age gap in any other competitive sport, with the possible exception of curling. The most common rationalization I hear is that table tennis is simply more interesting than tennis. I agree, and I've admittedly used precisely this argument to justify my own turn toward table tennis, and away from tennis, in my youth.

What makes table tennis interesting, so the argument goes, is the diversity of styles. There are blockers, loopers, flat hitters, choppers, fishers, lobbers, combinations of these, and many other styles. Table tennis is a game of spin. Spin is also important in tennis, but tennis rackets do not have the ability to grip the ball the way that sticky table tennis rubbers do. The rubbers that players use—which vary in the amount and types of spin that can be imparted to the ball—also vary widely. Chinese rubbers, for example, are renowned for their tackiness. Some rubbers, which have long pimples, or in table-tennis vernacular, long pips, actually reverse the spin on the ball. Other rubbers remove spin entirely. Much of table tennis involves deceiving your opponent about the amount of spin on the ball. The art of deception is especially important when serving, and service styles vary widely across players. Indeed, serving offers an arena of creativity and originality that is rare in competitive sport. *Time* magazine evidently recognized this when they ranked German Olympian Dimitrij Ovtcharov's backhand serve one of the top fifty inventions of 2008 (retail DNA tests were number one that year). In sport, successful styles tend to be identified and replicated and successful serves are of course mimicked as well, but every player puts their own unique stamp on their serves. Strategies to deal with the diversity of spins players encounter is complex and frustrating, but it makes the game endlessly interesting.

Nonetheless, revisiting my earlier comment, how can I suggest that my competitive stance with Eliel might have been the smartest thing I ever did? Rationalizations aside, the economic realities remain, suggesting some colossal dumbness on my part. But as I said, it is a matter of perspective, so I'll let the following pages speak for themselves. You can make the judgment.

MY SHARED JOURNEY WITH Eliel into the world of table tennis was just beginning. But before turning to the sinuous story I want to tell about our lives in this world, it is worth stepping back and getting some perspective on this marginal sport. How did the table tennis world that I will subsequently describe emerge? What is its history? Unfortunately, I'm not a historian, at least not yet. So in this book you'll have to settle for the following idiosyncratic chronicle and portrayal of, in my biased yet humble opinion, the world's greatest sport.

CHAPTER 3

Almost a Brief History of Whiff-Waff

Although I didn't realize it at the time, my babysitter and I were not the first to misuse a dining room table for ping pong passions. Indeed, the game was born on such tables, probably much fancier, in Victorian England. Table tennis began as a parlor game—that is, as entertainment for the English upper class, who in the mid- to late-nineteenth century found themselves with too much leisure time on their hands. In English parlors, table tennis competed with Blind Man's Bluff, Tiddlywinks, Twenty Questions, and I Spy for the attention of the wealthy elite. As marketers would soon be emphasizing, table tennis had an advantage over such classic games: it provided exercise for participants. The disadvantage, aside from the inevitable scratch marks on the dining table, was the continual scrambling and searching for balls that rolled underneath other expensive parlor furniture.

Like most sports, the historical origins of table tennis are murky. One thing we know for sure, though, is that it did not spring into existence fully formed. Table tennis, like all sports, evolved. Trial and error are the key ingredients in this process, and error seems to have been overly abundant in the case of table tennis. Early forms of the game were attempted on the floor rather than a table. Balls made of cork and rubber were tried and ultimately discarded; balloons were even used for a time. And the original paddles were stringed rackets, smaller versions of those used in tennis.

The use of stringed rackets, albeit awkward, is not surprising. Ball games with stringed rackets have a long history in the world. Many Native American groups played such games, although they were team contests—sometimes entire clans pitted against other clans—rather than individual competitions. The French were playing a tennis-like game with stringed rackets in the sixteenth century, a significant development from its earliest versions in the twelfth century, in which the ball was struck with one's palm, and appropriately known as *jeu de paume* (game of the palm). The word *tennis* itself is derived from the French *tenez*, or "take heed," which was shouted across the court to alert an opponent that a serve was on the way—a warning that, as I will describe later, would be entirely apt in table tennis. Table tennis serves don't reach the speeds of tennis serves, but service spins can be utterly confounding, even for experienced players.

The modern game of tennis, as well as badminton, emerged in mid-nineteenth-century England, several decades earlier than table tennis. Indeed, most accounts suggest that table tennis was simply lawn tennis moved indoors, stringed rackets and all, a logical development given the reliability of British rain and the difficulty of outdoor play during the winter months. Several clever Brits evidently arrived upon this idea independently, and a variety of similar games emerged in the 1880s, each with their own patented name: indoor lawn tennis, parlor tennis, Gossima, whiff-waff, and of course ping pong, to name a few. As you might have guessed, I'm partial to whiff-waff, but I didn't get a vote. Table tennis ultimately developed from these prototypes. Thus, the evolution of table tennis cannot be represented by a classic phylogenetic evolutionary tree, unless you envision that tree to be upside down, in which diverse branches lead into solid trunk. But even that image falls short since the modern sport of table tennis has spawned many intriguing offspring, including headis, table squash, and pingpongo. If these games haven't made it to your neighborhood, look them up. Human ingenuity never seems to rest.

I HAVE A FRIEND at the University of Oxford, a biologist by training, who enjoys reading American history. I'm personally fascinated by British history and we've often joked that in our next lives we'll come back as historians. When we initially discovered our mutual love of history, I pointedly asked him why he enjoyed reading American history. Without missing a beat, he responded: "You can't make this stuff up!" Such sentiments surely apply to the history of table tennis as well, although much of it took place on his own British soil. While the origins of table tennis may be murky, its early history and global spread are best described as "filled with intrigue." My aversion to politics aside, there has probably never been a sport whose history is more closely entangled with politics than table tennis.

The architect of the modern game was a Cambridge-educated Jewish British communist aristocrat who served as a Soviet spy. Really. Ivor Montagu, or Intelligentsia as he was known to the Soviets, was the third son of Lord Swaythling, an English baron and heir to Samuel Montagu, an exceedingly wealthy banker. Ivor had a passion for table tennis that was only matched by his passion for communism. He was easily recruited as a spy by the Soviets, often using his table tennis credentials and activities to travel to places otherwise forbidden to British citizens. The British secret services of course noted how the Soviets opened doors for Ivor that were closed to other Westerners, but he remained free to pursue his double life. It was preferable to keep close tabs on him rather than expose their knowledge of his duplicity and the clandestine spy network they had uncovered. Remarkably—and that is a word I could use in every sentence about Ivor Montagu's life—to claim he had a double life misses the mark; triple life might be more accurate. In addition to spying for the Soviet Union and spreading table tennis throughout the world, Montagu was an active filmmaker and founder of various film organizations and institutes. He was a close collaborator of Alfred Hitchcock and contributed significantly to many of Hitchcock's early films. As I said, you can't make this stuff up.

From its origins in Britain in the late 1800s, by the early 1900s table tennis was spreading throughout Europe and had even reached Japan by 1902, evidently courtesy of a Japanese student on his return from England. The game had reached the Americas before that year, but 1902 is notable as the year that the United States found itself in the grip of a ping pong mania. As one advertisement poetically describes:

> That's Ping Pong dear—it's all the rage,
> The Bar, the Church, the House, the Stage,
> All Ping Pong now—it's quite the fashion,
> And you don't know it? (with compassion).
> Such ignorance is quite a shame;
> Come, you shall see us play a game!
> Alas, she saw—she caught the fever—
> (And goodness knew when it would leave her).

The craze, perhaps inevitably, led to a shortage of ping pong balls. Newspaper notices in Chicago announced that precious jewels could be exchanged for ping pong balls and the headline of one article ran: "Chicago Society Dying of Ennui for Want of Ping Pong Balls." But like the Rubik's Cube craze of the early 1980s, the 1902 US ping pong obsession soon faded into history.

Ivor Montagu is credited with bringing the game of ping pong into the modern era. Indeed, he is the founder of the International Table Tennis Federation (ITTF), the world governing body that to this day regulates all international table tennis activity, including tournaments and rules. Founded in 1926, Montagu served as its president for the first forty-one years of its existence and it is hard to overstate his impact.

In the first half of the twentieth century, table tennis tournaments attracted thousands of entrants and tens of thousands of fans. For the modern player, who outside of Asia plays in complete obscurity, the accounts of the popularity and interest in table tennis in the early twentieth century read more like science fiction than history. It is not clear to me how thousands of spectators packed into an arena could see a thirty-eight-millimeter ball, and this was of course before large video monitors were enhancing our experiences at sporting events. Admittedly, the pace of the game was much slower then, but more on that in a moment.

Despite its success and rapid spread throughout the globe, Ivor understood as well as anyone that sports evolve. Maybe it was the fact that in addition to spying, serving as ITTF president, and chumming with Alfred Hitchcock, he was also a zoologist, a vocation he used as a cover when his table tennis activities would not do. Montagu evidently absorbed Darwin's insight that survivorship depends on an organism's ability to adapt and respond to environmental change. He appreciated that there are many pressures—social, political, technological, and economic—that stimulate change in sports.

Ivor's ability to adapt was tested fairly early in his tenure as ITTF president. While most modern changes to table tennis have been aimed at slowing down the world's fastest sport, in the first half of the twentieth century, Ivor faced the opposite problem: the game was too slow. Defensive play, what is known as chopping, chiseling, or pushing, became popular among players, but it wasn't much fun to watch. During the 1936 World Championships in Spain, Arnon Paneth from Romania and Alex Ehrlich, a Polish Jew, decided to force the issue. They agreed that neither player would attack, and while the several thousand fans were initially amused, within a half hour—while still in the first point—many of them began to head for the exits. Ehrlich's teammates set up a chessboard and he called out moves while playing. He also ate his lunch during this first point. Montagu, who was witnessing this charade, called an impromptu meeting of ITTF board members in hopes of instituting a rule change. Montagu and the board returned to the arena two hours after the match began and Paneth and Ehrlich were still in the midst of the first point. The point mercifully ended on a net ball after two hours and thirteen minutes. A clock—a chess clock, actually—was instituted, limiting the length of the match. The remainder took less than ten minutes, with Ehrlich the decisive victor. Incidentally, Ehrlich's success as a player saved his life. While at Auschwitz, despite his emaciated body, Ehrlich was recognized by a Hungarian guard who had seen him play. The guard pulled him from a line entering a gas chamber and Ehrlich ultimately survived the war.

Most modern changes to table tennis are motivated by attempts to make the sport more spectator friendly. Such changes include increasing the size of the ball: not only to make it more visible to spectators, but also to slow the sport down. Other technology-based rule changes are similarly aimed at slowing down the world's fastest game, such as proscribing glues and "boosters" used to attach rubbers to blades that increase the speed of the rubbers. You can look forward to a description of my perilous experiences attaching rubber to a table tennis blade in Appendix B.

Technology is often a major source of innovation in sport, and in table tennis the most significant technological change in the history of the sport occurred in 1952. The scene was the World Championships, held in what was then known as Bombay. Hiroji Satoh was by most accounts the weakest player on the Japanese National Team, yet he captured the 1952 World title with little resistance. Rather than thin pimpled rubber, Satoh glued sponge to his paddle, enabling him to play with more spin and speed than anyone had ever seen before. Despite protests to Montagu from the world's top players, there were no rules—at that point—limiting what could be used as a paddle. The old paddles could not compete with the sponged paddles, and rather quickly nearly all players adopted sponged paddles, although rules ultimately limited the thickness of the sponge permitted. The pre-1952 paddles, known as hard bats, are still used in what is referred to as the "classic game," and some tournaments hold hard-bat events in which sponge paddles are prohibited and classic rules, such as the twenty-one-point scoring system (see notes to Chapter 2), are employed. Satoh made his mark on history, but his moment in the sun was short-lived, as others soon adopted his technological advantage.

Nineteen fifty-two was a pivotal year in the history of table tennis for another reason. In October of that year, Ivor Montagu visited China. Montagu did not bring table tennis to China—the sport had been popular in China for decades prior to his arrival—but it could be claimed that Montagu brought table tennis out of China. Mao had long recognized the importance of physical activity in transforming the Chinese people and their image. Sport would thus naturally ally with politics for Mao throughout his rule. The main problem was that the banishment of Chiang Kai-shek to Taiwan isolated China on the world stage, preventing China from competing in international sport competitions. From Mao's perspective, Taiwan was a province of China, albeit a disobedient one. The West didn't quite see it that way, and Mao's legitimacy was always in question. Montagu came to the rescue.

Montagu had been making discreet overtures to the Chinese since 1950 in hopes of attracting them to the 1952 World Championships. Despite his efforts, the Chinese ignored his intimations; they accurately assessed that they were not ready to compete with the world's top players. To compete demanded victory because winning would not only be a victory for the players and nation; more importantly, it would be a victory for communism. When China ultimately entered international competition, winning is precisely what they did, probably in ways that are unprecedented in the history of modern sport, and table tennis has never been the same.

But in the early 1950s, China would not participate in any organization that openly legitimized Taiwan. Nor would China have official diplomatic relations with any country that had relations with Taiwan. Montagu seems to be one of the few diplomats, if he can accurately be described as such, who was able to circumvent this self-imposed isolationism. He did so by doing what other Westerners were unwilling to do: accede to Chinese demands and sideline Taiwan. As a lifelong ambassador of table tennis, with communist sympathies, he probably found the decision fairly straightforward. Montagu officially welcomed both China and Taiwan into the ITTF, but Taiwan would only be admitted under the name "The Taiwan Province of the People's Republic of China," which was acceptable to the Chinese but not the Taiwanese. China was in; Taiwan was out. To put this in perspective, consider that while China became a member of the ITTF in the 1950s and would ultimately be rewarded with hosting the World Championships in 1961, the 1950s also saw China leave Fédération Internationale de Football Association (FIFA) and the International Olympic Committee (IOC). Sport in China during the 1950s was all about table tennis.

And their single-mindedness paid off. Unexpectedly, in 1959 Rong Guotuan captured China's first Men's Singles World Championship. Twenty-one more Men's World Championships, which since 1957 occur every other year, would follow in the succeeding decades. The only non-Chinese male to win the World Championships in the twenty-first century is Austria's Werner Schlager, who in 2003 stunned the Chinese and the world with an unlikely run to the title. Chinese women would follow with a singles championship of their own, which Qiu Zhonghui captured on Chinese soil at the Beijing World Championships in 1961. The Chinese women have been even more dominant than the men, claiming twenty-three singles championships since then. The last time a non-Chinese woman won the World Championships was 1993; in fact, that was also the last year that a non-Chinese woman made it to the finals. In the last fifty years, there have only been three times that non-Chinese women have been crowned World Champion. World Championships for Men's Doubles, Women's Doubles, Mixed Doubles, and Teams (which consists of three players) are similarly lopsided in favor of the Chinese.

Chinese supremacy in the table tennis world has been so overwhelming that even the Chinese themselves have recognized it is unhealthy for the sport. They are of course not looking to relinquish their dominant status, but they have sought to train players in other countries so at least they have competition. The Chinese authorities also limit the number of players they allow to attend international tournaments. If Chinese players were free to enter any tournament they wished, in truth not only would the Chinese likely win every tournament, but it would also be rare to see a non-Chinese player even reach the semifinals in any event. There are that many good players in China. There is a wonderful story—surely apocryphal—of Sweden's Jan-Ove Waldner hanging around the playing hall late one evening while training in China. The janitor sees him and asks if he wants to play a match. Waldner obliges and in some versions of the story the janitor wins, which can't be true, but the fact that such a story is even told—and I've heard it recounted multiple times—is telling. China is a land in which those who sweep the floors can sweep away an Olympic gold medalist and two-time World Champion.

There are many, many strong players in China, but as everywhere there are limited roster spots on the National Team. Some top players—those who don't become janitors in the national training facility—serve as practice partners for the National Team. Sometimes these players are asked to mimic the styles of other top players in the world, a strategy the Chinese have been employing since at least the 1960s. One of the coaches at the club in Maryland where Eliel often trains during the summer was tasked with impersonating Jan-Ove Waldner. Some believe this coach, Cheng Yinghua, could have been a world champion, but that was not the role the Chinese team designated for him. Many players in recent years, such as Coach Cheng, have immigrated to other countries outside of Asia, immediately becoming the top player in their new home. Coach Cheng, well past his prime by the time of his arrival, captured the US National singles title four times. This Chinese migration pattern was on full display at the 2016 Rio de Janeiro Summer Olympics. More than 30 percent of the competing table tennis players were born in China, and they were representing more than twenty countries. Many Olympians are of course immigrants who represent their new respective homes, but the percentage of athletes born in one country makes table tennis an extreme outlier. There is no other sport dominated by one country the way China dominates table tennis.

SPORTS AS POLITICS BY other means was on full display during the one moment in US history when it appeared that table tennis might break out of the basement. At the 1971 World Championships in Nagoya, Japan, Glenn Cowan, a suburban Jewish hippie from New Rochelle, New York, unwittingly set in motion a series of diplomatic events that was ultimately dubbed "ping pong diplomacy." Like many of his fellow hippies from the sixties, Cowan got on the bus, but the bus he got onto was the bus of the Chinese National Team, which like the buses of all the national teams, was parked outside the playing arena waiting to transport the players to their hotel. As it turns out, what was an accident by Cowan was likely fully orchestrated by the Chinese. On the Chinese bus, three-time World Champion Zhuang Zedong presented Cowan with a gift that included a pin with an image of Mao, which was reciprocated by Cowan on the following day: a Beatles "Let it Be" t-shirt with an American flag displaying a peace symbol in lieu of the stars. Apparently, John Lennon's claim that "if you go carrying pictures of Chairman Mao, you ain't going to make it with anyone anyhow" was not quite right after all.

Following these encounters—Cowan's return gift was offered rather publicly—Zhou Enlai, the People's Republic of China's first Premier, extended an invitation to the US National Team to visit China after the World Championships, an unprecedented gesture at the time. The US State Department approved the travel and these unknown table tennis players—a computer analyst, professor, UN worker, dental assistant, and high-school and college students—were thrust into history. Despite a few hiccups, such as food poisoning, drug smuggling, and an entanglement with a prostitute, these unlikely ambassadors played their roles without major incident. Upon their return to the US, Nixon and Kissinger invited the Chinese National Team for an American tour. The diplomacy was a political success by most historical accounts; a dialogue between two countries without diplomatic relations was initiated. It was hoped that table tennis would ride its newfound exposure to success as well, popularizing the neglected sport.

It was not to be. The tour of the Chinese team was covered by the national media and some of the exhibitions were telecast on ABC's *Wide World of Sports*, the premier sporting program prior to the rise of ESPN. Eleven thousand fans packed Cobo Hall in Detroit, a place where I regularly competed as a teenager, but never with such a crowd. Sizable crowds also watched exhibition matches in California and at the Universities of Michigan and Maryland. But the US sporting world was not revolutionized by these events. Following the departure of the Chinese, American sports fans returned to football and baseball. American table tennis players returned to their invisible subculture. Cowan sought to capitalize on his fame, briefly appearing on various national talk shows, such as *The Dinah Shore Show* and *The Phil Donahue Show*. But interest in Cowan, like table tennis, quickly faded. Sadly, his life spiraled downward. He was unable to maintain employment and he ultimately wound up homeless on Venice Beach in California. He passed away, largely forgotten, in 2004.

"Ping pong diplomacy" was not the last time that table tennis would be used to heal political wounds. In 1991, North and South Korea—formally at war with each other—played as a unified team at the World Championships in Chiba, Japan. The unified Women's Team stunned the Chinese to capture the title. Over the last three decades the North and South Korean teams have united at various other tournaments as well, most recently in 2018. Table tennis is not the only sport in which Koreans have joined forces, but because of the political history of table tennis, the unification of the Korean table tennis teams had deep resonance among players and observers. Politics and table tennis do mix. While Mao saw table tennis in terms of political warfare, describing it as China's "spiritual nuclear weapon," it is Montagu's legacy which is most likely, I hope, to endure. For him, table tennis was "a weapon for peace."

MY TABLE TENNIS LIFE with Eliel did not begin on this grand international stage, although Eliel would eventually compete in international tournaments. Our journey out of the basement, my final one, began modestly and locally.

CHAPTER 4

For the Love of the Sport

On a whim I typed "table tennis clubs in Massachusetts" into Google, probably misspelling my home state, as I usually do. I wish I had a sense at that moment how this simple act of curiosity would change my life. But of course, at the time it was just one of the thousands of things I've typed into Google (frighteningly, Google can confirm this). The moment was not built up by dramatic music in the background—Dylan was likely playing on my turntable—nor were there bolts of lightning from the heavens. An ordinary moment on an ordinary day.

To my surprise, one of the table tennis club listings was in the same facility where Eliel attended soccer camp, or as we like to think of it, one of his favorite places to break an arm. It was also a popular place for his classmates to hold birthday parties, so the next time we were there I inquired about their table tennis club. As it turned out, they no longer had a table tennis "class," as they called it, but they were able to give me the contact information of the man who ran the class.

His name was Mozart. First name, in case you were unsure. I was. As a teacher I encounter an extraordinary diversity of names—an embarrassingly high percentage of which I cannot pronounce—but in my life I had never come across someone, with the exception of the musical prodigy, named Mozart. To be clear, I am not judging Mozart's parents on their name choice for their son. If anything, the evidence would suggest that I'm a huge fan of unusual names. Most people, including my mother, find my children's names to be not only unusual, but unpronounceable. While we are on the subject, Eliel is a three-syllable name pronounced: the letter L, the letter E, the letter L. If I had a dollar for every mispronunciation of his name, he might be playing tennis instead of table tennis.

I called Mozart and he told me his club had not disbanded, but rather relocated. His new club was actually closer to our home, in the neighboring town only four miles away. I inquired about the level of play and he assured me that players at all levels would be welcome. The club met twice a week at a fitness center and he invited me to stop by and play. I asked Eliel if he would be interested in checking it out, and he was.

New social situations make me nervous; actually, all social situations make me nervous. I am fully aware that this is an unfortunate trait for a professional anthropologist. While we are on the subject of traits that do not help my professional life, I'm not only terrified of humans, especially in large numbers; I'm terrified of public speaking. More than twenty years of standing in front of classrooms of students has not diminished that terror, at least not much. So it is a fair question to ask how I got into this business: Why would I choose to study people? And if I was so compelled to study humans because I find them to be such curious creatures, why on earth would I study them employing a methodology that requires social interaction? The truth is, it was the theoretical aspects of anthropology that captured my imagination. Humans are indeed a puzzle to me: Why is Frodo an appropriate name for a pet, but as my wife assured me, not for a child? Why aren't elven cloaks fashionable? And why aren't we all living in hobbit holes? Admittedly, anthropology has not solved these enduring mysteries, but it did offer some theories that helped me understand other behaviors of my conspecifics.

Or it might have been the beards. After beginning college as an engineering student and realizing that I didn't want to spend my life on a computer—mind you, this was before the age of the personal computer—I went through various majors until in my junior year I was intrigued by one of my anthropology courses. I decided to attend a lecture in the anthropology department's speaker series that was being delivered by my favorite professor. I'd like to say the talk was so brilliant that it changed my life and inspired me to become an anthropologist. The lecture probably was brilliant, but as an undergraduate I didn't understand much of it. Nonetheless, I did notice that all the men in the room were sporting beards. So was I, and I realized that I felt comfortable in such a crowd. I had found an academic home.

I mention all this because although I normally would have been terrified to enter a new social situation, I realized as I was driving to the club that I was not anxious. I was too busy being excited. Although I had no idea what awaited us at the end of our four-mile drive, I had a sense that I was returning to a comfort zone I had not known in a long time. The world of table tennis had changed dramatically—in equipment, rules, and clientele—since the last time I had been to a club in the early 1990s, but at the time I was unaware of these changes. I had been to many clubs in my youth, so I thought I knew exactly what to expect.

And indeed, the club was not all that different from the club I attended regularly as a teenager, at least in terms of the physical space. Rather than a community college campus, this club was located on the second floor of a fitness center. But both clubs were situated in dance studios that held four tables.

After being escorted upstairs and through a long corridor, we opened a door and found ourselves in the middle of one of the long sides of a rectangular room. The entrance was immediately in the playing area, between the two middle tables; consequently, when members would enter the club, balls would sometimes exit, sending players chasing down the hallway to retrieve them. The long wall opposite the entrance was entirely mirrored. This was convenient for watching yourself shadow-stroke (after a missed shot, of course) but less convenient for tracking the ball, as sometimes the ball's reflection, or your opponent's reflection, would confuse matters. The ceiling was high, which was wonderful for lobbing, and the floor was a soft and lightly colored wood that I would later appreciate as being easy on my knees. The room was much cleaner and brighter than the club I grew up in. I did not realize it at the time, but I had stumbled across the best playing conditions in the Boston area. Technically, I should probably say second best, but the club with the best playing conditions at that time was located in a renovated warehouse without heat or air conditioning, which made it unplayable for much of the year. Boston is not San Diego.

One table was separated from the other three with a row of barriers. Dozens of balls were on the floor of this court, and it was clear this was the space where Mozart gave lessons. There were no barriers between the other tables. Folding chairs were set up against the long non-mirrored wall where we had entered. The width of the room was large enough that players could sit at the ends of the courts without interference, even without barriers. I would later learn to situate my seat strategically so that I did not spend the evening catching winners or missed balls.

There were no kids, just Asian and Russian men, and Mozart, who is from Haiti. One of the Chinese men introduced himself in broken English and asked if we wanted to play. They freed up a table so that I could hit with Eliel, but after a bit I moved to one of the other tables and one of the men kindly agreed to hit with Eliel. When I began to hit on the other table the club members could see that I was a player—or at least had been a player—not just one of the many basement enthusiasts to pass through the club with his children. These folks show up once, maybe twice, recognize that neither they nor their child will be magically transformed into a tournament player, and return to the basement from whence they came to continue as king of their neighborhood. Some things about table tennis haven't changed in forty years.

After Mozart's lesson he invited Eliel to hit with him. He showed him how to hit his forehand and how to correctly position his feet. Eliel was definitely enjoying himself, but I was wary. I worried that Mozart was only hitting with Eliel so that he would sign up for lessons, but at sixty dollars an hour that was not an option for us. We were raising four kids and sending them to Jewish day schools; private lessons for anything were not feasible. My wariness, however, was not only unfounded, but in hindsight I find it shameful. Mozart loved the sport and while he did make a living coaching, he was also endlessly generous with his time and knowledge. Over the next several years he never hesitated to hit with Eliel and instruct him, and he never asked for a dime. Mozart could be tough and a little impatient with his students, including Eliel, but there was never a doubt that he cared. For years at tournaments other players and parents would ask whom Eliel took lessons with and I would answer honestly that he had never taken a private lesson. But in truth, Mozart was giving him free lessons almost every time we went to the club. Remarkably, this pattern has continued. Just yesterday we were at the club we now regularly attend, which I'll describe later, and Eliel cumulatively hit for four hours with the two coaches at the club, in between their lessons to paying customers. The head coach worked with Eliel extensively to keep his elbow up on his backhand, which is a problem he has been trying to fix for several months.

In his youth, Mozart played on the Haitian National Team and after his competitive days he served as the head coach for the team. He began playing when he was eight years old and has never stopped since. Sort of. By last count, he's been forced to stop at least nine times for shoulder, wrist, and knee surgeries. Ever since we've known him he has played with pain, but he rarely complains. Retiring, even briefly, to let his body heal is unthinkable. Surgery rather than rest has always been the solution.

In 1985, while in his late twenties, he came to the US and decided he wanted to share his love for the sport with others. At that time the number of full-time table tennis coaches in the country could probably be counted on two hands. Mozart has founded several clubs that have moved around the Boston area, and his two extant clubs are now incorporated as the Boston Table Tennis Academy. The club by our house is essentially the satellite club. His main club is closer to the center of Boston, but he had some students in our area, so with their help he opened this local club on Monday and Thursday evenings. The other five days he spends at his main club, which meets in the gym of an elementary school.

Mozart's munificence is not limited to his adopted country. He regularly returns to Haiti to run school programs to promote and teach table tennis to underprivileged Haitian youth. In 2017, Mozart founded the USA Friends of Association Haitienne de Tennis de Table. The goal of the association is to provide support to the AHTT, which opened the first sports center in Haiti where children could play table tennis. The center provides children with food, clean water, and a safe space to meet. They have also been instrumental in organizing leagues and providing coaching at the center as well as at schools. For more than twenty years the AHTT has supplied Haitian schools with table tennis equipment, including tables.

Eliel is not expressive, but during the car ride home he made it clear that he would like to return to the club. And so we did. Again, again, and again. We were regulars at the club for several years, attending two evenings a week, and occasionally they would open up the room for us on Sunday. The other men unreservedly hit with Eliel and he quickly improved.

LIKE ALL TABLE TENNIS clubs, this club had its share of personalities. While the club we currently play at is curiously filled with software engineers, this club, inexplicably, had an inordinate number of radiologists. The most talented player at the club, one of the radiologists, was a Korean man, Benjamin, who was debilitated by a degenerative muscular disease. He was in constant pain and could not move while at the table, but he compensated for his lack of movement with extraordinary hand speed. Benjamin couldn't practice much because hitting the same shot over and over—the essence of practice—was too painful. He could play matches, but rarely did he have the strength to play two in a row. Unfortunately, during our time at the club his condition worsened until he was unable to play at all, which was tragic for many obvious reasons. While he was able to play, he constantly spoke about his love for the game and although it was physically painful to play, he insisted it was worth it. His wife could not understand his devotion to the game, but I could. I imagine that all activities have some addictive potential, yet I also presume that some activities have greater potential for addiction than others. Our hardwiring seems to make many of us susceptible to overuse of Facebook, email, and certain video games because of the constant positive feedback we receive (likes, messages, killing zombies, etc.). Table tennis might provide such repetitive positive feedback when winning points. Moreover, I suspect there is meditative comfort when hitting the same stroke over and over.

Addiction or not, Benjamin had a deep love for the game. Throughout the time he played he had a friendly but fierce rivalry with Eliel. At first he would spot Eliel points, but as Eliel improved and Benjamin's condition worsened, the roles reversed and Eliel would give him a seven-point lead in an eleven-point game. In addition to being a good player, Benjamin was also one of the nicest people I've ever met inside or outside the table tennis world. He is a *tzaddik* (a righteous person), which is a label I do not bestow lightly. Indeed, I typically reserve it for my children, using it as a term of endearment. Benjamin, however, possesses an unquenchable optimism that brightens everything around him, making the world a better place. The term *tzaddik* implies a sense of holiness and, in my mind, there is nothing holier than improving the world around you—intentionally or unintentionally—so I think Benjamin is deserving of the appellation.

One of Benjamin's fellow radiologists was the Chinese man, Donghai, who first greeted us. His English was unpolished, and throughout our time at Mozart's club he would ask us the meaning of English words. He was an all-or-nothing offensive player with a wicked forehand smash. Whenever he hit a forehand winner he would quickly exclaim "Lucky!" If this happened every once in a while you might believe him, but he could win five points in a row, blowing each ball by you with his vicious forehand, and after each one he would shake his head, hold up his hand as a gesture of apology, and say "Lucky!" I said to him many times that an occasional winner might be lucky, but he hit such shots routinely so it could hardly be luck. I assumed his exclamations were expressions of his characteristic humility, but in this case I think there was a translation issue. Chinese and American concepts of luck are not identical. When an American describes something as lucky they are referring to a quality that is random and beyond control. But if my Chinese friends have not misled me—and I would not be the first anthropologist to be misled by informants—the Chinese concept of luck acknowledges that skill can create luck. This would also explain a comment frequently heard at tournaments when a player wins or loses because of an imbalance of unreturnable net and edge balls. Better players, it is acknowledged, get more nets and edges.

As it turns out, others have made a similar observation regarding different conceptions of luck. In *The Metaphysics of Ping-Pong*, Guido Mina di Sospiro writes:

... if a Western player deliberately chooses to execute a particularly technically challenging shot, and if that shot does land on the table, in his view it has nothing to do with luck, but everything to do with skill. For Chinese players, on the other hand, the concepts of "lucky" and "deliberate" aren't mutually exclusive. In their view, a technically demanding but deliberate shot that works is, in fact, a lucky shot. It's a high-risk shot that paid off, and luck had its part in it. So it seems that for a Chinese mindset accidentality and causality are still interrelated, precisely as described by the I *Ching*.

Donghai's passion for table tennis rivaled Benjamin's. When Donghai inevitably tore his rotator cuff while hitting one of his patented forehand smashes—probably for a winner, but obviously not lucky this time—he stopped playing for a few weeks after his surgery. Nonetheless, he would still visit the club twice a week, just to be around table tennis. Spectatorship wouldn't last, however. One day, with his right arm in a sling, he began to play left-handed. We tried to discourage him since we didn't want him further injuring himself, but our pleas fell on deaf ears. He missed the game too much and couldn't tolerate not playing. He played left-handed for nearly a year, and quite respectably toward the end, until his right arm healed. He was not the last table tennis enthusiast I met who, after injuring their playing arm—sometimes permanently—learned to play with the opposite hand.

The only drama in this club involved one of the Russian players, Igor, affectionately known as Iggy. Like all the Russian players, Iggy was Jewish. An accountant by trade, Iggy was in his mid-sixties when we met, but he had the physique of a twenty-five-year-old. Not an ounce of fat, just muscle. Russian men at every club I have visited like to bare their chests. Not all of them should, but if I had a chest like Iggy I wouldn't even bother owning shirts. Aside from being a fitness freak, Iggy was always reading something interesting—history, science, philosophy, or religion—and he would regularly ask me whether I had read his current book; if not, he would launch into a detailed synopsis. I'm an avid reader, so his oral reviews were greatly appreciated. He introduced me to a number of good books, and hopefully he enjoyed a few of my recommendations as well.

Some players compete like they are playing in the World Championships. Mozart *did* play in the World Championships, but he is not one of those players. Iggy is. Envisioning yourself at the World Championships is actually an excellent approach to competition if you wish to win, and the point of competition, usually, is to win. The problem is, most players who compete at a club do so, not only for the competitive excitement of winning and losing, but also for comradery and exercise. And there is a fine line between playing competitively and playing too competitively. Iggy's competitiveness, occasionally, would cross that line. Everyone wants an opponent to play his or her best, but a club match should not be so serious that it is no longer fun. Iggy demanded a lot of himself, and when he would lose points he would become frustrated, often blaming himself, but sometimes blaming others, especially those who were talking too loudly and disturbing his concentration. Players learned quickly to keep their voices down and not enter his playing area if their ball happened to bounce there. Every so often, conversations were too loud and Iggy would just leave in frustration. There were definitely players who tired of his outbursts, particularly those who liked to schmooze.

Mozart was not blind to the drama, but he and Iggy were longtime friends and Mozart was able to separate Iggy's behavior on the court from his behavior as a person. Mozart is clearly one of those fortunate souls who sees the good in everyone. And yes, these people are fortunate—seeing the bad in others, at least in my experience, invariably leads to a cranky day. One of my rabbinic inspirations, Levi Yitzchak of Berditchev, was evidently incapable of seeing faults in anyone. One Levi Yitzchak story, among the many I used to share with my kids on Shabbos, relates:

> On the eve of the holiest day of the Jewish Year, Yom Kippur, when Jews repent their sins while fasting from food and drink, Levi Yitzchak was walking to synagogue with his *gabbai* (helper) when they got caught in a downpour. They took cover in the overhang of a tavern until the storm passed. Through the window, the *gabbai* noticed two Jews with questionable reputations eating and drinking in the tavern, seemingly oblivious to the oncoming fast. The *gabbai* commented on their audacity but Levi Yitzchak dismissed the remark.
>
> "They are surely eating heartily to prepare for the fast."
>
> "Rabbi, I don't think so" the *gabbai* countered. "I can hear them talking and they are boasting to each other about recent burglaries they have committed!"
>
> Levi Yitzchak admiringly exclaimed, "What holy Jews they are! They are obviously confessing their sins before the holiday!"

Not judging people for how they behave in the heat of competition is an important skill in the table tennis world, one that I have had ample opportunity to cultivate. I try my best to emulate Mozart's example, but I struggle, especially with certain people. It seems to come naturally, though, to Eliel. I wish I could claim he inherited his generous view of humanity from me, or that he is like this because of my parenting prowess, or even better, due to my storytelling and anthropological preaching. But I know it is not so—since early childhood he has always been trusting and kindhearted. It is me who learns how to see the good in others from him, rather than the other way around.

Back to the club. Each of these players, as well as the other club members we would eventually get to know, utterly amazed me. Not as players, but as human beings. Eliel and I were the only regular players at the club who were born in the US, so each of them experienced the challenges of life as an immigrant. Some came here when they were young; others attended college here and never left. On more than one evening I feigned being too tired to play so I could just sit and listen to their extraordinary stories. What these men accomplished in successfully building their lives in this country is nothing short of a miracle. Or maybe more accurately, it is Chinese luck. Frankly, I felt quite small in their presence, even though I was physically taller and actually a better player than all of them.

The club, sadly, is now essentially defunct. When I last spoke to one of the Russian radiologists he told me the tables were still there and Mozart occasionally goes to the club, to give a lesson or play with another Haitian player. Unfortunately, table tennis did not bring in enough money—a theme I hear at every club in the US—so the owner of the fitness center rented out the dance studio to a yoga class and moved table tennis to another room. But the new room had carpeting, dim lighting, and insufficient space. In the blink of an eye the club went from having the best playing conditions in the area to the worst.

By the time of the room change Eliel and I were no longer regulars at the club. I suspect when Eliel gets older he will have fond memories and appreciation of this club, Mozart, and the other men who nurtured his interest in table tennis, similar to the sentiments I have for the first club I regularly attended. But Eliel needed better competition; hence began my life in the car and my continuing battle with Boston traffic as I take Eliel to more distant clubs. We spend an inordinate amount of time together in the car, not just navigating Boston traffic, but driving up and down the East Coast for tournaments and training opportunities. We typically pass the endless car hours by listening to *The Lord of the*

Rings trilogy, again and again. Of course we know the ending, but like the stories my mother tells at every family gathering, the enjoyment is in the listening; some tales never get old. We believe *The Lord of the Rings* should be read on an annual cycle, similar to the way Jews read the Torah. Eliel, with layers of irony, refers to *The Lord of the Rings* as The Good Book.

So, what sparked Eliel's enthusiasm on that first evening at the club? He didn't see twenty table tennis tables spread across a large gymnasium, the sight that left me speechless. He saw four, yet he was equally smitten. Eliel will tell his own story someday—his recent response to my query was his patented shoulder shrug—but I think he was attracted to the club because there were no other kids there. It is not that Eliel dislikes humans his own size and age—somehow, he seems to like everybody. Rather, being in an environment without children suggested to him that this sport was serious. Indeed. Players at Mozart's club had fun, but like every club I have ever visited, they were constantly trying to improve so there was a seriousness to their play. Eliel seems to have observed and understood that aspect of the table tennis scene, and he liked what he saw. With such observational skills, maybe a life in anthropology awaits? As it turns out, excepting Mozart, Eliel's dedication to table tennis has been more serious than that of anyone who was there that first evening. But before further exploring Eliel's journey in the world of table tennis, we should take a brief tutorial, filling in some details about competitive play in this magnificent yet marginalized sport.

CHAPTER 5

A Guide for the Perplexed: Serves, Sounds, and Status

Most people who change their residence based on the season fly south for the winter and return north for the summer. Our family, however, had a habit of reverse migrating. That is, we are New Englanders who headed southward in the summer. The reason is simple: air conditioning. My sister and her husband, who lived in Maryland, had it and we didn't. So, until their recent move up north, we always visited their bi-species family during the hottest weeks of the summer. In addition to the comfortable air conditioning, we enjoyed the countless museums Washington DC offers, free family haircuts courtesy of my brother-in-law (he is not a barber, but he was willing and we are not too discerning), and constant entertainment of the various canines my sister brings home from the dog shelter she volunteers at.

And yes, although I'm not a dog-person I've come to appreciate that dogs are endlessly entertaining, at least in comparison to my staid Israeli-born cat, Jumpy. Maybe it's because dogs, as archaeologists inform us, have been domesticated for nearly twice as long as cats—more time to breed for a sense of humor? Whatever the reason, for the promise of a treat my cat would never dance, chase his tail, or adorably tilt his head bearing an endearing expression; indeed, he scoffs at such self-abasement. Jumpy is a mice-exterminator, not an entertainer. Nor has my cat ever eaten anyone's underwear and then regurgitated it days later at the kennel, obliging one of the employees to sheepishly ask, "Umm ... sir, would you like your wife's underwear back?" Only life with a dog can furnish such experiences.

One day while at my sister's home, after our daily dose of dog amusement, Eliel and I got online to see if there were any table tennis clubs in the area. We discovered, to our good fortune, that one of the premier clubs in the country, the Maryland Table Tennis Center (MDTTC), was located near her home. While the rest of the family continued to play with the dogs and museum-hop during our visits, Eliel and I invariably headed to MDTTC where he would attend summer training camps. And our trips to stay at my sister's home got longer and longer each summer—or as we would say, they became two-haircut visits.

IN ONE OF ELIEL'S early camp sessions, the coach asked the players: "What is the most important shot in table tennis?" A campmate confidently responded that the forehand loop is the most important shot. Indeed, as mentioned earlier, one dividing line between basement players and tournament players is the development of a strong forehand, especially a forehand loop. So this response to the coach was not unwarranted. But it was incorrect.

That's because it was a trick question and coaches, like professors, know that trick questions are useful educational tools for creating therapy-inducing self-doubt among students. The correct answer is the serve, which most players understandably do not think of as a shot. Technically, however, it is, and as coaches correctly point out, a player's serve begins half the points of the match. It is the one moment in each rally that one of the players can entirely dictate the shot. Of course, the corollary to this is that the second most important shot in table tennis is the service return.

Unfortunately for beginners, serving and returning serves takes years of practice just to become mildly competent. Back in New England, an entrepreneurial father and his two sons often organize tournaments at large local companies, bringing tables to the workplace. Before the tournaments the sons give an exhibition, and as part of their routine the father holds up a crisp one-hundred-dollar bill and offers it to anyone who can return one of his sons' serves. They've been using the same bill since they started giving exhibitions. The challenge of returning serves is reading the spin. For a beginner, the service spins of advanced players are extremely "heavy" and the ball simply flies uncontrollably off the racket. In my experience, the extraordinary amount of spin on competitive players' serves never fails to shock novices. But even once a player becomes accustomed to the heaviness of service spins, serves are still difficult to read because opponents use various deceptions to disguise the spin they are imparting to the ball. For top players, the same service stroke can produce topspin, underspin, or no spin, depending on where they contact the ball in the stroke, as well as where they contact the ball on their paddle. Service motions are quick, so for the untrained eye it is very difficult to see where contact is being made. Indeed, even advanced players can be fooled, so returners often rely on multiple cues, assessing service spin from the sound of contact, as well as the trajectory of the first bounce on the table. The second bounce is less helpful because by then it is too late to react.

Returning serves is so challenging, in fact, that the ITTF has regularly instituted new rules to help receiving players, which also makes the game more watchable. Fans want to see rallies, not missed service returns. Service rule changes over the last few decades include requiring the ball to be tossed at least sixteen centimeters (about the height of the net) before contact. Moreover, the toss has to be from a completely open palm and must be nearly vertical, without any spin imparted from the server's hand. As it turns out, it is extremely difficult to return serves when an opponent has a spinny toss. A former Chinese National Team member, Olympic quarterfinalist, and one of the most decorated players to ever play for the US National Team, is regularly accused of tossing the ball with spin. I've seen verbal fights break out during more than one of her matches. One year at the US Nationals, after a heated argument with the umpire about her service toss, she simply walked off the court and right out of the tournament, defaulting her quarterfinal match. She hasn't won over fans by these uncomfortable episodes, but in my mind her unprecedented accomplishments as a US table tennis player entitle her to a little petulance. I grew up rooting for John McEnroe; with his theatrics as my benchmark, most table tennis competitors seem tame.

Heated arguments appear to be the unintended, but primary, consequence of one particular service rule change: servers are not allowed to shield the point of contact of the serve with their body or non-playing hand. Prior to instituting this rule, skilled players would essentially contact the ball behind their bodies and move out of the way after contact. Needless to say, if you can't see the contact point, it is nearly impossible to return the serve.

But this rule is very difficult to enforce, thus it is a continual point of contention at tournaments. Players regularly complain, especially after losses, that servers are "hiding the ball." Video replays have recently been used to assess service visibility on the World Tour, which has helped considerably, at least among professionals. But without video replay, two additional officials—beyond the standard umpire and scorekeeper—are needed to effectively enforce the rule. Umpires and scorekeepers sit opposite each other across the long sides of the table, so they have a poor angle to determine whether a player is shielding his or her serve. To monitor serves, the additional officials are positioned behind each player outside the court, securing a view similar to that of the service returner. But most US tournaments do not have the resources to employ four officials per match. Arguments inevitably ensue, and Eliel has had his share. Despite his quiet demeanor, from an early age Eliel firmly advocated for himself when he thought servers were hiding the ball. His steadfastness and confidence in these animated debates has always surprised and impressed me.

Serves are incredibly variable. There are some standards, such as the "pendulum," "tomahawk," and "shovel" serves (the names reflect the arm motions of the server), but good players also put their unique stamp on whatever serves they use. For me, the evolution of serves has been a blessing in disguise. When I returned to the sport after twenty-five years away from competitive play, my slower body and mind were unwelcome limitations. In contrast, my twenty-five-year-old serves turned out to be an advantage, especially when playing younger competitors who are not regularly exposed to old-fashioned serves. I've watched the father who holds the hundred-dollar bill beat higher rated Juniors (players under eighteen years old) because they were unable to return his windshield wiper serve, in which his service arm moves quickly from right to left in the motion of a windshield wiper. I once had this serve in my arsenal as well, but the serve requires a vigorous knee bend to maximize the spin, and the strain on my knees forced me to give it up. Every once in a while I'll pretend I'm fifteen years old again and try it, only to be scolded by my unforgiving knees and a caring teenager who needs a bipedal practice partner.

One counterintuitive service technique employed at the highest level of play is the no-spin, or dead ball, serve. Elite players are accustomed to heavy spins, and they can use those spins against the servers themselves. But no-spin balls, especially if they are unanticipated, don't give the opponent any spin to work with. Such serves are easily popped up or hit off the table, so top players, including Eliel, regularly mix no-spin serves into their repertoire. I've had my fair share of mishaps with no-spin serves. They look so easy to return; it is as though the ball is tempting you, taunting you: "Here I am! Just hit me!" Being mocked by a spinless table tennis ball, as you overhit it off the table, is utterly demeaning. But I am usually comforted by the knowledge that my size-thirteen feet have spent a lifetime flattening many of its forebearers, and that is the likely fate of any ball that goads me. Revenge is sweet, although it can get expensive.

Competitive players regularly spend time during their training sessions with a bucket of several dozen balls, serving to no one but the floor. One of Eliel's friends from Chicago, another top Junior, practices his serves for a half hour before school every morning. And many top players bring a bag of balls to tournaments to practice their serves before each match. Players are constantly tinkering with their serves, trying new variants and honing their regular serves. Serving is one of the most fun (because it offers the potential for genuine creativity) and frustrating (because returning other players' creativity can be a headache) aspects of the game. Life is never straightforward.

Just as serves evolved during my absence from the game, service returns have developed in ways that were unimaginable several decades ago. The changes are aptly described as fruity, which will make sense in a moment. Although throughout the twentieth century novices learning the sport of table tennis were regularly disabused of basement tendencies to hit backhands from the forehand side of the table, at some point in the 2000s, players began to disregard the wisdom of the sages. It is not clear who initially developed the shot—like any good story, there are competing narratives—but former World and Olympic champion, Zhang Jike, is credited with mastering what is known as the *banana flip*. The shot gets its name from the motion of the paddle in which a player hits a backhand, with their elbow up and wrist down, fully rotating the wrist in a crescent-like or banana-shaped motion while grazing the ball. The shot is used to impart topspin on an underspin serve, enabling players to return short underspin serves with an offensive shot.

Notably, players use this backhand service return everywhere on the table, including serves to the forehand side, which had previously been unthinkable since it was believed that a player would be out of position for the return, exposing his wide backhand side. But banana flips can be spinny and powerful, so players are able to control the point with a good banana flip and recover their position on the table, even when executing the flip on the forehand side. Indeed, Eliel can devour my serves with his banana flip, and all the current top players now regularly use this service return.

Some players have added a variant of the banana known as the *strawberry*, in which the wrist moves in the opposite direction of the banana flip. Mima Ito, Japanese star and the only genuine threat to complete Chinese hegemony in the women's game, has the most effective strawberry on the World Tour. Nobody seems to have a good explanation for why it is called a strawberry; someone evidently wanted to keep with the fruity theme. One of my favorite older players, who has refused to adopt these new strokes, regularly yells at opponents when they try such shots on him, "Get that fruit out of here!"

THERE ARE SOME ASPECTS of table tennis, like all sports, that cannot be taught directly; rather, they must be experienced and perceived. The study of sensory perception—how we perceive the world around us—understandably falls under the domain of psychology. But anthropologists have also spent considerable time studying the senses, specifically trying to understand how our cultural surroundings influence our sensory perceptions. We can easily appreciate how growing up in different cultures leads to associations with certain tastes, resulting in diverse food preferences. Nor are we surprised, as many anthropologists have documented, that hunter-gatherers can see things on the forest floor—such as evidence that a jaguar passed this location about three hours ago—that those of us who did not grow up in the forest simply cannot see. But as some anthropologists have argued, different cultures emphasize and develop sensory perceptions that most of us do not even recognize are possible. For example, anthropologist Nathaniel Roberts describes how during his fieldwork in impoverished Indian slums, people in the community could tell with uncanny accuracy when he had not eaten for a while. They claimed they could see it in his eyes. At first he assumed it was coincidence, but it happened far too often throughout his fieldwork to be mere coincidence. Moreover, when they pointed out that he looked hungry, they were never wrong in recognizing that he was long overdue for a meal. This was even the case when he himself had not realized it; on many occasions he was so caught up in his work that he simply forgot to eat.

Like the community Roberts worked with, elite-level table tennis players seem to know the unknowable. Table tennis is obviously a game of vision, but players are not just watching the ball. Similar to tennis and badminton athletes, table tennis players are using cues from their opponents' body movements to determine where the ball will be hit. Baseball hitters and boxers do the same in order to prepare for a pitch or a punch. In table tennis, most shots leave too little time to respond if a player waits until the ball is hit before reacting. One of the most extraordinary—and uncomfortable—experiences of playing a table tennis professional is that they always seem to be ready and waiting for your shot *before you even hit the ball*. Through hours of practice, professionals are able to determine where a ball will be hit just by observing an opponent's preparation for a shot. This is why the Japanese professionals that Eliel played, whom I described earlier, were able to be in position with their forehands on every shot. Yes, they had exceptional footwork, but it was their ability to read Eliel's body movements that allowed them to use their superior footwork to such great effect.

A GUIDE FOR THE PERPLEXED: SERVES, SOUNDS, AND STATUS

But table tennis is not just a game of vision; it is also a game of sound. When my daughter Aviva first went to see Eliel play in a tournament, she commented that the most striking aspect of the day was how violently the players stomp on the floor. This was an interesting observation since I had assumed that she would be most amazed by the extreme speed at which the sport is played. However, I guess she had anticipated the fast pace but was unprepared for the noise of the stomping, which players do, especially on serves, in order to cloak the sound of the paddle contacting the ball.

Competitive players, it turns out, use both sight and sound to read the amount of spin on every shot. The ball coming off a racket makes different sounds depending on how much the ball has been grazed. Or as players like to say, "you can hear how much wood is on the ball." A lightly grazed ball will generate a lot of spin, whereas a ball that is not grazed—that gets more wood—will be flatter. Competitive players use sound to help read the amount of spin on the ball. And many players will complain about not being able to hear the ball in certain venues, usually because of the acoustics and too many players playing within a confined space. Table tennis players have no shortage of excuses for losing.

The other notable sounds that fill tournament halls are celebrations after winning a point. Eliel is a muted player, rarely showing any expression, but in recent years I've been making up for his reticence, cheering a bit too loudly when he wins a point. By far the most common exclamation heard at tournaments is the Chinese expression "*Hao qiu!*", which literally means "Good ball!" Yes, a little self-congratulatory, but a literal translation doesn't fully capture its meaning in the context of a match. Anthropologists have long observed that dominant societies tend to spread their cultural practices, and this is definitely true in the table tennis world; everybody copies whatever the Chinese are doing. Although "*Hao qiu!*" obviously began with Chinese players, today players of all ethnicities—most of whom do not speak a word of Chinese—shout "*Hao qiu!*" after a triumphant shot. I considered attempting to start a trend by shouting "Mazel tov!" and dancing a little *horah* after Eliel's victorious points, but I thought better of it.

A COACH WOULDN'T BOTHER to explain the rating system to his or her new students; in fact, the coaches at Eliel's summer camps in Maryland often told players not to worry about ratings. This is something I repeatedly stressed with Eliel and thankfully the message sunk in. But on this matter he is unusual, particularly among Junior players. For better or worse, players often worry about their ratings; indeed, how the rating system works is one of the first things that new players learn from their friends.

While sporting communities create social bonds—brotherhoods, sisterhoods, and deep lifelong friendships—they are not egalitarian. Sporting communities are about competition, and competition breeds hierarchies. Well, that is usually the case. Nineteenth and twentieth century colonization has brought native peoples many unsolicited Western cultural "gifts" such as political structures, economic organizations, transportation infrastructures, religions, foods, and, last but not least, sports. Interestingly, while in the West we think of competition as a—if not *the*—core feature of sport, when sports were introduced to many indigenous populations, they embraced the sporting activities of the colonizing culture but not the competitive nature of the sports. In a classic anthropological example, Trobriand Islanders of Papua New Guinea adopted cricket, but they adapted the sport to suit Trobriand culture, treating it as a ritual rather than a competition. In Trobriand cricket, there is no limit on team size so entire villages can compete against each other. And home-field advantage takes on new meaning among the Trobrianders. In Trobriand cricket the home village is *always* the victor. The home village is also responsible for throwing the post-match celebratory feast, which is attended by both teams; thus, there is some logic to this practice—it's hard to imagine the Red Sox throwing a party for the Yankees at Fenway after losing to them. Trobriand reconfigurations of cricket are not unique. In other places where cricket has been introduced the competitors play until the score is *tied*. In our culture, of course, even beer pong is competitive. But I digress.

In table tennis, a player's level of play is quantified through ratings. Quantification, as historian Allen Guttmann argues in his landmark study *From Ritual to Record*, is the sine qua non of modern sports. And quantification is getting more sophisticated from year to year. Don't get me started on how sabermetrics is ruining baseball.

In table tennis tournaments, players gain rating points when victorious—the higher the rating of the opponent, the more points—and lose rating points accordingly when defeated. For all the problems with the current rating system, it is a vast improvement over the previous ranking system in the US. In 2017 I met the creator of the US rating system, Jack Howard, while visiting the Las Vegas Table Tennis Club. As I'll discuss in Chapter 9, we were there so Eliel could acclimate to the conditions in Vegas prior to the US Nationals. I knew of Jack Howard through stories and articles, but it was only partway through our conversation that I realized I was speaking to the living legend himself. In the 1960s and early '70s, Jack was among the top players in the US and served as the captain of the US ping pong diplomacy team. Sadly, he passed away during the COVID-19 pandemic.

When we spoke, he claimed he developed the rating system, borrowing from the Elo rating system in chess, to give people something to talk about. By that measure it has been a smashing success. Prior to the adoption of his rating system, rankings were determined by the board of the United States Table Tennis Association (USTTA), ostensibly based on players' win-loss records. To clarify what may be thought of as a typo, USTTA is the predecessor of the current United States of America Table Tennis (USATT); that is, USTTA morphed into USATT for some opaque reason, as though altering the letter order of our governing body's acronym would catapult American table tennis out of obscurity. In any event, voting was highly subjective and if players were disliked, USTTA board members would not rank them highly, even if their record warranted a high ranking. Maybe the name was changed to dissociate from such practices.

The current rating system has certainly created discussion. It is one of the first things players ask each other when they play: "What is your rating?" And players often sort themselves, at tournaments and clubs, based on their ratings. Ratings are a badge of honor, and bizarrely, USATT has come out with color-coded pins that players can wear on their garments to indicate their rating. Gauche table tennis at its best.

Ratings have become not only badges of honor, but they also have become goals, which is the primary problem with ratings in any sport. Players aim to break certain benchmarks, often losing sight of the more basic goals of improving and winning tournaments. T-shirts proclaim "The Road to 2500," and there is even a book titled *Breaking 2000*—respectable content, unfortunate title. Setting goals is essential to progress, but I've seen too many players drop out of events—even events they would be seeded to win—because they did not want to risk losing rating points gained earlier in the tournament. And of course, there are players who avoid some tournaments altogether if they believe their rating will be at risk. Yet ratings are artificial and often an inaccurate assessment of the quality of a player. At best they are an assessment of how a player fared at their last tournament. The variety of table tennis styles is so diverse that oftentimes players lose matches because they struggle against a certain style, or they win matches because they play well against certain styles. I'm a case in point. I play well against loopers and choppers, often beating higher-rated players with these styles, but

I can lose to flat hitters—those with more level strokes, whose shots consequently lack spin—who are rated several hundred points lower than I am.

I don't want to give the impression that ratings are entirely inaccurate; they are not. Despite some manipulation, they do capture the general level of play among competitors, sometimes surprisingly well. But like baseball batting averages, where fans often mistakenly judge slight differences as significant when comparing hitters' skills, slight differences in table tennis ratings are also not a good indicator of comparative playing level. Although the problem with perceiving ratings as end goals themselves is widely recognized within the US table tennis community, the rating system is necessary for tournament competition and it is not going anywhere. Maybe we can draw on the wit of Winston Churchill to best sum up the current rating system. Paraphrasing his assessment of democracy, I think it is fair to say that the rating system is the worst form of ranking and assessment, except for all the others.

ELIEL'S FIRST SUMMER CAMP at MDTTC essentially constituted our first step out of the local table tennis community in New England and into the Northeast table tennis scene. But when we returned home after visiting my sister, our table tennis life continued as before: playing twice a week exclusively at Mozart's club. Eliel's exposure to elite-level play in Maryland, however, stirred a desire for more. There simply are no coaches in New England like those at MDTTC, who, when they were younger, competed at the highest levels nationally and internationally. Nor were there many other children to play with in our community, as there were in Maryland. Yet, despite his inherent passivity, Eliel took some initiative to bring elite-level play, even briefly, to our remote corner of the country.

CHAPTER 6

The Letter

As far as I know, Eliel has never watched Tiger Woods or LeBron James pursue their crafts. He's never seen the Super Bowl nor expressed any interest in doing so, even though we live a bike ride away from the home of the six-time Super Bowl champions. The athletes who populate his imagination have names like Ding Ning, Koki Niwa, Xu Xin, and Ma Long. It just dawned on me that I am making Eliel sound like Dwight Schrute. In his enthusiasm for table tennis, yes; otherwise, no. But if the comparison sticks, let's just call it even. Smashing balls off my head was bound to have karmic consequences.

In the fall of eighth grade, Eliel received a school assignment to write a letter to a famous person. He asked me if I had any ideas. During the previous summer we had discovered the Maryland Table Tennis Center, and we had been playing a few times a week at Mozart's club for the past year and a half. But Eliel had not played in a tournament yet and he continued to play other sports. Nonetheless, I suggested he write to a table tennis star.

"Who?" he asked.

"How about Danny Seemiller? He's a five-time national champion who has his own grip named after him. You can't get more famous than Danny in the table tennis world."

Surprisingly—teenage contrariness was still a few years away—he agreed with my suggestion. Danny was my table tennis hero, but I wasn't sure how Eliel felt about him. I had certainly mentioned Danny many times to Eliel, but I thought he might be more interested in writing to a younger star. Personally, I wondered if Danny would recognize Eliel's last name, or remember me at all. It had been about twenty-five years since I had last seen him.

DANNY SEEMILLER IS A hidden national treasure if there ever was one. Born and raised in Pittsburgh, he grew up in a fertile Catholic family, one of nine children. One of his siblings, younger brother Randy, was the coach along with Perry Schwartzberg at the first clinic I attended when I was eleven. Another brother, Ricky, was the head coach at the Olympic training camps I attended for several summers as a teenager. Ricky was always among the top players in the country while I was growing up, although his achievements were overshadowed by Danny's national and international success. However, as Danny acknowledged in his autobiography, he couldn't have accomplished anything without Ricky. That's because in the late sixties when the Seemiller brothers began to play in their backyard barn, they did not have access to professional coaches like today's youth players. They had each other. Danny and Ricky spent hours together practicing in the barn and figuring out the sport of table tennis on their own. I still marvel at their underappreciated genius and dedication.

Admittedly, part of my admiration stems from my anthropological understanding of humanity. Humans—all of us, no matter how asocial—are cultural creatures. As a species, we survive and succeed on cultural information that is transmitted across generations by family and friends, as well as experts and specialists. Without the collective wisdom transmitted through culture, not only would most of us be unable to feed and shelter ourselves, we would never even figure out how to turn coffee beans into coffee. Actually, we'd never even realize that coffee beans could be turned into coffee. And yes, I appreciate the Catch-22 here: most modern minds, my own included, can hardly complete a sentence, let alone create a new beverage, without an infusion of morning caffeine. Regardless, the point is that we habitually and unconsciously rely on cultural information in all aspects of our lives, and the knowledge required to play sports is no different. Yet Danny and Ricky Seemiller didn't have access to this knowledge. They had to figure out how to turn coffee beans into coffee on their own.

In any sport, professional coaches offer years of accumulated collective wisdom. As I've taken on the role of Eliel's coach, I've been awed at what "real" table tennis coaches—those not professing anthropology for a living—know and can accomplish. But coaches, understandably, believe there is a "proper" way of doing things and their job is to correct improper movements, timing, thinking, and so forth. This is generally effective, although coaching often creates homogeneity and tends to eliminate creative variation, some of which has the potential to advance a sport.

Creative variation could have been Danny's middle name, and he didn't have anyone around to tell him his creativity was in error. As he describes his approach to serving, for example, "I always try the weirdest serves I can think of in practice." Not all of them worked, of course, but he fine-tuned those that did to devastating effect. His unique serves, though, are just one of the reasons he dominated US table tennis. The most distinctive feature of his game was his grip. Without instructors, nobody had told Danny how to properly hold a paddle. Instead of shaking hands with the paddle, as most players do, he held it with his thumb and pointer finger wrapped around the base of the blade, with these two fingers leaking over each side. Thus, rather than hit a backhand with the backhand side of the paddle, which would be very awkward with such a grip, he hit his backhand and forehand with the same side of the paddle. He would switch from forehand to backhand with a windshield wiper motion of his arm. No coach would have let him get away with this, but when he started to play he didn't know any better, and it was a grip and style of play that he and his brothers perfected. To this day, there are three main ways to hold a paddle, with variation in each of the styles: *shakehand, penhold*, and *Seemiller*.

The advantage of the Seemiller grip is that it offers a very powerful forehand. Like the penhold grip, which also elicits a strong forehand, the Seemiller grip allows for greater forehand wrist rotation than the traditional shakehand grip. The other advantage of the Seemiller grip is that since the backhand and forehand utilize the same side of the paddle, an alternative rubber can be used on the opposite side. In 1971, after reading about how a French player had defeated World Champion Stellan Bengtsson—who would eventually coach against Eliel during the US Olympic Trials—with a rubber known as anti-spin, Danny attached a sheet of anti-spin to the side of his blade that he was not regularly using. He taught himself to flip his paddle between shots, known as *twiddling* in table tennis jargon. Twiddling sounds easier than it is; after years of trying I still can't do it effectively. Danny can, which enables him to alter the pace of the ball during a rally. Indeed, anti-spin rubber, as the name implies, kills the opponent's spin and enables a player to drop the ball short even on spinny topspin shots that would otherwise be returned long. It is also useful for neutralizing service spins and directing service returns where they are not anticipated. Anti-spin rubber can be very difficult to play against, especially if the user knows how to capitalize on its benefits, and the Seemillers were masters at it.

Like all wonderful things though, the Seemiller grip has a downside, and the downside is the backhand. The Seemiller backhand is excellent for blocking, especially right in front of the body, but it is difficult to generate world-class power on the backhand side. It is also particularly weak wide to the backhand. The Seemiller brothers compensated for these shortcomings with exceptional athleticism, relying on quick footwork to cover the table with their formidable forehands. Indeed, Danny's athleticism extended to other sports: most notably, baseball. He was scouted by the Pittsburgh Pirates and offered a contract to join their farm system. Danny declined the offer—as he would write years later, the buzz of ping pong diplomacy was in the air—and he invested his athletic gifts in table tennis. It is hard to overstate the value of that investment for the sport of table tennis in the US.

When I was growing up there were many players, especially in Pennsylvania, who adopted the Seemiller grip. In 1985, four of the five men on the US National Team who attended the World Championships played Seemiller style, including two-time National Champion Eric Boggan, the top US player at the time. Boggan's father, Tim, had traveled with the ping pong diplomacy team, ultimately reporting on the experience for the *New York Times* and other news outlets. But 1985 would be the zenith of the Seemiller grip. The following year the International Table Tennis Federation required all rackets to have two distinct colors, and the Seemiller grip declined precipitously in popularity. Prior to this rule change, the Seemillers and others, like their teammates Eric Boggan and Brian Masters, used an anti-spin rubber that was red, like their opposite-side tacky rubber, and it was very difficult for players to determine which rubber they were using on any given shot. The best way to tell the difference was by listening to the sound off the racket, but players like Boggan were quite adept at stamping while hitting, thus masking the sound of their shots. Needless to say, if the players had difficulty determining what rubber was being used on a given shot, the fans were utterly clueless, which is likely why the ITTF instituted the rule change. It was a change that had been brewing since two Chinese players, Liang Geliang and Huang Liang, twiddled their way to the semifinals of the 1977 World Championships using *long pips*, a rubber that reverses the spin on the ball. Once the ITTF required paddles to have different colors on each side, it was impossible to disguise the use of anti-spin, long pips, or other so-called "junk" rubbers. The Seemillers continued to use the Seemiller grip, and Danny passed it on to his son, who was also a strong player, but very few new players use the grip. It's a shame; diversity makes the world interesting.

WE FOUND DANNY'S ADDRESS online. He was living in Indiana and serving as a full-time coach in South Bend. His coaching career has been as successful as his playing career. His students from South Bend went on to play on the US Junior and Men's National teams, and one of his students was an Olympian and four-time runner-up at the US National Championships. In addition to coaching in South Bend, Danny coached many US National teams, as well as the US Olympic teams in 2000 and 2004.

In Eliel's letter—we unfortunately did not save a copy—he told Danny he was learning to play and wondered if Danny would be able to come to the Boston area and give a clinic for a week or even a weekend. While there were private coaches in our area, there was nobody of Danny's caliber. Eliel described how the overall level of play in our area was low, and would benefit from Danny's expertise. Moreover, Eliel was the only kid who regularly played at his club. The Boston area was admittedly a table tennis backwater (no, Eliel did not use that phrase), but maybe a visit from Danny could inspire others to play? We may not have saved a copy of Eliel's letter, but Danny's handwritten cursive response has been kept in the top drawer of Eliel's nightstand, right next to his bed, ever since he received it.

THE LETTER

1/29/15

Hi Eliel,

Your letter was a nice surprise. It made me feel like a champ again. Eliel, I am a full-time coach at South Bend TTC and don't travel as much as I used to.

I do give 3 and 4 day camps in South Bend. You could even stay at my house if you can travel here. I usually allow 3-4 juniors to stay.

If I can make it to Massachusetts someday for a camp I'll let you know. Our club is SBTTC.org on the web and my email is xxxx@gmail.com.

You can still achieve great things in table tennis in Brookline [where Eliel's school is located]. It just won't be easy. My brother Rick and I trained in our backyard barn to beat the Chinese someday, and we did.

Good luck,

Dan Seemiller

A champ and hero indeed. Danny never did make it to Massachusetts, nor did Eliel travel to South Bend. But a year and a half after their exchange, Eliel and Danny met at our first US Nationals. I was delighted that Danny remembered me and that Eliel was able to meet him. Eliel was understandably shy, but Danny has great people skills—he's genuine, passionate, and a gifted storyteller—and was able to connect with Eliel. We would cross paths many times at national tournaments over the next several years, and when the opportunity arose Danny would offer Eliel advice on his game. I've been touched that Danny has paid attention to Eliel's progress in the table tennis media over the years, as was evident each time we saw each other.

As a parent I've shared much of my knowledge and experiences with my kids—heck, I've even unwittingly shared my nickname. One evening, returning from Mozart's club I stopped at the local gas station. As I was filling up the tank I was startled to hear "Sos! What's up dude?" I couldn't figure out for the life of me how this teenager, whom I did not recognize, knew my nickname. It's a name my childhood and college friends still lovingly use. But this teen walked right past me to embrace *his* Sos: Eliel.

Back to the point I was making. In addition to knowledge, experiences, nicknames, passions, and good books, I feel quite fortunate that I have also been able to share a friendship with a childhood hero.

CHAPTER 7

All That Is Gold Does Not Glitter

When Eliel had written to Danny we were playing exclusively, while in New England, at Mozart's club. It was convenient, friendly, and I felt the competition was good enough for Eliel. But when Eliel began to improve, players at Mozart's club suggested that I take Eliel into the city on a weekend to play at a club with more competitive players. So, one Sunday we drove an hour to play at the New England Table Tennis Club (NETTC) located in Malden, Massachusetts.

    Finding NETTC is no easy task. Indeed, the club website advises: "Please note that if you use MapQuest, Yahoo! Maps, or AAA TripTik, the directions they provide will get you close to the club, but won't get you all the way there." The club is hidden in one of a series of grim rectangular office buildings and warehouses that lie off Malden's main thoroughfare. Finding the right building requires meandering through an unsigned parking lot, avoiding potholes, and a bit of luck. Fortunately, I had Eliel with me. From the beginning of our travels together, he has been my navigator, and he is the best navigator there is, or at least he is the best navigator in our family. The importance of this role should not be underestimated. Although it is admittedly stereotypical, I am, apparently, an absent-minded professor. I never thought of myself as such, but as a non-academic friend recently pointed out to me, I am the only person he knows who has ever driven away from a gas station with the hose still in the car. And I've done this twice. The first time, regrettably, I drove several miles down the highway before finally pulling over to try to make sense of why the passengers of every passing vehicle were gesticulating wildly at me. The second time I was only spared this extended spectacle because the station attendant chased me down before I merged back onto the highway, although this affair too attracted its fair share of amused onlookers. In short, the world is probably a little safer when I have a reliable driving companion.

Eliel—aka, Mr. Reliable—ultimately found the club for us and NETTC quickly became our second table tennis home. The club is located in a three-story, 1970s-style cinderblock building. The exterior is decorated with a thick coat of unflattering pale-yellow paint. The structure is remarkably long—several hundred yards—but it is conveniently broken up into isolated sections. The building entranceway is narrow, with offices situated immediately on both sides, and a very steep stairwell lies directly in front of the entrance. Sturdy metal handrails flank the stairs and serve as life support, at least for me; Eliel sprints up both flights. The stairs are worn and discolored in the middle, but discoloring in this grey environment is almost charming. As you climb the remaining stairs toward the third floor, the loudness of the bouncing balls usually provides some indication of how many people are at the club, and Eliel and I invariably offer our guesses as he waits for me at the top of the stairs.

There is a small platform at the top, adorned with two tattered mats, one in front of each black metal door. A single plastic black chair sits between the mats and before a window that overlooks the parking lot. On the left is a mysterious business with an unpronounceable name, and on the right is NETTC. The NETTC door holds a white paper sign fastened by scotch tape; elsewhere on the door, tape marks memorialize the location of previous signs. The current sign offers "Opening Hours," listing the daily schedule, but the schedule has probably never accurately characterized the club's hours of operation.

When we open the heavy metal door all the tables are visible, so we can immediately determine whether our guesses on the stairwell were correct. The entrance is several feet from the back end of Table 4, so to enter the club players must walk to the right on a grey concrete floor. When one does so, the tables are on the left; on the right are a standing metal cabinet and refrigerator, which are followed by four folding chairs. A bulletin board hangs above the chairs with a few business cards and assorted news articles celebrating the tournament successes of club members, most notably, a ninety-two-year-old who received some well-deserved attention after winning the over-90 doubles event at the World Veteran Championships last summer. It also contains a sign with the message "Carry In/Carry Out," nearly identical to signs I've encountered on backpacking trails, encouraging players to take their trash with them when they leave. After the bulletin board and chairs there are two small bathrooms and then a more "spacious" sitting area, roughly thirteen by seven feet. This space has plastic shelves on the side next to the bathrooms and at the far end sits a display case that Eliel and I carried up the treacherous stairs after it was discarded by another club. The case contains rubber, blades, balls, shoes, and other table tennis accessories for sale. In between the shelves and the display case are two rows of six plastic and metal folding chairs, as well as a stack of five broken chairs that lean folded against the wall. The aforementioned shelves contain gym bags, random articles of clothing, extra toilet paper and paper towels, and a working microwave. There are also pegs at the top of the shelves where players hang their coats, although they are frequently knocked off by passersby because of the tight space. The walls of the sitting area are adorned with large pictures, cut out of annual table tennis calendars, of famous professionals who are either hitting a winning shot or posing awkwardly with their racket in hand. Also posted on the wall are the weekly updated ratings of Wednesday and Thursday nights' leagues.

Behind the display case is a stool and small shelves with files and a chess set. On top of the display case rests a former tissue box wrapped in pink paper with the words "DRINKS – FOOD DEPOSIT HERE THANK YOU" on all four sides. It is not a trash receptacle, as I had first thought, but rather a place where players drop their dollars if they take a drink, ice cream sandwich, or burrito from the refrigerator. Also on the display case is a clipboard that holds the sign-in sheet and a rectangular metal money box. Players can put their fees in the metal box and take their own change, or one of the volunteers, if they are not playing, will operate the cash box. The top surface of the glass display case is also cluttered with pens, pencils, scissors, reading glasses, forgotten water bottles, old paddles that players can use if they did not bring one, and the club cell phone. Regulars regularly answer the cell phone; in fact, I did so in the midst of writing this paragraph. The call was from a father wanting to know if there was a table free for him and his son to play on. I said no and tried to be friendly but also somewhat discouraging, as the club was already crowded. I was unpersuasive and he said he was on his way. Unfortunately, as happens all too often, when he did arrive, he stayed to watch for about fifteen minutes but left without him or his son ever getting on a table. Friendly or not, seeing the speed at which high-level table tennis is played for the first time is intimidating.

The club has six tables that are set up in two rows of three. The tables are separated by freestanding ball barriers which consist of blue or green sheets of plastic, somewhat thicker than a shower curtain, draped over metal frames. The barriers are roughly two and a half feet high, seven feet long, and adorned with the logos of respective table tennis companies such as Donic and Butterfly. I have a bad habit of knocking these barriers down when I try to step over them—evidently, it is always the tall people who knock them down. The cement floor gives way to a wooden floor—raised an inch or two—upon which the tables reside. In addition to the movable barriers, at the back ends of each court are floor-to-ceiling mesh that help keep the balls within the courts. The two rows of tables are also separated by a floor-to-ceiling mesh. The twenty-two square windows in the club are covered with black garbage bags to keep out the sun, which can cause glares on the table, and the mundane world. The walls are painted light blue and there is a decorative yellow stripe above the windows around the entire playing area. At some point there must have been an attempt to remove the paint because on half the playing area there are dozens of brown and white marks the size of grapefruits.

Club members are inured to the condition of the walls—and the club itself—and generally only notice such things when they bring a guest to the club. One player, after watching a videotape of himself playing, was shocked to see the discolored wall in the background. When recording he had planned to send the video to his friends, but then he thought better of it. Such incidents clearly expose the process of habituation in which the physical condition of the club becomes normalized for regular members. Videos fail to capture how regular members experience the club, especially its familiarity, hominess, and warmth.

The club prides itself as a place that is open to players of all levels. Low-level members regularly comment that they like the fact that they can play against high-level players. And when so-called basement players, in contrast to table tennis players, show up, there are efforts to find them a table they can hit on, undisturbed. Admittedly, this is as much for their benefit as the benefit of regular members. Yet the club most definitely distinguishes itself as a place of sport, a place for serious play, not the basement game that most Americans are familiar with. So it is with some irony that the painted cinderblock walls, tin ceiling with nails sticking out, exposed heating ducts and water pipes, permanent dust in every corner, and complete shutting out of the outside world produce a basement-like experience, despite being on the third floor of an office building.

It is only fair to note that the conditions of NETTC would have been considered paradisiacal in the 1950s and '60s. During that time, many of the best players in the US, including previously-mentioned Dick Miles, Marty Reisman, and Sol Schiff, played at Lawrence's in Midtown Manhattan, located above an automobile showroom. A former speakeasy, Lawrence's was essentially a table tennis gambling den, with gangsters as interested patrons and walls decorated with bullet holes. Further uptown was no better. Journalist Nicholas Griffin describes Bob Gussikoff's club on Seventy-Third Street, where Glenn Cowan of ping pong diplomacy fame learned to play, as a:

> ... smelly, filthy, undersized playing area, [with] poor lighting, and a bathroom that looked like it hadn't been cleaned, ever. Parents who dropped their children off for the afternoon were horrified to return to find their teenagers playing poker with men in their thirties and forties.

Griffin continues that some saw the sorry state of table tennis clubs as a benefit, a view that was promoted in *Table Tennis Topics*, the official magazine of the USTTA:

> Most table tennis locations [are] in skid row type locations. This naturally produces good table tennis. In order for players to get to their clubs, they inevitably develop great reflexes. They can't help it—avoiding muggers, rioters, falling buildings, etc., can't help but improve your footwork, coordination, and general speed of reaction.

ON WEEKDAYS NETTC OFFICIALLY opens at six p.m. and on weekends at noon, but on most days not only will the club fill up by the official "opening" time, some players will be on their way home by this time, having already spent several hours playing. The club's real opening time is when someone with a key arrives. This requires a bit of explanation.

The club might be the most successful cooperative venture I've ever encountered, and I've encountered quite a few. One of my areas of academic expertise is collective societies, utopias, intentional communities, and communes, and I've spent several years of my life living in such places and probably an equal amount of time reading and writing about them. What is most remarkable about how NETTC functions—different from every other cooperative I've experienced—is that its members seem to be completely oblivious to its achievement as a functioning cooperative enterprise. Most successful cooperatives are quite self-aware and understandably proud of their achievements. Cooperation is not easy; if individuals can freeride on the efforts of others, they will tend to do so, despite high ideals and moral imperatives suggesting they should behave otherwise.

How does NETTC do it? It might be a brilliant scheme by the owner, a quirky Yale-educated Venezuelan who married into wealth, or so I've been told. But this scheme seems unlikely as he is the dictionary definition of an absentee owner, evidently taking a laissez-faire business model to an extreme. Months can go by without his appearance at the club, and when he does show up it is usually for a brief visit, exchanging jokes with players he has known for years. Occasionally he brings his paddle and plays. It is always amusing to watch new members, who have been at the club daily for months, meet the owner for the first time and assume he is a potential new member. At one point the owner attempted to work repairs on the club, rather than hire someone to do the job. He set up a workspace in the far corner of the club, reducing the playing space for one row of tables much to the annoyance of the club's regulars. But his attendance went from infrequent to nonexistent and the work never got completed. After two years the dormant workspace was finally dismantled.

NETTC's success, as with all successful cooperative ventures, lies in the efforts of a small group of highly committed members. There are at least eight of these unpaid table tennis altruists who enable NETTC to function. Aside from being unstinting with their time, they are all retired or semiretired men who enjoy table tennis and kibitzing, with the latter being at least as important as the former, if not more so. Behind the scenes, without any fanfare, these men keep the club relatively clean, stock the fridge with drinks and snacks, purchase paper towels and toilet paper, and deal with maintenance issues, including stuffed toilets, air-conditioning malfunctions, and replacing dead florescent lights.

Every week these volunteers split up the official club hours into shifts, lasting two or more hours. But in fact, if one of the volunteers is late or unable to make it, regular members will step up and fill the gap. For the most part, being in charge of a shift entails minimal responsibilities. The volunteers should answer the phone, but if they are playing, someone else will answer it. Their main responsibility is to ensure that everyone signs in and pays, but regular players often sign themselves in and if they don't have a monthly or yearly membership, they deposit their nine-dollar daily fee in the unlocked money box, taking their own change if necessary. Other than these tasks, the volunteers are there to make sure players are getting on and off the tables appropriately. Usually this takes little attention, but if new players without experience come, they are often given a table of their own, and this requires a little finesse. Indeed, a recent incident highlights the potential hazards created by this unofficial policy. I only learned of the incident because I ran into the aggrieved party at another club.

It was a surprise meeting, to say the least, as the club where we crossed paths is the least welcoming club I have ever played at. It is hard to believe the owners of this club are actually trying to run a business. Rumor has it they make their living by selling kitchen equipment that is stored in one of the side rooms of the renovated warehouse that serves as the club. Why a table tennis club would be serving as a front for a kitchen equipment business is a mystery, but such mysteries are useful fodder for lurid gossip at the other clubs. Kibitzers need something to kibitz about.

It is widely acknowledged that this club has the nicest facilities in the Boston area. Its only drawback, as mentioned earlier, is that the temperature of the club is a little too closely linked with the temperature outside, making the conditions unplayable in the heart of winter and summer. But the playing area is spacious, ceilings are high, lighting is good, tables and nets are of professional quality, and the floor is covered with the red rubber matting that is standard at all high-profile tournaments. Moreover, they have a carpeted and comfortable lounge, changing area, and even separate restrooms for men and women.

If only appearances were everything. And if only the owners wanted anyone to play there. The club fees and lesson rates are more than 50 percent higher than any other club in the area, and the owners also have a bad habit of using the fewest lights possible: the second you step off your table they are likely to turn the lights out on you. More times than I'd like to remember we've had to change our shoes and put our stuff away in the dark. I've thought about suggesting to the owners that they could save on electricity altogether if they provided players with glowing florescent balls, but I worried they might take me seriously. And if I had any doubt about their interest in having players frequent their establishment, they were answered on this visit. We were there because a French player who had lived in Boston but relocated to Germany with his German girlfriend was back in town for a brief visit, and he wanted to hit with Eliel to prepare for a tournament. When he lived in the area he would play with Eliel once a week at this club because it was close to his workplace. We had not been to this club in over a year, and I was curious what kind of reception we would receive. The owners did not disappoint: there was no reception at all. No "Hello." No "Hi, how have you been?" Not even a smile. I smiled, but it went unreciprocated. I simply paid and Eliel went to the court.

So I was surprised to see this player, a young Israeli engineer, who had been a mainstay at NETTC. He explained that he no longer went to NETTC because he'd had a fight with one of the volunteers. When basement players come, the volunteers often kick people off the table so the newcomers can play undisturbed with players at their level. Apparently, he was getting kicked off more than his fair share. He complained in a way that probably would have been culturally appropriate in the Middle East, but it didn't fly at NETTC, and he hasn't been back since. He said he planned to write a letter to the owner, but he had never met the owner. We both acknowledged that the owner was unlikely to care; one of the advantages of his laissez-faire ownership was not getting entangled in such dramas.

At yet another club I received, unsolicited, a different account of this affair. In this version, admittedly told by a detractor of the aggrieved player, he did not voluntarily leave the club but was kicked out. Like most tales, the various versions of this drama coexist and transform with the different audiences who retell it. If this version of the story is accurate, it is somewhat extraordinary because, with the exception of one player who was suspended for two months from a New Jersey club for disparaging the club's playing conditions on Facebook, I cannot recall ever hearing of someone getting officially barred from any club. And at NETTC I've seen behavior that would warrant such excommunication, including kicking tables, throwing barriers, and attempted but thwarted physical altercations with other players.

So, back to the hours of the club. While the kitchen-supply club has precise hours—they turn the lights off fifteen minutes before closing even if you are in the middle of a match—NETTC will open when any of the key-wielding volunteers wish to play. On nearly every day at least one of them opens the club several hours early. Moreover, players never have to worry about the lights being shut off. If the last volunteer is heading home for the evening, they will simply ask whomever is there to turn off the lights and lock the door behind them when they leave. It is not unusual for play to continue past midnight, and I know of several occasions when players decided to play all night before catching an early morning flight out of Boston's Logan Airport. Table tennis addiction on full display.

The club has open play every day, but on Wednesday and Thursday evenings the tables are reserved for league play. The Wednesday night league began about a decade ago, but after seven years it grew too large and spawned a second league on Thursday night. The Wednesday night league is reserved for players rated over 1800 and Thursday is open to players rated less than that. Coach Gui runs both leagues. Gui is what you might call an uber-volunteer; his earnest dedication to the club and the sport never ceases to amaze me. It is hard to imagine his life prior to NETTC, but he has a PhD in physics and made sufficient money on patents from his research to retire. Without others telling me this, I would have assumed his mother gave birth to him at the club—on a ping pong table of course—and left him there for the past sixty years. He is simply part of the atmosphere of the club. And like the ceiling, you don't really appreciate his importance until he is not there. A yearly vacation to visit his wife's family in Malaysia often leaves the league nights in disarray for a few weeks.

Running league night consists of matching up opponents, keeping warm-ups to a minimum, and getting players on a table once a match has finished. None of these tasks are easy, as those who replace Gui during his travels can attest. Matches should be against players of similar level—the point of league-night is to play competitive matches—but certain players don't like to play each other and Gui has to be sensitive to these preferences. Some players simply don't like each other, but some players are avoided because of an awkward style, such as long pips, or because they scream too much or play too slowly. And although warm-ups are supposed to be limited to two minutes, similar to professional matches, who can really warm up in two minutes? Players of course come to play, so you would expect them to eagerly get on an open table when Gui calls their names; but players are also there to socialize, and a player in the middle of a juicy story is usually reluctant to prematurely end his conversation. Gui is there to nudge.

Overall, the club's operations, thanks to folks like Gui, are extraordinary. And to be clear, by all measures, NETTC is the most successful club in New England, despite holding only six tables. The club is home to the region's top players, it is open more hours than any other club, its tables are almost always in use, and it has more patrons by far than any club in the area. For me, it is these patrons who give NETTC its distinctive personality, and it is to them I now turn.

CHAPTER 8

Where Everybody Knows Your Name

On our first visit to NETTC we were, initially, treated as basement players: the volunteer who was in charge, Mark, cleared a table for Eliel and I to hit. I have vivid memories of those first moments at the club because Mark's friendliness made a strong impression on me. It is no small accomplishment to make two introverts feel immediately welcome, and I am still grateful for the warmth and kindness he extended to us on that day. I would later realize that Mark was a mainstay at the club—ever-present, even when he was not the volunteer on duty. Over the next few years we would often play at the club during off-hours so Eliel could train undisturbed, and invariably Mark would be there, alone on one of the back tables, practicing his serves. Not even a global health crisis could diminish Mark's steadfastness. Throughout the pandemic, Mark would arrive at the club daily between six thirty and seven thirty a.m. to get a few hours of practice in before anyone else arrived, serving and training on the club robot. This sport grabs a hold of people.

And yes, most clubs own a table tennis robot, as do many competitive players, including Eliel. Table tennis robots shoot balls across the table and the return shots are caught in a net, which then recycle through the robot. Table tennis robots have been around since I was a teenager, but as with all technology, there have been considerable advancements since the days of the dinosaurs, as my kids refer to my childhood.

It is possible that on our first visit Mark cleared a table for us because we were a father-son duo, which at the time was surprisingly uncommon at the club. Recently, more children have been playing there, primarily because one of the coaches is teaching his daughter and son how to play. But in the first years we attended, it was almost exclusively an adult club. Needless to say, on our initial visit Eliel attracted some attention, and when we began to hit people realized that this was not our first time out of the basement.

The first person who asked to hit with Eliel was a middle-aged Korean penholder, Jeffrey, who I would later discover frequented the club every day. Jeffrey had apparently learned to play as an adult and was now one of the top players in Massachusetts. Achieving such expertise at table tennis, or any sport, late in life is rare. But if Jeffrey's account is accurate—given his limited English I always wondered if I was misunderstanding him—it seems he was able to achieve his success, at least partially, because of his highly unusual playing style. He is a flat hitter, playing with long pips and short pips, which he regularly twiddles. It is very difficult to return long-pip flat hits; normal strokes will send the ball into the bottom of the net—if you are lucky enough to reach the net at all. Players have to adjust their strokes, often quite uncomfortably, and the minute you begin to tinker with your strokes in the middle of a match, it is very easy to lose your timing, touch, and ultimately your temper. To add to the frustration, Jeffrey's long-pip flat hits generally drive players back from the table, which sets up his devastatingly shallow short-pip drop shots. Playing him can be a humbling experience, and at tournaments I've watched him infuriate and ultimately defeat much higher-rated players who were encountering his unique style for the first time. To add insult to injury, while playing at the club Jeffrey is habitually drinking beer, which he claims helps alleviate his back pain.

Whatever the rationale, while other players bring water or a sports drink to the table when they play, Jeffrey brings a lager. Five-game matches often require two.

Even before our visit to NETTC we were apparently not unknown to Jeffrey; rumor of us had passed through the Korean grapevine via our friend Benjamin, the radiologist who suffers from a degenerative muscular disease. Eliel would eventually become a much stronger player than Jeffrey, but on this first visit to NETTC Jeffrey's willingness to hit with Eliel was quite generous. Over the years I watched Jeffrey's generosity in action countless times, most notably in training a chemistry graduate student from China, Eleanor, who was studying at Harvard. After years of training, Eleanor began to teach Jeffrey's wife how to play. Perhaps that was the plan all along; countless stories circulate in the club of players who have attempted to teach their significant others table tennis. Heated arguments seem to be the inevitable outcome of such well-meaning efforts.

While Eliel was hitting with Jeffrey, one of the Chinese coaches, who awkwardly goes by Luigi, asked where I learned how to play. But before getting to my response, this seems like as good a place as any to note that the Asian, especially Chinese, habit of adopting American names when living in the US is frankly embarrassing. They are changing their names on the advice of compatriots who have preceded them, recognizing that Americans have difficulty with Chinese names. Should native-born Americans be insulted? Do foreign-born Asians think Americans are too parochial to remember or pronounce their names? Well, yes, and they are right. As Eliel will attest, I am among the worst culprits. I need to do better.

Back to Luigi, who I insist on calling Qingshang, his Chinese name. I described my background to him and good fortune lent my story some credibility. Tim Boggan, father of two US Men's National Champions and media liaison for the US ping pong diplomacy visit to China, is the official historian of USATT. He has written an unwieldy multivolume compendium on the history of table tennis in the US. The material is mostly drawn from the now defunct monthly magazine of the USTTA, *Table Tennis Topics*, which Boggan skillfully and colorfully edited for many years. It so happened that on a shelf at NETTC there were a few volumes of this meandering historical source. I opened a volume from the early eighties and showed the coach my name in several places, including an award I received at an Olympic training camp and a picture of me competing on the US Junior Team. I'm fairly confident that anyone who played in a tournament at this time—regardless of skill level—would have been included in this volume, but I failed to point that out in our conversation.

THE AREAS OF MY ignorance are vast and often don't seem to overlap with others' knowledge gaps. For example, I know nothing about financial matters, technology, or popular music, and I wouldn't trust myself to change a tire. Nor do I know how to tie a tie (my wife pre-tied several ties for me when I visited universities for job interviews, which is the last time I wore—or owned—one). I should point out that it is not exactly every Jewish mother's aspiration to have a son who knows how to wrap and wear a loincloth but doesn't know how to tie a tie. Sorry Mom. For what it's worth, I've been told I don't look too bad in a loincloth. In any event, regarding relevant knowledge gaps, I'm honestly not sure what most Americans do on Christmas Eve. I know they are celebrating Christmas, but I don't know what that entails exactly. I do, however, know what two peoples have been doing on Christmas Eve ever since their ancestors landed on the shores of this country: the Chinese have been opening their restaurants and the Jews have been frequenting them. As it turns out, table tennis clubs are also a popular venue on

Christmas Eve, as well as Christmas Day. With its abundance of Jewish and Chinese members, NETTC tends to be crowded on both these days.

By the way, if you are unfamiliar with the Jewish celebration of Christmas Eve at Chinese restaurants, or Jews' general affection for Chinese food, I think a recent episode at a Chinese restaurant in Brookline, a Jewish neighborhood in the Boston area where Eliel attends school, will tell you all you need to know. Several years ago, this restaurant, owned by a Chinese family, suffered damage to its roof and front awning. Most businesses would take out a loan to pay for damage not covered by insurance. But when news about the damage spread, the Jewish community—led by the local rabbis—initiated a fundraising campaign to cover the costs of the damage. Seriously. It was as though the Jewish community was treating the Chinese restaurant as an extension of the synagogue, and maybe for many it was. Of course, given the importance of the cause, the fundraising efforts were successful and the damage was repaired. Unfortunately, no good deed goes unpunished. Within a year of this charitable gesture, the owner of the restaurant was arrested: a hidden camera, which had apparently been there for years, had been discovered in the restroom. The owner was imprisoned, but presumably out of fear of losing a local Chinese restaurant, Jewish community members came to the defense and rescue of the remaining family members, who had distanced themselves from the convicted husband/father. Jewish leaders, including rabbis, successfully supported the family's efforts in the courts to retain their restaurant. What would Jews do without egg rolls, moo shu, and lo mein? The restaurant is still in business—tragedy narrowly averted.

One Christmas Day, Gui said he would be opening up the club as usual and Eliel arranged to play with one of the Jewish Russian players in the morning. By the time we arrived, four others were already there. Rebecca, a prolific author and illustrator of children's books, was hitting with Jacob. They had both eaten at a Chinese restaurant on the previous evening (Gui had asked).

I believe it was in graduate school where I first heard the comment that "lotteries are a tax on people who are bad at math," and I've heard it many times since. A math-challenged close relation once mentioned in earnestness that if he ever had enough money he would win the lottery by placing a bet on every possible number. Point proven. Or so I thought; Jacob has forced me to reconsider the validity of this aphorism. Jacob is an MIT graduate and a successful science entrepreneur. Every time we cross paths at the club he tells me of his latest invention, but I'm a mere mortal and I have no real understanding of what he is talking about. Anthropology, thankfully, has taught me how to smile and nod politely. Over the several years I've known Jacob he has won the lottery twice. Let me rephrase that. He has won a multimillion-dollar jackpot, twice. Despite his obvious brilliance he thankfully does not attribute his good (and now, large) fortune to any mathematical wisdom on his part—pure luck. We've never played a match, but I wonder if he also benefits from an inordinate number of nets and edges.

On one of the other tables two Russian Jews were playing, Alek and Sergei. They were in a heated battle, albeit one-sided, when we arrived. Alek was visibly annoyed at himself and was hitting the ball wildly in frustration. Gui, who gives lessons to Alek every week, advised Alek to take a break and cool off. Incidentally, Sergei is a chopper and this is what choppers can do; they frustrate their opponents and mentally crush them. Alek of course refused to follow Gui's sound advice and he continued to scream and play poorly. He knew as well as anyone that he needed to be patient, but the mental discipline to maintain patience had been lost. To everyone's relief, they finally took a bathroom break and I sarcastically asked Alek, knowing I can joke with him even when he is upset, if he's ever played a chopper before. He responded that they usually play evenly but today Sergei was returning everything. Alek, in his Russian accent, continued,

> I wouldn't be so frustrated but I spend more time here than with my family. I'm going to go home and my wife is going to ask "Any results?" What can I say to her? When I tell her that I lost every game she's a Jewish wife and you know what she'll say? She'll say, "For this you are spending one hundred dollars a week on lessons? We could be sending this money to Israel! We have relatives there who are starving, and you spend money on this?"

WHILE THROUGHOUT THIS CHRISTMAS DAY many Jewish and Chinese players showed up, one regular at the club was noticeably absent: a Taiwanese jokester who many consider a token member of the tribe (that is, Jewish). Jokester doesn't fully capture Kuan-Yu's personality, or more importantly, his role at the club. He is better characterized as a trickster. He invariably greets Eliel and I with "*Shalom*," as do many of the Jewish Russian players, but unlike Kuan-Yu, they are all Israeli citizens, having first immigrated to Israel before relocating to the US. He departs from us also in Hebrew—"*L'hitraot*"—and he wishes us "*Shabbat Shalom*" every time he sees us, regardless of the day. Kuan-Yu regularly asks Eliel to teach him Hebrew words, and Eliel obliges. When asked about his interest, he responds, with as much seriousness as he can muster, "I'm training to become a rabbi."

Our interactions with Kuan-Yu are not exceptional. He has his particular ritual greetings for everyone. When he sees Mark, the ever-present volunteer who greeted us on our first visit, Kuan-Yu always asks when he arrived at the club. Whatever Mark's response, Kuan-Yu counters that Ma Long, the world's greatest player, didn't even start training until an hour or two after Mark.

A trickster is a cultural figure who crosses boundaries; they break the expected behavioral norms within a community. Tricksters appear in the myths of countless cultures in every corner of the world. In the West, Loki of Norse mythology (and Marvel movie fame) might be the most recognized trickster, crossing the boundaries between humans and the gods. He not only breaks behavioral norms, but like many tricksters he also breaks physical norms, relying on shapeshifting to pull off his ruses. My kids were raised on stories of a Jewish trickster, Hershele of Ostropol (located, now, in Ukraine), whose tales and schemes I would occasionally relate at Shabbat dinners on Friday night. Hershele lived at the turn of the nineteenth century and worked as a *shochet* (ritual slaughterer), but evidently lost his job and subsequently was forced to live by begging and his wits. For example, one story relates:

> Hershele once visited a restaurant, sat down, and ordered two rolls. When the rolls arrived, he changed his mind and asked for two doughnuts instead. He promptly ate them and walked out of the restaurant without paying. The owner chased after him and demanded payment for the doughnuts.
>
> "But I gave you the rolls for the doughnuts," Hershele insisted.
>
> "You didn't pay for the rolls either," the owner responded.
>
> "But I haven't eaten the rolls, have I?"
>
> Having settled the matter, Hershele walked away, satiated, in at least two senses of the word.

Hershele ultimately gained some stability for his family when he was hired as what can essentially be described as a court jester for a Hasidic Rebbe. His job was to lift the spirits of the Rebbe and prevent him from sinking into depression. His antics were legendary and he was able to flout Jewish law and poke fun at the Rebbe with impunity, breaking otherwise sacred social norms like all tricksters do. In addition to tales about his adventures and deceits, many classic Yiddish expressions are attributed to Hershele, such as "Never wish a doctor or an undertaker a good year" or "What does God think of money? Just look at who he gives it to." My favorite, and one that has come in handy: "Stay out of the way of mad dogs, runaway horses, and fools with an education."

According to anthropological wisdom, tricksters are important, and thus prevalent, because by crossing boundaries they highlight social rules and practices, making them real and salient for people. And Kuan-Yu is indeed a boundary crosser. Not only is he a rabbi in training, but he is a token Korean, Brazilian, Indian, Frenchman, Iranian, and probably an unofficial member of many other cultures represented at the club. In a community with so many national orientations, racial identities, religious commitments, and political leanings, there is certainly value in someone who can cross the various cultural and ethnic boundaries in the club. He achieves his chameleonesque adaptability through language—learning just enough phrases to talk to nearly everyone in their mother tongues—but also through humor. He is probably the only one at the club who can make jokes about Mao with impunity and he won't hesitate to imitate someone who is being a poor sport, invariably turning a tense situation into one everyone can laugh about. But he doesn't only rely on humor; he is also one of the few who doesn't hesitate to point out racism when he sees it. His personality obviously suits his role as trickster: he is very clever, naturally comedic, and has a great ear for languages. But I suspect as a Taiwanese in the US he understands marginality and ambiguity, having feet both inside and outside the Chinese community.

Kuan-Yu might also be a successful trickster because, like many others at the club, he is a software engineer. He can thus relate to many players through shared work experiences, regardless of cultural background. That said, I don't want to give the impression that everyone at NETTC is a software engineer. There is actually quite an odd assortment of occupations, aside from the quirky Jewish anthropologist: auto mechanic, physician, ethnomusicologist, hostler, jazz pianist (who had his own show in Vegas for years), distinguished linguistics professor, realtor, tennis instructor, priest, and of course, Chinese restaurant owner.

There is no shortage of brain power at the club. I don't know what the relationship is between education and table tennis—the oft-quoted claim that "table tennis is chess on steroids" strikes me as self-aggrandizing and gratuitous—but NETTC is certainly an overeducated community. This may be a function of the location; Boston is home to an abundance of universities and high-tech industries. Or it may be a consequence of US immigration laws that favor those who are educated. The Russians at the club are particularly noteworthy. It seems that either they, their kids, or their grandkids—sometimes all three—have been educated at Harvard or MIT. I've seen the whiteboard that serves as a signup list for tables be entirely erased when two Russians got into a vigorous conversation and needed the board to solve some equation they had initially been working through in their heads. They were essentially speaking two languages I didn't understand. And the Russians, characteristically, are often playing chess on their cell phones between matches. But they are not alone; many of the players play chess between matches. Eliel, who after Naftali was my second child to win his school's chess tournament, would occasionally play chess between points when competing against a Pakistani player at the club. In his youth, Ali had been a member of the Pakistani Junior National Team, and he was still a very strong player, often beating Eliel. But he suffered from painful back problems—his doctor advised him never to play table tennis again—so from time to time he was unable to play a match all the way through. When his back was flaring up, he and Eliel would play six points and then take three moves on a chessboard they had set up next to the table. If chess boxing can succeed—and it has—maybe this form of table tennis will attract a following as well.

SPEAKING OF OVEREDUCATED PLAYERS, one day a retired math professor, Ken, told me about an article he published that he thought would interest me. He was correct. He related that years earlier while in Madrid he was eating Shabbat lunch with a local colleague when one of the other guests at the table commented that he had learned from a rabbi to always boil an odd number of eggs, evidently, a little known *halacha* (Jewish law). Ken was curious. As his article, titled "Odd-Boiled Eggs," describes,

> According to the laws of *Kashruth* [keeping kosher], Jews may not consume eggs containing blood spots. When observant Jews make an omelet or bake challah, they break each egg separately and discard any that are bloody before they add them to the rest of the ingredients.

Actually, not all observant Jews discard their bloody eggs. Our cat Jumpy's insatiable fondness for non-kosher animals, such as mice, snakes, and squirrels, suggested to us that he was opting out of our family's kosher vegetarianism. Indeed, Jumpy expresses no moral qualms about blood spots, so he gets our blemished eggs. Ken's article continues,

> But when you boil eggs, there is no easy way to tell beforehand if the eggs you are cooking have blood spots or not. Once the eggs are boiled and opened, the spots can be

seen, but by then it is too late ... Because of the hardship caused by throwing out already-cooked eggs and needing to make cooking utensils kosher once again (a tedious and time-consuming process), by rabbinic decree it was decided that if the majority of eggs in a pot are free of blood spots, all the blood-free eggs may be eaten and the cooking utensil remains kosher.

In the article Ken was able to show the mathematical logic—how adding an egg to an odd number of eggs lowers the probability of a blood-free majority—behind this obscure practice (one I was not familiar with) of boiling an odd number of eggs among some traditional Jews.

Ken and his wife followed their son, Jonathan, when Jonathan was diagnosed with cancer and he and his family relocated to the Boston area for treatment. Jonathan was a regular at the club and I had known him for at least a year without any knowledge of his diagnosis. Like his father, he was a truly kind and gentle soul. We often talked about tennis, as he had played competitively while growing up in Minnesota. One of his childhood friends was a well-known table tennis player, Cory Eider, who fell one match shy of being a US National Champion. Cory is now a highly regarded coach in New Jersey and he has worked with Eliel on various occasions. In their youth, Jonathan and Cory competed against each other, and Jonathan enjoyed recounting how he had beaten Cory at tennis and table tennis before he became exceptional at both sports.

One day when we were talking I asked Jonathan if he wanted to hit, but he said he needed to rest. He casually mentioned that his treatments were becoming more difficult and it was challenging to play. I asked him what he was being treated for and he said he had terminal cancer. He hadn't been hiding his diagnosis from me or anyone—indeed, he had assumed I was aware of his situation—but he was so full of life that he simply never brought it up in conversation with me. His passing within the year was devastating, leaving a wife with young kids and both his parents. I remember sharing the sad news, awkwardly, with Cory. They had lost touch years earlier, but at least I was able to relate that Jonathan often spoke fondly of him.

Since Jonathan's passing I have long thought about the fact that despite constant pain and limited energy, he chose to come to the club and play. And, remarkably, he sought to improve. How am I to understand this game, a sport that people will play, and play with goals in mind, even at the end of life? I recall talking to Ken at the club after Jonathan's passing and he mentioned how coming to the club meant a lot to Jonathan. In their book, *All Things Shining*, philosophers Hubert Dreyfus and Sean Dorrance Kelly posit that "Sports might be the place in contemporary life where Americans find sacred community most easily." But for Jonathan, it wasn't just about socializing and seeing friends or finding community; he really enjoyed physically playing. I'm honestly unsure what to make of that. I do know, however, as I get older and think about my own mortality and what I want to be doing with my remaining years on the planet—may they be many, healthy, and filled with grandchildren—I have increasingly turned to table tennis. I can't explain why this strange little sport should have such a hold on me, but evidently it does and I know I am not alone. Is it really possible to derive enduring meaning from a game?

I'll speculate more on this question later, but for the moment the work of sociologist Ray Oldenburg may provide the glimpse of an answer. In Oldenburg's terminology, The New England Table Tennis Club, and similar clubs throughout the world, can be thought of as a "third place." These are places outside of home and work (hence, third place), where people congregate and make community. Oldenburg's work largely focused on cafés and bars and did not consider sport communities. However, NETTC shares nearly every defining characteristic of Oldenburg's third places: it is a space that is inclusive, local, fun, and playful; unimpressive to the uninitiated; and lacking individual anonymity—everyone knows everyone. Unlike Oldenburg's third places, conversation is arguably not the primary activity at NETTC; table tennis is. Yet conversation is clearly a close second, and there are people who occasionally visit NETTC just to spend time there, with no intention of playing. And it is not uncommon for injured players who are taking time off from competing to heal to drop in and hang out because they miss the camaraderie.

It is likely that Oldenburg did not include sport communities in his analyses because in contrast to third places, sport communities are not, or are at least not entirely, status-leveling, which is another one of his defining characteristics of third places. Sports create status differentials on the court, table, field, track, and so on, but like third places they do level other forms of status, such as education, class, and income. Interestingly, this minor difference between third places and sport communities reveals a highly significant and informative facet of the social conditions that can foster meaning-making. Oldenburg's classic work on third places, *The Great Good Place*, notably does not discuss meaning; it is not a critical factor in motivating and sustaining third places. While third places are about community and friendship, they support friendships in which "people do not get uncomfortably entangled in one another's lives." Third places encourage relationships in which people can "easily join and depart one another's company." Friendships at sporting communities like NETTC are similar, except that structured competition, which is avoided in third places, also cultivates meaning. Almost every NETTC member is striving—with different levels of commitment—toward improving their table tennis skills. Even club members who are over ninety years old, even Jonathan. Maintaining and pursuing these goals invariably contributes to their identities and elicits meanings for players in ways that the purely social atmospheres of third places do not. In our rapidly and endlessly transforming world, we seem to seek meaning in historically grounded environments that, while stable, are also changing and afford opportunities for us to grow. After all, to be human is to grow.

Pardon my sci fi and fantasy side from seeping through, but it's impossible for a Trekkie and wannabe hobbit to pass up an opportunity to discuss *Star Trek* and Middle-earth when pondering the human condition; there are no better sources, in my humble opinion, to think with. In *Star Trek*, every encounter with another life form contains a tension in which the Enterprise crew is at pains to clarify what makes humans unique. Episode after episode, the captain and officers explain to "alien species" that humans differ from other life forms by their need to grow. The entire mission of the Enterprise, to explore distant galaxies, is derived precisely from this need. And to the surprise of the many species they encounter on their journeys, for the Enterprise crew, life deprived of growth is not worth living; the denial of growth is death itself. As science fiction writer Kurt Vonnegut observes, "We have to continually be jumping off cliffs and developing our wings on the way down." If denied possibilities for growth, we create challenges for ourselves that provide us with opportunities to learn, solve, and grow. In the *Star Trek* universe, revealingly, the most dangerous nemesis of the United Federation of Planets is not the Romulans, Cardassians, or Klingons, but rather the Borg, a cybernetic species who share the human desire for perfection but mistakenly believe they have achieved it, thus denying themselves the possibility for growth.

Tolkien was similarly attuned to the fact that growth is essential to what it means to be human. In Middle-earth, what distinguishes "the race of Men" from other "races" is specifically the need to grow. Hobbits may "share a love of all things that grow," but hobbits themselves do not change. They are anachronistically forever stuck in Tolkien's nineteenth-century English countryside. Orcs are interminably evil; repentance and redemption are never considered as an option for them. And the Elves, Ents, and Wizards of Middle-earth are depicted as eternal and unchanging, barely ever senescing. In Tolkien's mythology, lack of growth for the "race of Men" is inherently evil. Notably, the One Ring, the epitome of evil, not only prevents its bearer from physically aging, but also thwarts all aspects of human development and growth.

And *Star Trek* and *The Lord of the Rings* are not alone. *The Lego Movie*, for example, explores the same theme: ultimate evil is depicted as permanently gluing Lego worlds in place, preventing the possibility of change and growth. It's also a movie that, like *Star Trek* and *The Lord of the Rings*, holds a special place in my heart, albeit for a different reason: it supported my contention—often contested by my children—that I am sane. With four kids and limited living space, we always had a couch problem on Shabbat, when the entire family would spend the afternoon absorbed in the books they were reading. As the youngest, Eliel would usually lose out and be relegated to the floor. My solution? I constructed a double-decker couch. Although the couch was very precarious, short-lived, and admittedly the source of many family jokes, when I encountered a well-constructed, functional double-decker couch in *The Lego Movie*, I felt redeemed. Despite my family's sentiments, perhaps I am not so crazy after all.

While double-decker couches were obligingly introduced to audiences in *The Lego Movie*, there is no evidence of table tennis in the Lego and *Star Trek* universes, nor in Middle-earth—an unfortunate oversight by the creators of all three worlds. For like the theme of growth underlying life in these fictional worlds, table tennis is about growth. Indeed, the opportunity for growth that table tennis affords throughout one's lifetime may explain why people are continually able to draw meaning from it. Those who have been marketing table tennis as "The Lifetime Sport" are on to something more accurate and insightful than I think they realize.

I HAVE NEVER ASKED Eliel about the meaning he draws from table tennis, but his actions tell more than his words ever would. Playing table tennis is a central part of his identity, and his commitment to the sport is unwavering, despite the many challenges he faces competing as an observant Jew. If you get him started he can talk for hours about professional matches he recently watched, or he'll tell you about the matches of the latest tournament in which he competed. And even when he is not playing he customarily wears table tennis shirts, almost as a reminder to others that he is a table tennis player. Eliel essentially grew up at NETTC. He improved as a player there, but more importantly, his social and competitive interactions with everyone at the club—all adults—nurtured his development as an individual. At NETTC he transformed from a quiet and reserved child to a confident and engaging teenager.

But meaningful growth is about transcending, and it was outside of Massachusetts on the national table tennis scene where Eliel really came into his own. Admittedly, he has had plenty of teenage moments along the way, but thankfully those are less painful when viewed in the rearview mirror as simply steps along the path toward the responsible, independent, and considerate young adult he is today.

CHAPTER 9

The Pilgrimage

Shortly after we began playing regularly at NETTC, our table tennis adventure entered a new phase, one that would categorically alter our life in this sport. We passed into the world of table tennis tournaments, and we haven't left it yet. I describe it as a transition to a different world because it does indeed differ considerably from club life. Tournament players are only a small subset of all table tennis players; there are many active club members who never compete in tournaments, and thus the US tournament scene is largely unknown to them.

Eliel's first tournament was in Rhode Island, and it came with everything you would anticipate from tournament competition: unexpected wins and spectacular defeats. Even at this young age—he was thirteen years old—he showed a maturity in defeat and grace in victory that amazed me. I certainly had not been so gracious at his age, and I am probably not as well mannered as Eliel even now. I watched as other children got frustrated and had uncontrollable meltdowns—the kind of train wreck you want to look away from, but can't. For most young kids, tournaments and tears are natural bedfellows. Eliel wanted to win as much as these other kids, but for whatever reason he never let his emotions boil over during or after a match.

I should note that I had ample opportunity to watch other children compete, meltdowns and all, because early in Eliel's tournament career I was banned from watching his matches. Not being permitted to watch Eliel, I watched other kids. The ban wasn't imposed by the tournament officials but rather by Eliel himself. I had done the same to my parents, something I deeply regret to this day because they never got to see me play at my highest level. Indeed, when they finally did get to see me play as a middle-aged adult—warming Eliel up at a tournament—they were surprised at how good I had gotten since beating their friends in the basement decades earlier.

I was jealous of parents who were permitted to watch their children compete, but my fate, and my parents' fate, was not unusual. Often the decision not to watch is mutual. Smart parents, probably those who read the advice books, know when it is time to make themselves scarce. Blaming parents for a loss—"Why did you look at me that way?!"—seems to be one facet of the sport that hasn't changed since its inception. At many of Eliel's early tournaments I sat in the parking lot during his matches while other parents kept me apprised after each game, letting me know whether he had won or lost. At one point, Eliel permitted me to watch his matches as long as I stayed out of his line of sight; he did not want to see me and get distracted. So when possible, I hid behind walls and other obstructions and stole glances, rooting in my heart, if not out loud. My days of overt cheerleading and coaching were still a year away.

We were fortunate that living in the Northeast we were in driving distance to many tournaments. After Eliel's first tournament in Rhode Island, we began to frequent tournaments about once a month, regularly traveling to Connecticut, New York, and New Jersey. There were also many tournaments close to home in Massachusetts (which as usual, I just misspelled on my first try). During these tournaments it became evident that the interesting characters who inhabit Mozart's club, NETTC, and the other local table tennis clubs Eliel and I had been playing at—there are about a dozen small clubs in the area—were not unique to Massachusetts; table tennis players everywhere were, well, harmless and well-meaning, but a bit eccentric. Here is one example.

At one of Eliel's early tournaments, a player about my age, who was shortly scheduled to play Eliel, excitedly approached me.

"How can I beat Eliel?" he inquired, with seeming innocence.

"Huh? Sorry, what did you say?" I responded, startled and confused.

"How can I beat Eliel?" he repeated. "What are his weaknesses? What serves give him trouble? Can he handle dead balls?"

I protested, reminding this player that I was Eliel's father and I wanted him to win.

"As a father it is your responsibility to provide Eliel with opportunities to develop as a player," he countered, unfazed by my protests. "Eliel will learn a lot more from a loss than a win. This is just one tournament. In the long run it will be better for him if you tell me how to beat him."

"Are you serious?"

He was. And he was relentless. I held my ground, despite his persistence and earnestness. Thankfully, Eliel won the match.

Regardless of eccentricities, Eliel was making friends with the other players—children and adults—at the tournaments we were attending. One of these friends eventually convinced Eliel that my presence at his matches might actually help him win. Eliel agreed and decided that at our next tournament, which was in New York, I could watch and coach his first match. He would assess the situation afterward.

The table tennis gods blessed me on that day. I watched, I cheered, I coached, and Eliel won. I did the same for all his matches at that tournament and Eliel had his best tournament, up to that point, in his playing career. Remarkably, my coaching advice was actually effective. I was no longer just the chauffeur and chaperone; I was now officially his coach—a title I wear proudly to this day. It is an honored position that comes with a level of stress that only a parent can fully appreciate, but like most parents in similar situations, I wouldn't trade my courtside seat for anything in the world.

BY THE SUMMER OF 2016 Eliel had been competing in tournaments for about a year, and he was learning and improving at every tournament. We decided he was ready for the national scene, which meant he was ready for Las Vegas. Las Vegas is a special place for table tennis players. Nobody would confuse it with the Holy Land, but the pilgrimage to Las Vegas for the US Table Tennis Nationals is a ritualized and sacred annual journey for many players. There is nothing quite like the experience. For Eliel and I, attending the Nationals felt like a rite of passage for legitimate entry into the US table tennis community. Rites of passage are a favorite topic of study for anthropologists because they capture cultural experiences that socially transform individuals, turning girls into women, boys into men, and outsiders into insiders.

Every anthropologist partakes in a rite of passage, whether official or unofficial, to gain acceptance into the group they are studying. I vividly recall arriving at the atoll in Micronesia where I conducted my dissertation fieldwork and being told by the chief that I would need to explain my presence to the council of elders. If they did not approve of my research, I would have to leave. After spending more than a year acquiring the necessary government research permits and more than two months traveling to this remote Pacific atoll—their contact with the outside world, at the time, was limited to a supply ship that serviced the atoll roughly six times a year—needless to say, I was terrified. And, I should add, I was terrified in a loincloth, as I had been instructed by the chief that such was required attire on the atoll. Skimpily clad, with my career hanging in the balance, I explained to these elders in my broken Woleaian (nothing like spending two months waiting for a ship to afford the time to learn a local language) that I had come to study how they cooperate. I explained that I knew that they cooperatively fished together every day and that they also cooperatively built and repaired their canoes and huts regularly.

Fortunately, after hearing my purpose and consulting among themselves, one of the elders responded, "Yes, you have a lot to learn from us. We have heard that some people in your country have no home and live on the streets without food. We will teach you how to cooperate and you can teach others in your country, so everyone will have food and a home."

Wow, I did have a lot to learn. I certainly haven't lived up to my end of this bargain, but my entry into their world was secured and my anthropological career was successfully launched.

And I did indeed learn much about cooperation from living with my gracious hosts, especially how seemingly trivial acts can create social expectations and obligations to care for others. For example, I observed that ritualized greetings are a simple yet underappreciated weapon against hunger and homelessness. On the atoll where I lived, residents didn't greet each other by saying "Hello!" or "Hi, how are you?" or other niceties that have become empty expressions in our society. Nor did they wish each other "Good morning!", risking a debate between a cantankerous wizard and a befuddled hobbit about the meaning of this ambiguous salutation. Rather, residents of the atoll greeted each other with a clear command: "Come and eat!" And they could be quite insistent. Who knew that living in Micronesia would be like visiting an island of Jewish grandmothers?

I guess stories about rites of passage for entry into indigenous communities have a way of taking on a life of their own. Recently I got together with some college friends I had not seen in years. My friend Jerry told me that he always recounts the story of how his good buddy, an adventurous anthropologist, was accepted into a tribe of hunter-gatherers from Brazil. I looked at him curiously and asked what he was referring to.

"You know, how you had to shoot a monkey with a bow and arrow, climb a tree to fetch it, and then break open its skull and eat its brains in order to be accepted into the group," Jerry responded casually, taking another swig of beer.

"Huh? What are you talking about?"

"You know dude, that whole rite of passage thing you had to do so you could live with those hunter-gatherers."

"Jerry, what on earth are you talking about?" I exclaimed with genuine confusion. "There is no way I could have shot a monkey with a bow and arrow. And I never had to climb a tree and crack open a monkey's skull and eat its brains. In fact, I've never even been to Brazil!"

"Really?"

"Yes, really," I responded with a mix of exasperation and amusement. "I did visit hunter-gatherers my advisor works with, but that was in Paraguay. I did indeed eat monkey and armadillo, breaking over a decade of vegetarianism, but this was to avoid starvation, not to gain acceptance into the group."

"Didn't you have to do something in order to go hunting with them?" Jerry stammered in disbelief.

"I suspect eating larvae won me some friends," I said, recalling the entertained faces of my hosts as I swallowed my first grub, "but as a student of my advisor I would have been tolerated no matter what I ate."

Jerry shook his head. "You have no idea how many people I've told that story to!"

"Well," I consoled him, "it's a good story, better than any story I could have come up with, and certainly better than any story I have ever lived. You should keep telling it."

That evening we had a lot of laughs, especially about my hunting prowess, tree-climbing skills, and the taste of monkey brains. At one point the conversation turned toward having kids, and Jerry, always happy to share a tale, related how the wife of his friend Charlie gave birth to their child in the front seat of their Mazda. He recounted in great detail how Charlie and his wife had been staying with his in-laws for the summer before he began a new job. It was their second child and since the labor for their first child had been quite long, they didn't rush to the hospital when contractions began. However, once they decided to head to the hospital, Charlie realized after about two blocks that they weren't going to make it, so he turned the car around and pulled up in front of his in-laws' house. As Charlie rushed inside to call 911 (pre-cell phone days), his father in-law ran out to the car and literally caught the baby.

"Jerry, that wasn't Charlie and his wife. That's how my son Naftali was born!"

Ever since that evening, Jerry, who can't resist spinning a good yarn, begins every story with "This may not be exactly true, but ..."

And speaking of stories, fanciful or not, this brings me back to the point I was making about rites of passage. Part of the reason the Nationals served as a rite of passage for us, and presumably for others, is because at clubs throughout the US players tell stories of past Nationals: the great victories and upsets they witnessed, as well as their own embellished triumphs and dramatic losses. This turns out to be common of religious pilgrimages throughout the world as well, whether the Hajj to Mecca or the Buddhist Shikoku pilgrimage in Japan: the experience of one journey provides a lifetime of stories. Now Eliel and I would have our own stories to tell. At times, following Jerry's lead, I've tried to take poetic license with some of my own, but there is nothing like children to humble parents and keep them honest. Thanks Eliel.

THE DIFFERENCE BETWEEN THE NATIONALS and most other US tournaments is vast. Many tournaments Eliel and I attend are held on five or six tables; the largest tournaments we attend have between fifteen and twenty tables. Most tournaments typically last one or two days; a few span three. The Nationals, in contrast, last an entire week, have between 130 and 150 tables, and attract players from nearly every state in the country. Also at the Nationals, table tennis companies set up large booths to sell their products (see Appendix A for an account of my greatest purchase at one of these booths), creating a carnivalesque atmosphere. Moreover, all the top players in the country compete, so for spectators it is a rare treat. For players, it is a table tennis paradise, or perhaps table tennis Disney World, depending on your age.

The Nationals, however, are not the largest tournament of the year; the US Open and the US Teams are larger. It is also not the most competitive in terms of skill level. The US Open and US Teams both attract elite foreign players, thus the quality of play is higher at these tournaments. Even the monthly tournaments at the Westchester Table Tennis Center (more on this club later) have stronger players than at the Nationals since many Chinese coaches who are not eligible to compete at the Nationals—they are not US citizens—regularly compete at Westchester.

That said, the Nationals is probably the most intense tournament of the year. Not only are players competing for national titles, they are also competing for coveted spots on the US National teams. Consequently, the tension at the Nationals is palpable. Many parents have spent tens of thousands of dollars on their child's training and adopted a foreign player to live in their home, not to mention the hours on the table that the child has invested. As one mother put it, "I could have bought a second house with the amount of money we've put into our son's training." And they live in California's Bay Area, home to some of the highest real estate prices in the country. The Nationals is the time when parents and children find out whether their mutual efforts and sacrifices have been worth the price.

The first US Nationals, also known as the US Closed (limited to US citizens, whereas the US Open is "open" to citizens and foreign players alike), was held in 1976 at Caesar's Palace in Las Vegas. By all accounts it was an amateurish affair. The tournament was held on carpet, probably not dissimilar to the carpet in Timmy's basement. Today, not even the lowest-level tournaments can be played on carpet; to suggest the possibility is unthinkable. With the exception of a few years, the Nationals has remained in Las Vegas, although it has long moved from Caesar's Palace to the Las Vegas Convention Center.

Typically, around 750 to 850 players attend the Nationals and compete in almost one hundred events. Like most US tournaments, there are many rating events (Under-1600, Under-1800, etc.), although in recent years these events are split into Adult rating events and Junior rating events, with eighteen years of age being the dividing line. Most adults strongly prefer to play other adults, who are not only slower than youth players, but also less likely to have overly aggressive fans, that is, parental spectators. And they are less likely to cry after a loss. Comedian Frank Caliendo, a competitive player, jokes that his goal in table tennis is to get good enough to make a kid cry, and Eliel's oldest sibling, Rivka, assesses Eliel's success at a tournament by whether or not he made an opponent cry (affirmative equals success in her mind, if that was unclear). In addition to the rating events, there are also many gender-specific events separated by age, including Under-11, Under-13, Under-15, Over-40, Over-50, and so on, with the age events peaking at Over-85. Moreover, there are also doubles events (for example, Over-75 Men's Doubles, Under-18 Girls' Doubles, etc.), including some mixed-doubles events.

The playing conditions in Las Vegas are unlike those of any other place in the US, which is a constant source of conversation and consternation among players. The ball simply does not bounce in the same way it bounces elsewhere. Most notably—and I know this is confusing, but

Vegas conditions are confusing—it is both easier to keep the ball short and difficult to keep the ball from going long. For example, serves that players normally struggle to keep short (players aim to serve short in order to prevent an opponent's attack), can triple and quadruple bounce on the opponent's side in ways that are unimaginable elsewhere. At the same time, when looping, players are forced to adjust their racket angle to cover the ball more than usual to prevent it from flying off the end of the table. There are apparently two factors involved in the unusual "Vegas bounce." First, the altitude in Vegas is over two thousand feet, thus the air density is lower, enabling balls to travel further than they do at lower altitudes. Like playing baseball at Coors Field in Denver, playing table tennis at higher altitudes can be an adventure. The trajectory of shots is different than at sea level. The second factor concerns the size of the playing hall. The enormity of the Las Vegas Convention Center results in greater air pressure on the ball, which is why even though the altitude makes it difficult to keep the ball on the table, when pushing or serving short, the ball stays unusually short.

WE HAD HEARD ABOUT the challenging playing conditions in Vegas from others, so when we decided to attend our first Nationals in 2016, we arrived several days early to adjust to the conditions, as well as the heat. But nothing could prepare us for the initial shock of that first step outside the airport terminal. I have lived and traveled in many hot places—including New Mexico, Arizona, Israel, Egypt, and Jordan—but I have never experienced anything like a Vegas summer. The similes—like sticking your face in a blow dryer or walking into an oven—all fall short.

We spent the next several days visiting each of the three active clubs in Las Vegas. It was exciting to be there early. We watched as the table tennis scene mushroomed over several days. Vegas went from a city with a few dozen competitive players to a table tennis mecca. Of course the one thousand or so table tennis players, family members, coaches, and spectators who descended on Vegas for the Nationals were unremarkable in a place of such size and ceaseless tourism. But once you know what you are looking for, table tennis aficionados are easily recognized, and we noticed the transformation of the city, even if most Vegas residents had no idea we were there. Arriving early to adjust to the conditions became our routine prior to every Las Vegas tournament we attended, so we got to know many of the local players quite well. In my humble and subjective opinion, the Las Vegas table tennis community is among the most welcoming on the planet. When we return, year after year, they greet us with a smile and warmth that makes us feel like we've been missed.

Each of the clubs has its own unique charm. The club that opened earliest in the morning was owned and run by a friendly woman who had been a member of the Chinese National Team. When we would arrive early to this club, we had the pleasure of watching the owner's preteen daughter mop the floor while riding on motorized rollerblades.

One of the other clubs kept irregular hours, but it was home to many elderly and once dominant players, who spent hours between matches kibitzing about the old days. I felt it was a great privilege to be in their presence, and much to Eliel's annoyance, I often preferred to sit and listen to them spin their tales rather than play. Indeed, this is where I met Jack Howard, creator of the rating system, and other US ping pong diplomacy team members such as Errol Resek, who sadly lost his battle with cancer during the first year of the COVID-19 pandemic.

One year we became particularly fond of the third Las Vegas club, simply known as Mr. Lee's club, which is hidden in a back alley of Chinatown. This is the only club I have ever been to that came equipped with its own ball boy, if the term is even appropriate here. An elderly Korean man stood in the back of the courts with a net and would race after balls following a missed shot. He only spoke a handful of English phrases, but hopefully "thank you" was one of them because I have never said it so many times in my life.

FOR OUR FIRST NATIONALS we were clueless. Having never been to Vegas, and feeling like the tournament hotels were a little pricey, we decided to stay elsewhere. So, we booked reservations online at the cheapest hotel we could find. It was not that far from the Las Vegas Convention Center—a ten-minute Uber ride—so we were feeling pretty good about the money we would save. That is, until we arrived at the hotel. We found ourselves staying in a room that was more suited for hourly rentals than a ten-day home for a father and his fourteen-year-old son. To say that the room was Spartan would be an understatement. It consisted solely of a bed, toilet, and a barely operational shower. I guess I should mention that it did have four walls and a roof, because after staying in such a place I've learned that nothing can be taken for granted. Missing were the clock, television, and typical complimentary accoutrements such as soap, shampoo, ice bucket, and coffee. The Gideons did not even bother to leave their trademark in this room. The door to our room was trapezoidal rather than rectangular, leaving massive gaps between the door and the door frame, gaps wide enough to stick our hands through, and my hands can palm a basketball. Since the hallway lights were bright, we had to stuff the large cracks with towels to darken our room before retiring to bed. We were there, regrettably, for an extended stay, so we asked whether we could obtain a refrigerator for our room. Of course: for a price you can get anything in Vegas.

Soon after our request, a hotel worker appeared at our trapezoid with a battered cube. I looked at her with a puzzled glance and offered "Can I help you?"

She responded matter-of-factly, "Didn't you order a fridge?"

"Yes" I responded, not fully comprehending her response.

"Here it is. Where do you want me to plug it in?"

This question, as it turns out, was not actually necessary; there was only one outlet in the room. After she left, Eliel and I burst out laughing. This refrigerator looked like it had been dropped from the roof of a skyscraper at least a dozen times. We tried to count the number of dents but it was impossible to keep track of what had or had not already been counted; every inch of the refrigerator was bashed in. Once it was plugged in, it rattled, but no worse than the room's air conditioning unit. Amazingly, it worked.

Against the sound advice of my children, and any editor worth their salt, I'm going to interrupt this narrative because I've written something that is untrue, that should be corrected before I go further. It is not necessarily accurate to claim that for a price you can get anything in Vegas. One year at Nationals, no lawyers, guns, or money could have secured a refrigerator for us; it turned out that only honesty would work. In that fateful year, there was a refrigerator in our hotel room—the fanciest hotel we had ever stayed at—filled with overpriced alcoholic and non-alcoholic beverages. A sign was posted on the refrigerator indicating that patrons would be charged for any item removed from the refrigerator and tampering would result in a three-hundred-dollar fine, so I called guest services and asked whether I could obtain a refrigerator for my food. They told me, nicely but firmly, that refrigerators were not available for guests. I didn't feel like I had much choice. I had already purchased all of our food for Friday night and Saturday, when we would not be able to go out to eat because of Shabbat, and I didn't want the food to spoil. So, I removed the several dozen beverages and stuffed the refrigerator with our Shabbos food.

The next morning, while Eliel was still asleep, I went to the fridge for milk, but the door was stuck. I pulled and pulled, yet I could not pry it open. I woke Eliel and he tried. We were baffled. Looking more closely I noticed that the door wasn't stuck; it was bolted shut. Then it hit me: removing everything from the refrigerator had triggered a sensor that locked us out of the fridge. I realized I had made a several-hundred-dollar mistake and there was no way to break into the fridge and recover our food. Despondent and without options, I put my tail between my legs and called the front desk to tell them that our fridge had been bolted shut.

"Good morning Mr. Sosis. How may I help you?"

"Well, my fridge seems to be locked. I'm sorry, I know I wasn't supposed to remove items from the fridge but I am here with my son and we keep kosher and we needed a place to store our food," I said honestly. "I had called guest services and asked about getting a fridge but they said the hotel does not provide refrigerators."

"Did you explain to them that you keep kosher?"

"Um, no."

"Well Mr. Sosis, I'm very sorry for this inconvenience. I really apologize. Had they known that you keep kosher they would have surely provided you with a medical refrigerator. I'll make sure a refrigerator is sent to your room immediately. Also, I'll send someone up to unlock your refrigerator. And do not worry, I will remove the charges that have already been added to your bill. Again, I'm really sorry about this inconvenience. Is there anything else I can help you with?"

Did that really just happen? My despondency had been transformed into elation in a heartbeat. I was stunned. I had never thought of keeping kosher as a medical condition, but I have ever since. And true to his word, within minutes a medical refrigerator was brought to our room and the beverage refrigerator was unlocked. Not only did I not touch the beverage fridge for the remainder of our stay, I kept a healthy distance from it, fearing my proximity might accidentally trigger some sensor or alarm.

Back to our first Nationals and our austere hotel room. During the week I had asked one of our Uber drivers about power outages. I found the heat so oppressive I wondered what would happen if there was a blackout. Without constant air conditioning, I reasoned, Vegas would be dangerous, our rooms exceeding one-hundred degrees Fahrenheit. Our Uber driver laughed and assured me that power outages were extremely rare and all the hotels had backup generators. He apparently never needed a hotel room for an hour because he was clearly unfamiliar with our fine lodging establishment. On Saturday morning we woke up and were surprised to hear the conversation in the neighboring room. Our air conditioning unit and maltreated refrigerator were so loud that they drowned out all other noises (in my mind, this was the room's most redeeming quality). But the air conditioner was not on. Nor was the refrigerator. I stepped into the corridor and the blinding hallway lights were also off. So much for the backup generator. I looked down the hallway and others were emerging from their rooms, likewise wondering about the electricity. One man, looking groggy in his underwear, summed it up perfectly: "Well, you get what you pay for."

On subsequent trips to Vegas we decided to stay at the official tournament hotels, which curiously changed from year to year. These hotels were certainly a step up from our first experience, but we never quite got used to the smoky lobbies, five-dollar coffees, and excessive resort fees that were invariably tacked onto our bill when checking out. Not to mention the constant fear of staying next to a party room and pointlessly explaining that it was vital that my son go to sleep because he was playing in an important table tennis tournament early in the morning. "Cool, your son is playing in a beer pong tournament? Awesome dude! Where can we sign up?"

WE WERE IN VEGAS for Eliel, but I had signed up for several events as well. After more than a two-decade hiatus, I was nervous but excited to return to national competition. On the first day of the 2016 Nationals I faced a player who was rated about 2100, slightly lower than my own rating at the time. He had a very strong forehand attack but he was inconsistent. I was able to keep the ball on the table and simply wait for him to miss, which he did plenty during the first two games. I lost the third game but he had scored six points from nets and edges, and it was still a close game, so I was unconcerned. As I expected, without his abundance of net and edge points in the fourth game, I maintained control. Up 10-5, I had five match points and assumed the match was over, but he had other plans. Without the help of a net or an edge I don't think he had strung together more than two consecutive points the entire match, yet down 5-10 in the fourth game he became an unstoppable freight train and I dropped the next seven points. Eliel, who was coaching me for the match, called a timeout during this stretch, but even this did not break my opponent's momentum. In the fifth game, however, I regained my composure and took a comfortable 7-3 lead. But clearly I had not learned the appropriate lesson from my game four loss: no lead is comfortable. I managed to lose eight out of the next nine points. My opponent was justifiably elated at the improbable victory; I was in shock and furious at myself.

I was ready to drop out of the tournament. Who needs this stress, pain, and self-loathing? I had known for a while that I had difficulty holding onto leads. My mind has a will of its own, so to speak, and it wanders toward thoughts of spectacular defeat as I approach the finish line. This was not a problem I had as a Junior player—in fact, I used to pride myself on my mental toughness—but as an adult my mental game was as firm as miso soup. At this time, 2016, I was still able to beat Eliel on occasion, but only if I gave him a lead. If I had the lead I would consistently lose it, but if he had the lead at least sometimes I was able to claw my way back into the match and emerge victorious. So rather than drop out of the tournament, I decided that for my next match I would play from behind for the entire match by literally giving my opponent the first two games. I of course would have to play the games, but I would make no effort to compete. I told Eliel that I would not need his coaching services for my next match—he would surely disapprove of such tactics—and I set my plan in motion, scoring less than five in each of the first two games. Now that my back was against the wall I decided to play, much to the astonishment of my opponent, who was the top seed in the round robin and rated more than one hundred points higher than me. Before he knew what happened I won three straight games and had my best victory of the tournament.

Later in the day, in another event, I played a Junior who was much stronger than me (rated nearly two hundred points higher), but my style is a little unusual and I was giving him considerable trouble. I had won the first game and was up 10-7 in the second. I was on the verge of taking a 2-0 lead in games when a cosmic force in the universe shifted. I lost the next five points to drop the second game, and in the third game I quickly found myself down 0-4. I finally broke the string of consecutive points at nine, but my opponent had broken my spirit, and I knew it was over. Another match slipped through my hands like sand on a beach. Slightly less painful than my earlier loss, yet I could not help but beat myself up for my second collapse of the day.

Shortly after this match I noticed that the two players whom I had blown big leads against were talking to each other. I walked over to them and said with a smile "Hey, are you guys telling stories about your amazing comeback wins?" The elder player looked at me, grinned, and said, "This is my son." Unbelievable. Cosmic forces indeed. At least I had a story to share at the club when I returned to Massachusetts.

OVERALL ELIEL HAD a successful tournament. As this was his first appearance on the national scene, he was unknown and able to surprise some players, especially since he was improving rapidly and playing better than his rating. He seemed to play better against better players, often unexpectedly challenging them, even if ultimately losing. But his level of play was inconsistent and he lost a few matches that he probably should have won. Indeed, it was at this tournament that he began a pattern of losing his first match of the day, almost by habit. For whatever reason, it takes him some time to gain his focus and get his body moving. Over the years we tried various strategies to fix these morning blues—arising early, arising late, heavy morning training, light morning training, and so forth—but ultimately, I just relied on prayer: please let his first match be against such a weak player that no matter how poorly he plays he'll still win. At this tournament, God was apparently listening to other parents.

Our doubles partnership was also a casualty of the morning blues. We had been practicing doubles together for several months and we thought we were quite good. We were confident, maybe naively, that we could win our event at the Nationals. At our club we were regularly beating doubles teams with combined ratings much higher than ours, so it wasn't an entirely unrealistic expectation. We practiced so much together we knew each other's games well, which helps in doubles because we could easily anticipate each other's shots. We were also both very steady players, rarely making unforced errors, which is helpful in doubles. And perhaps most importantly, we trusted each other. But our first-round match was at nine a.m., against a lower-seeded team from Puerto Rico, and it was over before either of us broke a sweat. We didn't even win a game. I was particularly disappointed, as it was obvious that by next year Eliel would be at a higher playing level than me and require a better partner to be competitive. This premonition was correct. Over the next several years our doubles playing was limited to arranging unofficial matches with Eliel's friends and their fathers, solely for bragging rights. So, I'll brag: we remain undefeated.

Friendships, for both of us, were probably the most important outcome of our first Nationals. I was able to reconnect with countless friends I hadn't seen for decades, and I was repeatedly touched that they were as delighted to see me as I was to see them. But for Eliel, this was really the beginning of his journey. He knew some youth players from training in Maryland, where they had a strong youth program, and from tournaments throughout the Northeast. The Nationals, however, opened a whole new world for him. I found it extraordinary—and heartwarming—to watch how quickly and easily these kids, almost all of them children of immigrants, became fast friends. The cultural and ethnic boundaries that we as adults have to work to overcome seemed nonexistent for these kids, despite their obvious racial, ethnic, and religious differences. Maybe there is something to the rabbinic teaching:

> Many have come to teach the holiness of God, but there is still not peace in the world. Many have come to teach the holiness of men and women, but there is still not peace in the world. When many come to teach the holiness of children, then there will be peace in the world.

These kids were curious about Eliel's Jewish observance, an innocent and pure curiosity without judgment. And Eliel was the same with them, curious about the languages they were speaking to their parents and the piquant foods those same parents were providing for lunch. Some of the kids were extremely generous—maybe recognizing a kindred spirit in Eliel—not only sharing their backgrounds, but also giving Eliel tips about beating certain players, which often proved quite helpful.

I was thrilled that Eliel was meeting and interacting with such diverse children, as I had experienced when I competed as a youth. But as the kids hung out, laughing, playing, and roaming the tournament halls unencumbered by their parents, I admittedly experienced the first hints of a loss that would become more pronounced in years to come. These friends, as I seemed to intuitively realize, would ultimately replace me as doubles partner, practice partner, lunchmate, confidant, and even coach. This is as it should be, and of course I wanted him to build such friendships. But recognizing this as an essential part of his growth as a person didn't lessen the melancholy that these thoughts stirred. Evidently, acknowledging that we want our children to mature into self-confident independent adults doesn't make this transition, when it begins, any easier.

CHAPTER 10

Identity

Eliel's development as a player between our first and second Nationals was considerable. He was now recognized among the top players in his age category, Under-15, which is curiously known as "Cadets." The Under-13 age category is known as "Mini-cadets" and older age categories are referred to as "Veterans" so the military theme is pervasive. Military clichés at tournaments are also common—"It's a war out there!", "Keep battling!", and so forth—so maybe there is some value in conceiving of tournaments as battlefields. And certainly "table tennis" could replace "war" in Sun Tzu's oft-stated observation that "All war is based on deception."

We had spent the previous year regularly attending tournaments throughout the Northeast, especially the previously mentioned monthly tournament at the Westchester Table Tennis Center (WTTC) in New York. This tournament was a genuine blessing for us. Aside from the high level of competition and ideal playing conditions, the top events were played on Sunday (lower-level events on Saturday) so we did not have a conflict with Shabbat as was true for many other tournaments. WTTC is one of the largest table tennis clubs in the country and one of the most welcoming. It is owned by Will Shortz—yes, that Will Shortz, of *New York Times* crossword puzzle fame. Will is almost the antithesis of the absentee New England Table Tennis Club owner. Not only is Will at WTTC daily, it is not unusual to see him sweeping floors, picking up empty Gatorade bottles, taking out the garbage, cleaning the bathrooms, and straightening barriers the evening before a tournament. I don't know how famous people normally live, but I'd be stunned if any of them live with as little pretense as Will Shortz.

In mentioning that Will is at the club daily I glossed over one of Will's (many) extraordinary accomplishments: he is the Cal Ripken of table tennis. Actually, he has now passed Ripken's Iron Man streak by a large margin, although he has a way to go to catch my favorite broadcaster, John Sterling (yes, I'm a clandestine Yankees fan living in the heart of Red Sox Nation). Since his late fifties, Will has played table tennis every day. Not nearly every day, *every* day. As of this writing he has played for more than 3,500 consecutive days. The only thing I can say with confidence that I've done daily over the last 3,500 days is breathe. There are so many things to marvel about Will's streak. Avoiding sickness and injury surely top the list, but sheer focus, determination, and steadfastness are right beside them. As the most famous puzzler on the planet, Will has a heavy travel schedule. Yet, wherever he is—Honolulu or Helsinki—he finds a place to play table tennis. I've served as his hitting partner during the streak on a few occasions, and contributing to his world record is one of the greatest honors I've had in a lifetime of playing this sport.

While we are on the subject, Will Shortz is not the only celebrity table tennis club owner. Actress Susan Sarandon co-owns the Manhattan and Toronto branches of SPiN, the swanky table tennis nightclub, for which Eliel is too young and I am too old. Apparently, Sarandon was attracted to table tennis because it is a sport in which men and women compete on equal terms. She is correct. Although there is a gap between the top men and top women in the world, this gap is not as wide as in most sports. Indeed, two of the top ten players in the US are women, and at a 2019 exhibition at UCLA, the Chinese Women's National Team easily defeated the US Men's National Team, five matches to one. Moreover, there is no difference between the length of men's and women's matches, as there is in tennis, nor is there any difference in playing conditions, as occurs in basketball (smaller ball and closer three-point line in the women's game). At most tournaments in the US there is no separation between genders; everyone competes in the same events.

Aside from Sarandon and Shortz, other celebrities have also been enamored with the sport. Prince was a regular at SPiN. And the aforementioned Frank Caliendo and comedian Judah Friedlander are both active and accomplished players. Indeed, in season four of *30 Rock*, Friedlander's character Frank sports a "Seemiller Grip" hat in the Halloween episode, which presumably went over most viewers' heads. Henry Miller was also an enthusiast, and he evidently played with Bob Dylan when they met in 1963. George Gershwin and Arthur Schoenberg regularly competed against each other—Gershwin's violin case allegedly carried his paddle. Incidentally, Schoenberg apparently passed his passion for the game on to his grandson Randy, who owns a table tennis robot. My first anthropology professor was not a celebrity—although on campus he was famous for the consistency of his wardrobe (green turtlenecks every day, regardless of the weather) and his smoking habit (during lectures, he entered smoking, then lit one cigarette from the previous one until the end of class)—but he used to play avidly with his professor and advisor, Victor Turner, who although not a household name, is about as famous as anthropologists get.

Back to our protagonist. As I was mentioning, between the 2016 and 2017 US Nationals Eliel competed in many tournaments so he was, to continue the military theme, battle-tested. He also spent time training in New York, New Jersey, and Maryland, and his rate of progress was exceptional. There was nobody at his level of play who started as late as him: eleven years old. His fellow Cadets had been taking lessons at least since they were seven or eight years old, and many of them began lessons as early as age five. Despite his comparatively late start, by the summer of 2017—within less than three years of tournament play—he had caught up to or surpassed most of them.

The criteria for making the US National Team has varied over the years, but in 2017 finishing in the top eight in your age category at the Nationals guaranteed a spot on the team. Making the team was clearly the goal, but I usually tried to deflect conversations away from its importance to alleviate pressure that Eliel might be feeling. In truth, Eliel has always been as cool as a cucumber; deflection was to lessen my anxiety. We mostly spoke about having fun and improving, although securing a coveted spot on the team was unquestionably in the back, or maybe front, of both of our minds. The competition was stiff, but Eliel would certainly be a contender. And this would be his last year as a Cadet, so now was his opportunity. Hence the pressure. Next year he would be among the youngest in the succeeding age category, the Juniors, with no chance of making the National Team.

The Cadet event began on the first day of the tournament, a Monday morning. There would be no time to ease into the tournament, but we had been in Vegas for a few days so we were acclimated to the unusual playing conditions and unforgiving climate, or as acclimated as we were going to be. He was the top seed in his round robin, and the only player who could legitimately compete with Eliel was one of his friends from Maryland. But Eliel had played him many times during training sessions, including the week before the Nationals, and had never lost, so this was a welcome first-round matchup. Eliel would not have to adjust to an unknown style or unfamiliar serves. My only concern was overconfidence, so I reminded Eliel that practice matches and tournament matches can be different beasts altogether. It was vital that he stay focused. Eliel went through his first two matches without much effort, while his friend, although ultimately winning, struggled during one match, which falsely buoyed our confidence. Eliel and his friend then met in the final match of the round robin to determine who would advance.

It is not easy to write about matches whose sole cosmic purpose is seemingly to hasten my departure from this planet. Eliel's friend was confident and playing brilliantly; Eliel looked hapless and overmatched. He was down two games to one, but he managed to pull off the fourth game in a nail biter. But in the fifth and final game Eliel found himself down 8–2, and then match point at 10–5. I don't know if it was my heartfelt prayers to every omnipotent force I could conjure from the Valar to the Q Continuum, but in one of his greatest comebacks ever, he pulled out the match at 15–13 in the fifth.

This match solidified Eliel's well-earned reputation as an escape artist. He seems to play his best when his back is against the wall, and I know from my own battles with him that no lead is ever safe. His match also turned me into a coaching favorite among Eliel's friends. Ever afterward, many of Eliel's friends would seek me out to coach their matches, in lieu of the coaches on their parents' payroll. This did not endear me to the other ping pong pops. Coaches charge a daily or a match fee, and parents pay for their flights, hotels, food, and other expenses. Yet kids were asking their parents to let the professional coaches continue playing Angry Birds or Candy Crush on their phones and allow a neurotic middle-aged Jewish professor to coach them instead. In truth, my success as a coach, if I've had any success at all, is similar to a phenomenon I see in academia: since professors generally thrived when they were in school, they often don't appreciate the learning challenges some of their students face. Likewise, I was closer to the playing level of Eliel's friends and I had a better sense of what they could and could not do than their live-in or club coaches. I'm a better cheerleader than I am a coach, and sometimes, more than the analytical tactics of a qualified coach, these kids simply need the confidence boost that a vocal supportive fan can provide.

The next round robin for the Cadet Boys event was not until Thursday, but Eliel had various other events to keep him busy until then. Most notably, he competed in the Junior Boys event for those who are under eighteen. He had little expectation to do well or even advance in this event. He was the second seed in his initial round robin, and the top seed was rated more than one hundred points higher than Eliel and had beaten Eliel comfortably the previous year at the Nationals. But Eliel had clearly improved more than this Junior and Eliel stunned him, and me, with a 3–0 victory. Eliel had even fewer expectations in his next round robin, as he was by far the lowest ranked of the six players. But he ended up finishing third in the group, upsetting several 2400 players along the way in some brilliantly played and absolutely thrilling matches. And even against the top two players in the group, who were among the best players (not just Juniors) in the country, Eliel was competitive even in defeat.

After the round robin, Eliel was placed into a single elimination draw, which was followed by one last match to determine his final position in the Junior event. He would be competing against one of the top players in the country, a 2600-rated US Junior and Men's National Team member. As expected, Nick Tio obliterated Eliel in the first game, and yes, obliterated is the correct word choice. It was not just that Eliel only scored a handful of points; Tio has the most explosive forehand of anyone in the country, by quite a large margin. To experience the power of his shots is frankly scary. I was glad to be sitting behind a barrier, and that was at thirty feet away. After the quick first game, Eliel came to me for water and advice, but what could I say against such a player?

"Nice work," I grinned. "You've got him exactly where you want him."

What else could I do but joke? But apparently Eliel took me seriously because he went out and won the next game, convincingly. And the next one too. Could this really be happening? A small crowd was beginning to gather, apparently asking the same question. If there was to be a miracle, I thought it was essential for Eliel to take the fourth game before Tio's confidence was restored. I urged Eliel to keep the pressure on, but Tio won the fourth game without much resistance. I knew Tio would assert himself in the fifth and the match was essentially over, but as dad and coach I offered encouragement and tried to make Eliel believe that he could pull off the upset, even if my rational brain, which occasionally rears its head, knew that it would be impossible.

The fifth game had now attracted a sizable crowd. Tio is an extremely aggressive player and Eliel is a very steady player, with exceptional defensive skills. Eliel was staying in the match by returning shots Tio normally blew past players for winners. Tio was simply unprepared for Eliel's surprising returns. The fifth game was tight throughout and the crowd was treated to some spectacular points. Toward the end of the game Eliel went up 9–7 and I was barely able to contain myself. My heart was pounding through my sweatshirt and I squeezed a friend's hand and nearly crushed it before I realized what I was doing. The buzz in the crowd was tangible. But Tio took the next two points to tie it up at 9–9 and I realized that this is what happens: good players find ways to win, so I resigned myself to the comfort of knowing that Eliel had fought well and brought one of the country's best players to the brink. On this day, that good player, however, was Eliel. He won the next two points and the match. And to his credit, and my pride, he was a gracious winner. No shouting, racket tossing, or World Championship-type celebrations, despite this being the best victory of his life. A simple respectful handshake and finally a well-earned smile when he returned to me to gather up his belongings.

We realized afterward that this kind of upset doesn't go unnoticed. The first inkling came the following day when Olympian Wu Yue, who had probably never heard of Eliel twenty-four hours earlier, asked Eliel to hit with her to warm up for an upcoming match. Like all communities, even among so-called egalitarian hunter-gatherers with whom

I've worked, the table tennis world maintains distinct status differentials. As Victor Turner, the aforementioned paddle-wielding anthropologist, pointed out, status is an abstract concept and thus physical activities—often rituals—are required for status to become established within communities. One of the ways in which status differentials become manifest within table tennis communities is through the social rituals of seeking a warm-up partner at a tournament, and the unspoken rules about whom a player can appropriately ask. Specifically, warm-up partners assort themselves by skill level; at the major tournaments part of the evenings are spent texting other players about warm-up plans for the following day. If a lower-skilled player were to ask a stronger player to warm up, it would put the stronger player in an awkward position since it is difficult to adequately warm up when a player cannot return your shots.

Words cannot capture the excitement I felt when Wu Yue asked Eliel to warm up. I realize competitive table tennis is unknown to most Americans, but for table tennis players Olympians are our heroes. Eliel and I had watched Wu Yue play many times, nationally and internationally, and we could legitimately be counted among her fans. She is an exciting player to watch, with an extraordinarily quick table game in which she hits everything right off the bounce. Her asking Eliel to practice would be like Sloane Stephens or Madison Keys asking an unknown fifteen-year-old to help them warm up at Wimbledon. I know, unthinkable. But that is what it felt like. Incidentally, Wu Yue won her match after she warmed up with Eliel, which only added to my pride.

Eliel's success at the Nationals was, unfortunately, short-lived. During an Under-2400 rating event that same day, Eliel and I were scheduled to play our round robins simultaneously. Eliel was heavily favored in his round robin and I was the third seed in my group. In other words, I had low expectations for myself and I didn't think Eliel needed my coaching; I assumed he would breeze through the round robin, especially the way he had been playing. But sports are interesting because they are unpredictable.

Eliel was playing several tables away from me so I found it impossible to concentrate on my match. In between points I would steal glances at his table, and I could see something was wrong. I wanted to default my match and try to coach him out of whatever mess he was in, but defaulting a match is unfair to the other competitors in the round robin. Out of respect for the competition I had to continue, so I did. By the time I finished my match he had lost to someone who was rated several hundred points lower than him: by far his worst loss in months. It was unthinkable, but Tio probably felt the same way the day before.

For me, it was the last time I entered a tournament in which Eliel was competing. I realized that my role was to be by Eliel as his coach, and that is precisely where I wanted to be. Maybe there will be a time when I return to competitive play, but it won't be while Eliel is competing. I wish I could have figured that out before such an unfortunate loss. But Eliel is resilient and the loss was quickly behind him. And in truth, although it was an event that Eliel thought he could have won, it was not his main event. That was the Cadets, and play would resume in that event the next day.

His Cadet round robin had six players, of which two would advance and make the US National Team. The pressure was extreme and unfortunately such pressure did not bring out the best in everyone. Actually, let me rephrase that. The players rose to the challenge and generally played well; the pressure did not bring out the best in the parents. During one of the matches an argument between two fathers erupted because one of the fathers claimed his son's opponent was serving illegally, hiding the ball behind his shoulder during contact. Parents aren't allowed to get involved in matches, but it was too late. It became a volatile scene and umpires were called in to settle things down. The incident set the tone—tense and uncomfortable—for the entire morning. As is all too common in youth athletics, the parents all lost that day.

Afterward, other parents rationalized the poor sportsmanship of the father who instigated the fracas, suggesting that had his son not advanced out of the round robin it would have been too devastating for the family to bear. They had a live-in coach who had been training their son for nearly a decade; only making the US National Team could validate their extraordinary investment. The son did make the team but was not invited to play in any international matches. Within a year he had dropped out of table tennis entirely.

With this player's advancement secured, the final spot to advance from the round robin and make the team ultimately came down to Eliel and a player from California, whose father ranks among the nicest ping pong pops I've encountered. I often practice with this father while our sons are off running around at the national tournaments, and I've served as his coach on more than one occasion. I'll let Eliel describe the match and its repercussions in his own words, written for his school's traditional end-of-summer-return-to-school assignment: write a one-page essay about an experience or challenge you had this past summer.

> Seven more points and the match would be over, a quarterfinal place secured as well as a place on the U.S. National Team. My father, acting as my coach, had repeatedly told me not to think ahead like that: always take the match one point at a time.
>
> But it is never that easy while playing table tennis. The games are too short to lose concentration for even a moment. In an instant I had lost, knocked out of my main event. Making the U.S. National Team had been my goal for years, but as I sat with my towel in my hands and my water bottle on my lap after the match, all I could think of was every missed shot,

every lost point. An onlooker would have noticed nothing from my expressionless face, but my mind was in turmoil, an unusual experience for me. I had failed to make the team, but the tournament was not yet over, so I tried to shift my focus to the matches ahead. Despite the loss, I still had matches that would determine my final position, and I was resolved to continue fighting.

I would love to tell of how I rose up from my shortcomings to go undefeated for the rest of the tournament, but alas, such was not my luck. After walking back to my hotel room with my father, I checked the draws for the next round. It was Thursday night, and I was expecting an early start the next day in the consolation bracket; but written on the draw next to my first match was "Saturday. 9:00 AM. Table 7." That was a problem. Saturday was Shabbat.

I was stuck in a conflict of values. I had sacrificed so much for table tennis: completing my math homework on the bus ride home from school to make time for practice, missing a week of school to attend the U.S. Open, and leaving Thanksgiving dinner early to attend a tournament. All my hard work had led to this tournament, to this event, but at this moment table tennis came crashing into conflict with another major part of my life. As an observant Jew, Shabbat is an inviolable time. For me, Shabbat has always been a day of rest when I connect with my family, play board games, read books, and sit down for a delicious meal. On Shabbat, I also have time to develop a deeper connection with God.

A central theme in Judaism is constructing barriers to improve oneself, and Shabbat is one such barrier. To me, observing the laws of Shabbat is not just about following rules; practicing Judaism gives my life more meaning and purpose.

Judaism guides me in making myself a better person and the world a better place. Although table tennis provides me with a sense of achievement, I recognized it could not take priority over my core values.

I realized that with my choice, I would be setting a standard for all my future competitions as well as any future conflicts between careers, family, religion, and personal interests. I had to make the choice I felt was right, despite the difficulty involved. And if table tennis had taught me anything, I knew I had to step up despite the challenge I faced. As an observant Jew, I decided it was not right for me to play the tournament matches on Shabbat. This experience helped me solidify my values and better understand what I stood for. I need to live up to the standards I set for myself even if this involves making sacrifices along the way.

With disappointment on my face but pride in my heart, I defaulted my final matches of the 2017 U.S. National Table Tennis Championships.

Postscript

Eliel was indeed disappointed that he did not make the Cadet National Team, but his success in the Juniors did not go unnoticed. Eliel's schoolmates in Massachusetts had been following the tournament online, as well as most of the players at the clubs we frequent. One day in August, when we had returned to Massachusetts, we went to play at Mozart's club. Mozart was not there, but someone texted him to let him know we had shown up. He drove out to the club and he looked terrible: he was covered in a rash from poison ivy and was understandably in pain. But what a beautiful spirit. He stood next to Eliel and asked everyone to stop playing. He then congratulated Eliel and told him how proud he was of his outstanding achievements at the US Nationals. Everyone applauded as Mozart handed Eliel a stunning, engraved trophy in honor of his success. I was deeply moved.

Unfortunately, not everyone in the world of table tennis is such a gentle, thoughtful soul—myself included. Or maybe more fairly, sometimes other responsibilities prevent us from realizing the noble and generous inclinations we likely all possess.

CHAPTER 11

Ping Pong Popping

In 2017, USATT hired a new High Performance Director, following the firing of the previous HPD due to accusations of bias. Specifically, there were concerns that players from the HPD's own club were receiving special treatment, most notably being chosen to represent the US at international competitions ahead of more deserving players. Like most scandals, gossip and rumor outpaced verifiable information, and as an outsider I am in no position to assess the charges. I'm also fond of the previous HPD and appreciate what he has contributed to the sport, so I am not without bias. That said, not only was the HPD fired, the entire USATT board resigned at the same time, certainly giving the impression that something foul was afoot.

The new HPD, Tomas, was a former Austrian player without distinction, but he had considerable success as a coach. He also had institutional experience in Austria, leading their women's professional basketball program. More importantly, Tomas had an explicit goal for American table tennis and a vision on how to achieve that goal. His primary objective was a US Olympic medal. Table tennis is one of three Olympic sports in which the US has never medaled; badminton and handball are the others. The importance of achieving an Olympic medal is straightforward. The US Olympic Committee will not begin funding a sport until it wins a medal, and in a sport such as table tennis that is perennially cash-starved, such funding would be the golden road to paradise.

Even for the most skilled leaders, long-term visions are difficult to implement, and Tomas's vision was, if anything, long-term. He believed there were no current American players who could ultimately win an Olympic medal. By his assessment, our only hope was children who were just beginning to play, those under ten years old, who could be properly trained and nurtured into champions. But Americans are dreamers. Sometimes unrealistic, sometimes arrogant, sometimes foolish, but always dreaming. We are good at it. So to inform an entire generation of players that they have no shot at Olympic glory was bound to cause trouble, even if the assertion was realistic. To be clear about my own position, I suspect Tomas's assessment was correct, or at least nearly correct. But sometimes being correct misses the point, and Tomas seems to have missed the point. He didn't understand the way Americans think and dream, and that understanding was critical to successfully implementing his long-term plan. He needed parents and players to get onboard and trust his vision.

Tomas's vision included several radical changes to American table tennis. First, he was convinced that Americans could not succeed internationally if they remained in the US. Not only does the US not have the infrastructure to support elite-level table tennis; it does not have the culture that is necessary for our youth players to succeed. Therefore, Tomas encouraged our top players to relocate overseas if they wanted to compete seriously. Four-time Men's National Champion, Kanak Jha, who is now twenty-two years old, has been living abroad—first Sweden, now Germany—since he was fifteen years old. This commitment is precisely what Tomas wanted to see, and Kanak has accordingly received attention and support from the HPD and USATT. Kanak Jha recently moved from the second division of the Bundesliga to the first, and as of this writing he is ranked in the top forty in the world. In 2018, upon high school graduation, a second men's player, the aforementioned Nick Tio, joined Kanak in Germany. The HPD facilitated this move and Tio played in the third division of the Bundesliga. Other youth players soon followed, and in the 2019–20 season an unprecedented twenty-three Americans were registered to compete in German leagues, many of them training in Germany full-time.

Second, for those youth players who have not resettled in Europe, Tomas expected players to regularly compete in international tournaments. This was indeed a positive step for US table tennis, but international competitions pose two challenges, the two challenges that youth players face at every turn: school and money. International competitions minimally require missing three days of school, but more often a full week because of the travel involved. To deal with this obstacle, the HPD has recommended homeschooling for top players, and accordingly, an increasing number of youth players have begun homeschooling, freeing up their schedules for international travel. Finances are of course another obstacle. USATT provides very little financial support to players competing internationally unless it is a major event, such as the World Championships. Following Tomas's directive, we considered attending a tournament in Sweden during Eliel's spring break, but when I sat down to figure out the actual costs involved, I realized we simply could not afford it. The sad truth is, our top youth players have parents who can afford such travel, while those who can't have generally dropped out of the sport.

Third, Tomas instituted national ranking tournaments for youths and adults. At three tournaments a year—one on the East Coast, one on the West Coast, and the US Nationals—players can accumulate points, and those with the highest point totals are guaranteed spots on the National Team. Again, missing school is inevitable, as is the expense of flying to opposite coasts.

These initiatives were met with mixed response among players and parents. I was initially frustrated by these decisions because they all make it harder for a player like Eliel to reach the highest levels of competition. But it was actually Eliel who convinced me of the merits of Tomas's plan. As I've surely mentioned before, Eliel is more level-headed than I am, and he was able to assess Tomas's vision independently of its impacts on his own table tennis career. I, on the other hand, as a parent, could initially only see the negative impacts on my son. But I do appreciate Vulcan logic, even if my emotions frequently cloud my opinions.

The financial investment expected of parents was one obvious problem I had with Tomas's new agenda, and this concern was regularly expressed by other parents and even coaches (who cared about the future of the sport) at meetings with Tomas. But parenting, at least in the US, requires resources regardless of a child's pursuits, so for me this was not the most significant issue.

For my wife and I, the deeper issues were about education and identity. For two parents with PhDs (my wife's degree is in geology), we have simply assumed that our children would pursue a college education. But the commitment to international competition and training required by Tomas's plan would make attending university nearly impossible. Since there is no collegiate support for table tennis in the US, college was understandably not part of Tomas's plan. I have come to deeply appreciate collegiate athletics, despite its sundry flaws, as I see what happens to players of a sport that is not supported by the NCAA and other university institutional structures. Many parents of table tennis players are also overeducated and have similar expectations for their children, so we were not alone in this concern.

But we also had another concern that was not shared by other parents. It was hard enough maintaining Jewish observance while active in the US table tennis scene. And it is worth noting here that the USATT and the national coaches have been very respectful of Eliel's unwillingness to compete on Shabbat. Tomas has been particularly sensitive and considerate, even offering to provide Eliel with kosher food at national training camps, a thoughtful gesture that we declined. Eliel always brought or purchased his own food, with his excessive yoghurt consumption becoming a running joke in the camps. Europe, however, would undoubtedly be less accommodating of Jewish observance.

These were my biases against Tomas's plan. Nevertheless, once Eliel helped me see past them, I realized Tomas had a job to do and his strategy was a viable way to achieve his goals, even if it left us behind.

I offer this background because over the next few years, Tomas and I had our differences. Thankfully, Tomas is someone who listens to differing opinions. He rarely changes his mind, in my experience, but at least he always listens when I have a grievance, which I appreciate. Indeed, I have great respect for Tomas's organizational talents and his commitment to table tennis, and most importantly, he has helped me realize I can genuinely like someone who I disagree with. Our differing opinions are understandable and probably inevitable: we have different goals. I'm a ping pong pop seeking the best opportunities for my son; he is running a national program with the aim of bringing home an Olympic medal.

I initially contacted Tomas because it was evident that, having not made the Cadet National Team, Eliel would not be on Tomas's radar. Nevertheless, I strongly believed, with parental bias of course, that Eliel had among the highest potential of any young player in the country. What he had already accomplished without formal training in such a short time was simply unprecedented, and his fellow youth players recognized this as well. I've heard many of them ask how he got so good without a professional coach or high-level players with which to train. Eliel's response to such praise is always the same: "Practice." This is true, but he is naturally athletic, so his practice, even with lower-level players, has translated into success. And he is a smart player, or as a commentator recently described him during a live-streamed tournament final: "Eliel is a cerebral player." Indeed, at national tournaments

I've had many players—some I knew, some I did not—tell me that Eliel will someday be a national champion. I'm always surprised by such comments since despite some good wins, there has always been a gap between him and the top players, even the top players of his age. But when I press them, these fortune tellers invariably point to Eliel's intelligence during match play. During competition he quickly grasps not only his opponents' strengths and weaknesses but also their strategy, and he is able to make mid-match adjustments in response.

Thus, I contacted Tomas hoping he would see what I and others had seen in Eliel. In the short term, I sought an invitation to the National Team training camp, known as the Supercamp, which was running during Eliel's winter break. Eliel had not been invited to previous camps, although he was a stronger player than many who were invited. All these players trained at one of the major clubs—and thus were visible to the HPD—and had professional coaches who could advocate for them. Lacking both, Eliel was understandably less visible than his peers. He needed an advocate, and I realized I needed to add that to my list of responsibilities as a ping pong pop. So I emailed Tomas, asking whether Eliel was being considered for the upcoming Supercamp, and I listed several national coaches who could vouch for Eliel's strong work ethic and level of play.

Tomas responded graciously. Decisions about the invitation list had not been finalized yet, but he would let us know shortly. Unexpectedly, his response came with another invitation: Eliel was invited to participate in the North American Youth Olympic Trials, for the US and Canada, that would be held in Las Vegas in December. The trials were limited to each country's top eight fifteen-to-seventeen-year-old players, but several US players ranked higher than Eliel were unable to compete. The reason they couldn't compete, as it turns out, was that they had already missed too much school due to international competitions, and their respective principals made it clear that further absences would not be tolerated. If Eliel accepted the invitation, he would, for the first time, be representing the US on the National Team at an international event.

Tomas had indicated that we had about a week to decide whether Eliel would compete. It was an exciting opportunity, but it had to be weighed against the costs of flights to Las Vegas, ground transportation, a hotel room, and missed school. I responded that we would let him know before the deadline, and Tomas reminded me that I had not informed him about Eliel's training environment and goals, which he had requested in his initial response to me. I'll pick up the email exchange at this point.

November 8, 2017

Tomas,

Thanks, we will let you know in time. Regarding Eliel's goals and training, his routine is complicated. He attends a Jewish day school with a dual curriculum (half a day in English, half a day in Hebrew) so his school hours are long, but a typical week is as follows. He awakes at 6:00 a.m., leaves the house by 6:20, and returns from school by 6:30 p.m. When he gets home he finishes his homework (we've made a special arrangement with his school, because of table tennis, so that he has a little extra free time in school to complete most of his homework so that he is free to play table tennis in the evening), eats dinner, and at 7:30 p.m. begins to train. On most days that consists of playing on our robopong robot from 7:30-9:00. He does a range of drills on the robot and the specifics vary depending on what he is working on (after tournaments we discuss what he needs to work on and this often influences his drilling). Sometimes he serves during this time and he does about 15 minutes of core exercises. From around 9:15 to 10:00 he hits with me (I'm a 2100 player). During this time he mostly works on serve and attack or short game, as well as service return. He is in bed by 11:00. That is the weekday schedule with the exception of Wednesday. On Wednesday I pick him up early from school so he can play in a league at a club that is about an hour from our home. The league has a lot of 2200 players so although he is often (but not always) the top player, this is the one day a week that he gets in some good matches. On Saturday he plays at home for generally about 4-5 hours, half with me during the day and half with the robot in the evening. He also does physical training for about an hour. On Sunday he makes arrangements to meet players at the club for training. He is there for about 5 hours and he does drills with two or three players who are about 2200 during that time. On the weekend he also likes to watch videos and he regularly follows matches on the ITTF website.

Concerning goals, like most players his age he dreams of the Olympics and being the national champion. He has a long way to go but he loves playing—all his effort is his own (in other words, we never tell him to play or exercise). He has only had one (one-hour) private lesson in his life (a birthday gift from his aunt) but he has spent several summers in Maryland in the training camps at MDTTC, which have helped his game considerably.

His strength as a player is his mental toughness and steadiness. Everyone who plays him or watches him comments that he is a smart player. He is also a good athlete. His weakness is power. He has some power on his backhand but his forehand is weak and he lacks the power of other players at his level. His service and service return game also are low for his level of play. He unfortunately does not train with other kids so he is not sufficiently exposed to the quick play of other kids, so although he is quick he is unused to playing other quick players. Thanks again for your emails and we will get back to you regarding the Youth Olympics.

Best wishes,

Rich

November 8, 2017

Hi Richard,

Thanks for all the information and the details!

I must confess, it gives me very mixed feelings because on the one hand I can read that your son is investing a lot and put in so much effort. I mean the daily routine is really remarkable and demands respect from me. On the other hand, the circumstances and especially the training conditions you are describing, without wanting to be disrespectful to you or anyone, is not an environment which I would consider to have a chance to make it to the top. And I'm talking about international high level, because this is what I'm responsible and aiming for with our talents.

Best,

Tomas

One thing academic life has taught me: don't respond to emails when you are frustrated. And at this point I was frustrated. I prudently waited to respond until my temperature cooled.

November 12, 2017

Tomas,

Thanks for your response, although to be honest I'm not sure what to make of it. About three years ago Eliel was given a school assignment to write a letter to a famous person. He chose to write Danny Seemiller. He wrote to Danny that he was learning how to play table tennis but there were limited opportunities where he lived. He asked Danny if he would ever be giving a clinic in Massachusetts; if so, he would like to attend and learn from him. Danny graciously responded (in a handwritten letter) that he does not travel like he used to so he did not think he would be in the area anytime soon. However, Danny invited Eliel to South Bend where he would be welcome to stay at his home and train in his club. In the letter, he also told Eliel: "You can still achieve great things in table tennis where you live. My brother Rick and I trained in our backyard barn to beat the Chinese someday, and we did." Eliel keeps this letter in the nightstand by his bed. I don't think you should count out Eliel or any child with passion and a dream. Nobody would have expected that someone who had been playing for only four years (less than three years of tournament play), without private coaching, would beat a member of our Men's National Team, but Eliel did. You obviously know your job description better than I do, and like you, I mean no disrespect, but I suspect that the kids at ICC [a top club in California], Maryland, and New York have their share of high-quality coaches; the kids who fall outside the orbit of these major table tennis hubs, however, would really benefit from your expertise. I hope they have the chance to train with you. I know Eliel has much to learn and he would cherish the opportunity to learn from you.

Regarding the Youth Olympics, thanks again for the invitation. He will indeed participate and is greatly looking forward to it. I have cc'ed Gordon [USATT CEO] on this message, as requested. Thanks for giving him the opportunity to compete. Please let me know what else needs to be done to register.

Lastly, if you are inviting non-team members to the Supercamp, Eliel would also gladly accept such an invitation, if it was forthcoming. Thanks again and we really look forward to meeting you in Las Vegas.

Best wishes,

Rich

November 12, 2017

Hi Richard,

Thanks for the confirmation! Good to hear that Eliel will participate in this event.

I like the story with Danny Seemiller's handwritten letter, and I can "feel" the passion your son has for TT. This is great!

My intention is not to take this, but nevertheless I am perhaps a little more realist, because the times with training in the backyard barn and then beating the Chinese, as Danny did then supposedly, are over. But not everybody needs to beat the Chinese and goals are individually different.

I like to promote motivated players in general and hope we'll find a lot more players who are so dedicated to our beautiful sport. Of course, in my job, I have to demand and promote a certain level, but everyone has a chance to offer and show what *he/she can. At the same time, however, I also have to point out or address when I feel that training conditions are not sufficient for the big goal and then I have to look at how they might have to be improved and/or changed.*

By the way, I don't believe in the system of private coaching like it is common here in this country. It can be a part of training, maybe one third, but not 100% of the content.

Best,

Tomas

He was right, but at the time I could only see, and only cared about, the consequences for Eliel. The immediate consequence was that, as had happened in previous years, Eliel was not invited to the Supercamp. He was, however, invited to many subsequent National Team training camps over the following years, but not all of them. And he did compete in the North American Youth Olympic Trials. As one of eight US players to be invited, it was quite an honor. He represented the US and was given a full team uniform and multiple shirts with his name adorned on the back, as well as shorts and a sweat suit. Actually, there was a mix-up and they made four additional personalized shirts for him, which we gladly accepted. As Eliel's official coach I was also appropriately outfitted, so we returned from Las Vegas with a suitcase full of new clothes.

Although the trials were held in Las Vegas, which was quickly becoming our home away from home, the atmosphere was unlike anything either of us had experienced before. The trials were an international event, differing in striking ways from a typical US tournament. It was well organized and run punctually. The conditions (in terms of flooring, court size, lighting, etc.) had to meet international standards, which are much higher than US standards. There were also abundant officials, in marked contrast to their scarcity at US tournaments. Along with the players, these officials were introduced to the spectators ceremoniously at the beginning of the match. This was the big time, and neither of us was ready. And unfortunately, the trials were in a single-elimination format, everyone beginning in the round of sixteen. Eliel was quickly eliminated in a best-of-seven match in the first round. Our experience gave new meaning to the classic shirt, ungratefully complaining that an uncle/mother/grandparent/friend went to some vacation spot and all they got was this lousy shirt. That is indeed about all we got, although once the rawness of Eliel's uninspired performance dissipated, I think we both cherished our mementos.

The eventual winner of the event, Kanak Jha, went on to compete in the 2018 Youth Olympic games in Buenos Aires, where he had unexpected success, reaching the semifinals before losing to Tomokazu Harimoto, a young Japanese superstar (see Appendix A). In the bronze medal match Kanak shockingly upset Lin Yun-Ju from Chinese Taipei, currently one of the top ten players in the world. Four years earlier, Lily Zhang similarly placed third at the Youth Olympics in Nanjing, China. Those bronze medals are the closest American table tennis has ever come to an Olympic medal. Maybe we are not as far away as Tomas imagined after all.

CHAPTER 12

Invisible Things

We entered the 2018 Nationals with mixed sentiments of great anticipation and low expectations. Eliel had trained all year for this tournament, so he was prepared and clearly playing stronger than his 2300 rating. Moreover, this was his third Nationals so he would not be overwhelmed by the atmosphere; no concerns about my child transforming into the proverbial deer in headlights. Realistically, however, this was his first official year as a Junior and there was a group of eight players who were rated over 2500 and somewhat out of reach. Also, because of his exceptional run the previous year—finishing thirteenth in the Juniors—he would not be surprising anyone. It would be tough to follow last year's success.

We arrived in Las Vegas several days prior to the beginning of the tournament, as we had the previous two Nationals. This year, however, we were not the earliest arrivals. Before the Nationals, Las Vegas had hosted the World Veteran Table Tennis Championships (WVC). As intimated earlier, this tournament, despite its name, is not for military veterans but rather is open to male and female adult players over forty years old. It is held biannually around the globe—2016 in Spain, 2014 in New Zealand—and this was the first time it was held in the United States. It has the distinction of being the largest table tennis tournament in the world. More than five thousand players competed at the 2018 WVC and it was estimated that another five thousand attended to watch. Incidentally, you can add this to the list of Danny Seemiller's accomplishments: with his longtime friend and fellow USATT Hall of Famer, Dave Sakai, he was responsible for bringing the WVC to the US.

There was one week between the end of the WVC and the Nationals, and the playing hall had been rented out by the USATT for this time, which meant that the tables were available for practice. I had emailed USATT's ever-accessible CEO, Gordon Kaye, to ask permission to play in the hall during this week. In previous years it had been strictly forbidden for anyone to play on the tables prior to the three-p.m. check-in on the day before play began, but I assumed it would be different this year. Gordon responded that it was no problem and he mentioned that the National Team would be holding a training camp during the week, beginning on Monday, and he would ask Tomas if Eliel could participate. I responded excitedly, but my excitement was premature as Gordon wrote shortly thereafter that Eliel would be unable to participate because "it's too late" and the camp was filled. So Eliel would have to train with his old man until other players arrived in Vegas.

AFTER WE ARRIVED, SUFFERED through the outdoor sauna, and settled into our room (closely eyeing our neighbors to see if they were the all-night partying types), we made our way to the playing hall. The security guards remembered us from previous Vegas visits and they were genuinely glad to see us. And frankly, the feelings were mutual. This unexpected reunion made us feel like we were home, and in a way, the convention center would be our home for the next week and a half. Prior to the tournament it was not uncommon for the security guards to watch Eliel train during their lunch breaks, shaking their heads in amazement as they ate. They would regularly compliment both of us on his playing, and at least one of us would swell with pride.

When we first arrived in the playing hall it was mostly empty: just us, the security guards, and about 130 tables that we had all to ourselves. We had been hitting for about two hours when it became apparent that this would not be our private practice hall after all. The National Team training camp, from which Eliel had been excluded, had arrived.

The camp consisted of ten female and twelve male players of varying ages. The rationale for the training camp was to prepare the Boys and Girls Junior teams that would be competing in the Pan Am Games directly after the Nationals. Tomas had invited other players to train with the team members, but how these other players were chosen ultimately became controversial. Some of the players were invited because their siblings were playing on the National Team. Some were simply top players, so they were suitable practice partners. But the presence of others, who were neither elite players nor relatives, raised eyebrows.

In any event, Eliel and I continued to hit as the training camp began their stretching and jogging routine. We were several tables away from them, yet we had evidently unconsciously wrapped ourselves in Harry Potter's invisibility cloak, which incidentally, beat out Ovtcharov's backhand serve by eight spots on *Time* magazine's top-fifty inventions list of 2008. Quite a year for human ingenuity. Nonetheless, here we were, a decade later, insignificant and seemingly transparent. Of course, they were not invisible to us, and we were both distracted, constantly stealing glances at the camp to see what they were doing. They were the center of attention and they knew it. I found this hard to swallow. Eliel was friendly with a number of kids at the camp and although most of the players were stronger than Eliel, he had beaten two of the players at the last Nationals. Eliel was stoic, however, and if he felt any pain he did not show it. I, the immature one, was seething. If one of the coaches had invited Eliel to participate in the practice session, would it have hurt anyone? We were the only other players in the entire hall, so it was not as though they would be opening up the floodgates. I guess it was fortunate for them that our invisibility was not the result of Sauron's ring, the One Ring to Rule Them All, as I would have been dangerous had I possessed such an evil power on that day.

I tempered my concern, however, by remembering that they were supposed to have an even number of players so maybe it would have been impractical to include Eliel. But when they began to warm up and hit, it became apparent that not everyone was there (we would later learn that some were sick—more on that later). One player, Nick Tio, was left to warm up with USATT's media specialist, a 2200-level player allegedly there to write about the camp for the USATT's electronic magazine, USATT *Insider*. Back to seething. Eliel is a better player than this media specialist (in rating and head-to-head competition) and it was insulting that Eliel was stuck hitting with me when both Eliel and Nick would have benefited if they were hitting with each other. Eliel must have been hurt. I was. And I also realized that those who failed to invite Eliel over were not thoughtful or caring people. Human decency is not always a part of the competitive equation. When I later told the story to Barney Reed, an endlessly entertaining and outspoken table tennis coach for—get this—Google, he shuddered to think that the coaches who excluded Eliel are fathers themselves. How could a father do that to another father? I like Barney.

The same scene played itself out on the following day, but Eliel was unwavering in his focus. I, on the other hand, was completely distracted and had one eye on the ball and the other eye on the training camp, or so I wished (as Eliel would point out, most often two eyes were on the camp).

The Para US Open began that same day, which was a Thursday, so we were no longer the only players in the convention center. However, Eliel and I and the National Team training camp played in one half of the hall and the Para tournament was held in the other half. The Para US Open attracted more than two hundred players from all over the world.

It is simply a remarkable event, and I spent considerable time over the next three days watching these extraordinary athletes compete. There are eleven divisions in para competitions, and each division or class defines a particular set of disabilities. One day I watched a class-6 doubles match between the US and Korea. The US team consisted of a player without hands or legs and a player with dwarfism. The former player had prosthetic legs that he took off while he was resting. Without hands he of course could not grip his paddle, however, his paddle was strapped onto his forearm, essentially becoming an extension of it. On the Korean side, a one-armed player with unstable legs was paired with a one-legged player who supported himself with crutches. I watched in awe as these players battled it out, and I should mention that the level of play was exceptional. Despite the challenges they face at the table, they were all 2000-level players. The Americans prevailed in the match, but all the players won my unqualified respect.

ON THE FOLLOWING DAY Eliel finally got some company. Two clubs, the Maryland Table Tennis Center (MDTTC) and the Alameda Table Tennis Club, organized their own training camps. While in Maryland, Eliel had been invited to join the MDTTC camp, and while in Vegas the coach of the Alameda club invited Eliel to join their camp as well. Like the National Team training camp, these camps turned out to be controversial. It was unclear why these clubs were given preferential access to the playing hall. The USATT had not informed other coaches and clubs that space would be available, if they were interested, for pre-Nationals training camps. Adding fuel to the fire, the Alameda and MDTTC camps were organized and run by individuals who were part of the High Performance Committee. In other words, as detractors said, USATT's inner circle had special privileges. I had to agree with the accusations, but after the humiliation and frustration of watching my son watch his friends playing in a privileged camp, I was simply relieved that he could be part of something. I was also relieved that he would not need me to train with him any longer. My body was a wreck.

The camps cooperated with each other and interchanged players so that the kids could practice against diverse playing styles. Although we were no longer invisible, the exchange of players was facilitating exposure to something else that was: a highly contagious stomach virus. Players in both camps were dropping like flies. One of Eliel's closest friends from Maryland, Jason, caught it, and even one of the MDTTC coaches missed a day because of the flu. We felt terribly for Jason as his entire trip to Vegas could be in vain. We later learned that he did not consume any food for two full days. Even on the third day he was barely eating. The coaches repeatedly stressed to the children the importance of vigorously washing their hands. Indeed, the coaches required the players to wash their hands before they began to practice each day.

After camp I asked Eliel to wash his hands but he refused. He claimed he was too tired. Before I go further and write something disparaging about my son, I need to highlight a quality of Eliel that I have surely not emphasized enough: he is naturally nice. Really nice. I'd like to say he got this personality trait from me, but he is much nicer than I am. His generosity of spirit was driven home to me in a conversation we had about three Junior brothers—two of whom are fraternal twins—who are among the best players in the country. These brothers are fiercely competitive with, yet selflessly supportive of, each other. The twins were at the National Team training camp. One of the twins would be representing the US at the upcoming Pan Am games, whereas the other twin had been invited to the training camp as a practice partner. The former twin was the strongest player of the three brothers, and after he made the Olympic team in 2016 (although he did not get to compete in Rio de Janeiro) I remarked to Eliel that it must be tough for his siblings, especially his twin, to deal with the success of their brother. I assumed the natural instinct among teenage siblings was rivalry and jealously. Eliel looked at me curiously, unable to comprehend what I was saying. He finally responded, "I think it would be amazing to have a brother who was an Olympian." Yep, he is much nicer than I am.

Okay, with that prelude, now I won't feel so badly about disparaging Eliel. For me, Eliel's refusal to wash his hands was the last straw in a string of minor incidents that left me feeling completely unappreciated. I was sacrificing my time, money, and frankly my body for him; couldn't he do this one little thing for me? I know he appreciates what I do for him, but I was very anxious about him catching this stomach flu as I realized that it could ruin a year's worth of training. After all I had done for him, handwashing did not seem like too much to ask. I stormed off like a petulant teenager, fuming at his immaturity and irresponsibility, as I saw it. When I act like this, he reminds me that there is room for only one teenager in our relationship and he has priority on that status. I would have liked to have given him the silent treatment for the rest of the day, but I'm not disciplined enough for such tough love and his success quickly takes precedence over my anger in these situations. When I ran into him a half hour later I tried to make peace by asking him if he wanted to hit with me. He responded that he would find someone else to play with. Ouch.

ELIEL'S MAIN EVENT THIS year was the Juniors, which was comprised of three phases. In the first phase players competed in round robins of four or five players. Winners of their round robins advanced to the second phase. The second phase consisted of twenty-four players who were divided into four round robins of six players. The top four players in each of these round robins would advance to the third and final phase, which consisted of a sixteen-player single-elimination draw. It was vital that Eliel make it to at least the second round so that he would have an opportunity to show his abilities against some of the top players. Making it to the third round would be challenging, but not out of reach. Indeed, according to the current rankings he was in a three-way tie for seventeenth, although the difference in ratings between the fifteenth and thirtieth ranked players was marginal: any of them could make it to the third phase.

Eliel's first matches at the 2018 Nationals were on Monday at nine a.m. Unfortunately, he would not have an opportunity to ease himself into the tournament. His first round robin was for his main event, the Juniors. If he did not win his round robin, his year of training was for naught. One misstep and we might as well rebook our flight and leave Vegas Monday evening (one player actually did this). The setup of the Junior event was scary for a variety of reasons. First, as I mentioned above, Eliel has a bad habit of starting slowly and playing poorly during morning matches. Second, although he was the top seed in his round robin, he was only ten points higher than the second seed, Jinhong, who had beaten Eliel at the US Open in Las Vegas six months earlier. In that match, Eliel controlled the first two games and won them convincingly. At that time Jinhong was rated much lower than Eliel, so it seemed like the match was over. But Jinhong's coach got Jinhong on track and Eliel looked helpless for the final three games. I attribute Jinhong's success to his coach because the same coach had guided another one of his students, also a lower-rated player, past Eliel in that same tournament. In short, there were lots of reasons for concern.

Monday arrived. We awoke early and reached the playing hall as it opened at eight a.m. Eliel had thankfully arranged to warm up with someone else, so I was off the hook and we could avoid a pre-match argument. There were four players in his round robin. Eliel played the lowest-rated player first and his play was strong right from the beginning. Eliel won comfortably.

After the match, trying to be friendly, I spoke with the opponent's father, whom I had never met before. This fellow ping pong pop complimented Eliel on his exceptional play. He wondered why he was not more familiar with Eliel. I explained that we are from New England, somewhat removed from the major table tennis hubs. He was amazed that Eliel had gotten this far without formal private coaching; his son had been taking lessons regularly for years. I could not agree more. Then, unexpectedly, the father, apparently defending his son's play and probably rationalizing to himself the costs he had sunk into his son's play, remarked that Eliel's style was weird.

"Because of his weird style he must go up 2-0 on a lot of players until they figure him out."

What a lovely comment. I had heard similar sentiments before. In fact, on the previous day another ping pong pop had mentioned that he hoped his son did not have to play Eliel since he has trouble with Eliel's "unusual" style. Eliel's style is not unusual except for the fact that his backhand is probably stronger than his forehand, which is rare.

In my conversation with the father of Eliel's latest victim, despite my annoyance, I played along—nodding and smiling—not revealing my anger.

"Eliel's style might be weird because he was taught to play by an anthropologist." The father gave me that conversation-ending puzzled look that mentioning anthropology usually elicits, and then he turned his attention elsewhere. I had notched another victory, perhaps even more satisfying than the one over his son.

This father was presumably more pleased with his son's effort in his next match. Although a losing effort, he went five games with the third seed in the round robin, so Eliel and I were both confident that the third seed, Arnav, would not give Eliel much trouble. It was the confidence of fools. Arnav trains at one of the strongest clubs in the US, known simply by its acronym, ICC (Indian Community Center). Eliel was down in the first game but he fought his way back and won the game 11–9. The second game Eliel won easily and it seemed like Arnav knew he had no chance. But as often happens, after winning the first two games, Eliel lapsed in the third game. Eliel was down in the game but forced his way to deuce. He had match point but was unable to convert it and he dropped the game 13–11. The fourth game was tight throughout but again, Eliel lost in deuce, this time 12–10. Eliel was now forced into a fifth game that twenty minutes ago he did not anticipate. In fifth games, especially for young players, it is vital to start out strongly. Eliel did not. He looked helpless and I began my mantra of rationalizations: it is just a game, it is just one tournament, he's a good kid and none of this really matters ... Down 8–4, I called a timeout. I didn't have anything to say but Arnav had opened up a significant lead and the match was nearly over. I encouraged Eliel, telling him it was comeback time and to focus on every point. He returned to play and managed to win the next three points, primarily on ill-advised shots by Arnav. Perhaps Arnav was anxious, as this would have been a significant victory for him. Down 8–7, Eliel missed a high ball that he should have easily put away. You can't win matches if you throw away easy points. But Eliel is a fighter, and somehow he won the next four points to close out the match 11–9 in the fifth. It was a comeback for the ages, and it took at least a decade off my life. Big deep breaths and a sigh of relief, and to Eliel's credit, he sincerely apologized afterward. Actually, such apologies have since become a routine post-match ritual when Eliel makes matches that shouldn't be competitive, competitive. We always wind up laughing through the apologies, joking about the inevitable heart attack he will induce, but I appreciate that he seems to understand how stressful life can be as a ping pong pop. Or maybe more specifically, how stressful life can be as *his* ping pong pop.

After emerging victorious Eliel was still alive in the round robin, but now he would have to face Jinhong, who was also undefeated. No initial heart attacks here: Eliel came out blazing against Jinhong. He took the first game comfortably at 11-7. In the second game Eliel began strongly as well. Jinhong's coach took a timeout to stop Eliel's momentum. Thankfully, for what it was worth, Jinhong had a new coach, an elite French player. Nonetheless, the timeout did turn the tide and Jinhong pushed the game to deuce. Both players had their chances to win the game and it seemed that whoever won the game would have the decisive advantage moving forward. Mr. Cool-as-a-Cucumber, fortunately, pulled it out 14-12. Jinhong was demoralized and Eliel took a commanding lead in the third game. At 7-2 Jinhong served and Eliel held up his hand and caught the ball without trying to return it. This was the second time he had done this in the match and he told Jinhong that he was hiding the ball behind his shoulder, which is illegal. As I noted earlier, an opponent must be able to see the racket and ball at the point of contact on a serve. Jinhong's coach objected. It was Jinhong's point, he argued; you cannot stop the ball in the middle of play. He was an international player, he exclaimed, and this was outrageous. It was just the type of distraction that Eliel did not need. If there had been an umpire, Jinhong's coach would indeed be correct, but this was the US and unlike in Europe or Asia, there were not enough umpires for every match. As it turns out, an umpire was close at hand, and although he was not officiating the match, he had been watching and thought they should play the point again. As the umpire said, Eliel made no attempt to return the serve. In the end it was Jinhong who was distracted, and Eliel quickly won the next four points to close out the match. Eliel was through to the next round! Such a relief. No need to rebook our flights. The trip to Vegas would not be in vain, or so we thought.

LATER IN THE DAY we checked the draw for phase two, which, as mentioned, consisted of four round robins with six players in each round robin. The top four in each round robin would advance to the third and final phase, a sixteen-player single elimination tournament. Eliel was the fifth seed in his round robin. Because the seedings were based on Junior world rankings rather than USATT ratings, the round robins were extremely unbalanced. Eliel had been fortunate that his initial round robin had been relatively fair; some initial round robins had multiple players over 2300, whereas others did not have any players over 2150.

Despite the imbalances of the round robins in the first two phases, I was surprised to learn that the new seeding system had a few supporters. Maybe I shouldn't have been surprised; supporters were parents of kids who benefited from this system, even though the youth players themselves were unanimous in their disdain for the new arrangement. Kids can seemingly smell out unfairness better than adults, which is frankly a little discouraging. One would hope that our upbringings would make us more, rather than less, sensitive to injustice. Table tennis was challenging my naïve idealism.

In one uncomfortable conversation, a father defended the use of world rankings for seedings, arguing that it would encourage kids to compete abroad, which was precisely Tomas's position. Another father who I am friendly with was also part of the conversation, although he remained silent, probably too stunned to talk.

"Tomas wants the kids to play internationally and if parents are upset by the seedings it will encourage them to compete abroad." I protested that not everyone has the money to send their kids to international tournaments, but he was quick to point out that those kids who cannot afford to pay are not Tomas's concern.

"Tomas," he opined, "is trying to create world-class players and the USATT does not have money to fund everyone. Players need to be funded by their parents."

I countered, "Tomas's new policies are excluding players with talent who do not have the financial resources to compete internationally. Wouldn't table tennis be better served in this country if all players were given the opportunity to reach their highest potential?"

Admittedly, this wasn't exactly an objective, noble plea, as it might seem at first blush. And the self-interest of my comments was evidently obvious to my interlocutor. Even though I hadn't mentioned Eliel at all, he responded that it made perfect sense that Eliel was being excluded since, as he was aware, I did not have the money to pay for coaches or international travel.

"I'm sorry, but under such conditions," he continued, "Eliel has no chance of being a world-class player." I wondered if Tomas was paying him to be his promotional bulldog or if he somehow had access to my Gmail account. "Tomas needs to focus on the kids who can reach that level," he said, implying of course that his son had this potential. "Those are the kids who should be on the National Team and be invited to the National Training Camps."

I was shocked but just rolled with the conversation. Thankfully, at subsequent tournaments Eliel has handily defeated his son, despite the fact that his son receives six private lessons a week. Yes, I can be petty.

But at the time I did not know what to make of this conversation. Had he really just told me that only rich kids should be on the National Team? Perhaps I misunderstood. The next day I ran into my friend who had observed the conversation and he looked tired. He said he was up all night, unable to sleep.

"I just kept thinking about that conversation yesterday. I was so upset. I couldn't believe that he told you that Eliel should not be on the National Team because you aren't wealthy!" Yes indeed, I had heard correctly.

Back to Eliel's phase-two round robin, in which he was the fifth seed. His round robin included the top two seeds in the Men's draw, in other words, the top two players in the country: Kanak Jha and Nick Tio. This imbalance resulted from the fact that as high-level players neither of them competed regularly in Junior events when they attended international tournaments; rather, they entered the Men's draw. But it was the Junior world rankings that were being used for the Junior event. The positive spin on this situation, which is what we tried to focus on, was that if Eliel could make it to the third phase he would avoid running into either of these players in the early stages of that phase.

Eliel had never played the third and sixth seeds in his round robin before, but he had lost to the fourth seed twice at the Nationals the previous year; they were both painful losses, the latter preventing him from making the Cadet National Team. Fortunately, he was scheduled to play the fourth seed last, the only match for this event he would have to play on Wednesday. For better or worse, his first match on Tuesday would be against the reigning US Men's National Champion; in his second match he would face the second-ranked player in the country.

ELIEL WOKE UP TUESDAY morning ready to conquer the world, or in his own vernacular: "Let's go kick some butt." Unfortunately, butt-kicking was not quite on the early morning menu. Playing Kanak Jha, our nation's best by a wide margin, is not the ideal way to start your day. Kanak showed up with his professional coach, a former doubles World Champion, but after he breezed past Eliel 11–3 in the first game, his coach left to presumably watch others who might actually need the edge his coaching advice could provide. Eliel fought valiantly, scoring

7 and 5 in the next two games, but Kanak was at a different level. He simply did not miss or make mistakes. In case it ever comes up in a trivia game, or you just want to stump your friends, Kanak Jha is the answer to the following two questions: Who was the youngest American Olympian at the 2016 Olympics? Who was the first American Olympian born in the 2000s?

Eliel's second match, against the aforementioned Nick Tio, was a little more intriguing because Eliel had upset (in every sense of the word) Tio at the Nationals the previous year. Indeed, that win was, thus far, Eliel's claim to fame. Earlier in the tournament a young kid from California (I could tell by his shirt) unexpectedly greeted me, "Hi, Eliel's dad!" I extended a friendly response, but I had no idea who the kid was. When I later pointed him out to Eliel and asked who he was, Eliel also did not know. Eliel's friend Jason, who was talking with us, laughed: "Everybody knows Eliel because he beat Tio." It seems that Tio also remembered his match with Eliel because he brought everyone he knew, including most members of the National Team, to cheer him on. And they did. After every point Tio won they cheered and screamed, regardless of the quality of the point. As it happens, he did not need the extended fan base; Eliel was no match for him on this day. When it was over, Tio exhaled and smiled a huge smile of relief.

Eliel's next match was against the third seed in the round robin, a player whom he had practiced with but had never played in a tournament. I was nervous since this player's coach had led several of his lower-rated students past Eliel at recent tournaments. Eliel was confident, however, and it was quickly apparent why. Eliel jumped out to a 6-0 lead and won the first game 11-2. The second game was also lopsided. Eliel was simply too steady for this player; every attack was returned until this player missed. In the third game this player got his footing and they played a competitive game. Eliel missed some key shots at the end of the game to drop it 11–9, but the fourth game was all Eliel. A crucial victory.

The bottom seed in Eliel's round robin, Jianjun, was a puzzle. He lived in the Southwest, where there are not many high-level players, so he had a live-in coach who was with him at the Nationals. He was a puzzle because he was clearly much stronger than his rating, which was 2100. Indeed, when we looked him up, he had recently been around 2250 but recently had suffered a significant drop due to a poor tournament. He had upset some strong players to make it to the second phase, and he had very close matches with the third and fourth seeds that could have gone either way, although he was on the losing end of both matches. This was a match Eliel had to win. And win he did; unlike Jianjun's previous round robin matches, Eliel blew him away quickly in three straight games. Eliel was playing beautifully and although we had not realized it right after the match, because he had dominated in his last two matches, he was essentially guaranteed a spot in the third phase. Even if he lost against the fourth seed—and the way he was playing, that seemed unlikely—he would advance as long as he won at least one game.

THE JUNIORS EVENT WAS finished for the day but at three forty-five p.m. the Men's Open event began. Eliel's round robin for this event had two New York players with whom we were familiar. Eliel had played one of them before and he was a self-described "Eliel fan." Indeed, he openly rooted for Eliel throughout the round robin. Some former competitors, even in defeat, respect Eliel's sportsmanship and often subsequently vocally support him at tournaments. I've always been pleasantly surprised by those cheering for Eliel during matches. Indeed, the best friend I've made on the national scene is an Iranian mother of another Junior who I met when she was applauding for Eliel during one of his matches at our first Nationals, even though she had never met either of us. She simply liked the way Eliel played and his demeanor on the court. I should also mention that in addition to his overt supporters, Eliel has a secret fan club, known as the 51505 73173 Club. The name of the club arose when on a whim my brother-in-law asked Eliel what his favorite number was, which struck me as an odd question to ask a teenager, but not half as odd as Eliel's immediate response: 51505 73173. We looked at him curiously until he showed us on a calculator (type the number into your calculator and turn it, or yourself, upside down). My brother-in-law is the founding member of the club, and he affectionately designed club t-shirts, but they are hard to come by since the object of the club's adoration has banned them from being worn in public.

The round robin came down to a match between Eliel and Jinhong, whom Eliel had beaten in three straight games the previous day. But when an opponent is of similar strength, it is not easy to beat them twice in the same tournament. Maybe it is overconfidence. Or maybe the loser has had time to reflect on what went wrong, whereas the winner simply continues with what worked best in the first match. Whatever the case may be, I was concerned. That concern was only heightened after Eliel got blown out in the first game. He regained his form in the next two games and after an 11–5 victory in the third it appeared that Eliel had everything under control. At 10-7 in the fourth game, with three match points, however, Eliel wavered and dropped the game at 13–11. I was confident that Eliel was the better player, but anything can happen in a fifth game. Moreover, my Iranian friend who has been Eliel's good luck charm for years—he had never lost with her as a spectator—had to leave to watch her own son play. I was nervous. The fifth game was close throughout, but Eliel took a slight lead toward the end and held on to win 11–8.

Winning this round robin meant that he had one more match for the day, which was scheduled for seven thirty p.m. He would be playing another sixteen-year-old, Gregory, whom he had lost to in a close match at the Nationals the previous year. It was late, but a few of Eliel's friends came out to support him during the match. Eliel dominated the first game to take it 11–7. But that is where his run would end. Gregory overwhelmed Eliel in the second game and I noticed that Eliel was not moving like he normally does. Between games I told Eliel to keep his feet moving, and he commented that he did not feel quite right. I did not think much of his comment as we had now been in the playing hall for almost twelve hours, having arrived at eight a.m. Of course his feet were slow; whose feet wouldn't be slow after a full day of matches? But he was never able to get his feet moving and his reactions were noticeably slower and slower. Gregory won the final games of the match without much resistance. This was not the same Eliel who had fought hard for every point earlier in the day. After the match he was deflated. He sat down in a courtside chair and said his stomach felt "blubby." Again, I chalked it up to a long day of playing.

When we returned to the hotel room Eliel lay down on his bed and had no desire for dinner or anything. Next thing I knew he had rolled over and vomitted into a trash bin, which thankfully was located at the side of his bed. After throwing up several times he said, "I feel much better!" and he was ready to eat. I assumed the vomiting simply resulted from a toxic mix of exhaustion, Vegas heat, excessive Gatorade consumption, and a long day of playing. But I was wrong. Within a half hour Eliel was kneeling over the toilet and emptying everything in his body that was not a vital organ. I felt his forehead and he was feverish. He had caught the dreaded stomach flu. By eleven p.m. we assumed there was nothing left to throw up so I got him back into bed, hoping he could still get a full night of sleep and would wake up feeling better. But that hope would soon fade as within a half hour he was back in the bathroom, somehow emptying himself even further. In fact, this is how he spent the rest of the evening. He stopped vomiting at six a.m. and all told he had vomited well over thirty times that evening. I have never seen anything like it. He would have to default his Wednesday matches, and as it turned out, he was in no shape to compete on Thursday either. A year of training flushed down the toilet.

He was of course not alone in being affected by the flu. In fact, the "epidemic" was being investigated by the Southern Nevada Health District and had been picked up by AP News. Eliel was too sick to express his disappointment, but nothing needed to be said. We were both disappointed. Food poisoning is not uncommon at Las Vegas tournaments, and I have seen many players drop out of the Nationals entirely after getting sick from a hotel buffet or restaurant. But naively, I always imagined that such things only happened to other kids.

It is hard to say anything positive about the experience, but we did learn who were our real friends. One concerned friend from Massachusetts, a Harvard Medical School physician, spent hours on the phone Wednesday morning, trying in vain to get Eliel a prescription. Apparently only casinos are open on July 4 in Vegas, no pharmacies. Many of Eliel's fellow Juniors texted him repeatedly to see how he was feeling or asked me about Eliel's health when they saw me in the playing hall while Eliel was sleeping. But others I ran into never bothered to ask about Eliel, a little too absorbed, I felt, in their own tournament.

THE TRIP TO VEGAS, however, was not a complete waste. There were two very positive outcomes. First, one of the National Team coaches noticed Eliel. He had watched Eliel beat up on his students and invited him to join the National Team training camp in New Jersey the following month. Finally, some recognition!

The second outcome was that Eliel got sponsored. One of the under-the-radar issues that hangs over the heads of talented young players is sponsorship. Although table tennis expenses pale in comparison to skiing, the equestrian sports, or even tennis, it is not cheap. The most expensive pieces of equipment are tournament-quality tables, which cost at least fifteen hundred dollars, and table tennis robots, which cost about two thousand dollars. But other equipment is much cheaper. Blades, which can last a few years, are usually between one and two hundred dollars. Table tennis shoes—specialized sneakers that are light, grip the floor well, and have the support to allow quick lateral movement—need to be replaced every other month or so, but they cost only around seventy-five to one hundred dollars. And while table tennis balls, especially after switching to plastic balls (see Appendix A), break or wear out fairly quickly, we spend less than fifty dollars a month on balls. The real equipment expense in table tennis is rubber. Two sheets of rubber cost between one hundred and twenty and two hundred dollars and active high-level players replace their rubber at least once per month. On top of lessons, training camps, club fees, tournament registration, and travel costs, it begins to add up rather quickly. Sponsorship is the best way to offset these costs.

The reality for youth players, though, is that these costs are paid by their parents and are of little concern, although most would certainly prefer it if they did not have to hear about their parents' financial woes. For youth players, sponsorship has value beyond not having to endure parental complaints; it is a sign of status, clearly indicating to other players that you have made it. Compared to other sports, table tennis sponsorships of US youth players are meager, to say the least. Even Kanak Jha, the US's most decorated player, had to pay for his own training and most of his tournament travel when he was younger, although now as a member of the Bundesliga, his team pays for much of this.

Yet any sponsorship is a status symbol in the table tennis community. For players at the large clubs, sponsorship is fairly straightforward. The club itself is sponsored by a table tennis company and when a young player attains a certain level of play, the company will take on the player as an ambassador, so to speak, of the company. Joola, for example, sponsors ICC and supports more than a dozen of their top youth players. For others, it is not so straightforward and it is highly competitive.

One problem with sponsorships, however, is that players are committed to using the products of the company that is sponsoring them. Sometimes, those products are not what the player would choose to play with, and sometimes the products are simply poor. One company, which I will anonymize as "Fulya," as I have no desire to harm their business, offers coveted sponsorships—they are one of the largest table tennis manufacturers in the world—but their products are often not as good as competing companies. Several youth players sponsored by Fulya have confided that they often play with other top brands because the Fulya rubbers do not have the power, spin, or control of the leading rubbers on the market. Moreover, their Fulya blades break regularly, with the carbon and wood layers of the blade sometimes separating in the middle of matches. As these players have noted, Fulya always replaces their blades, so they do not care, but they would never purchase such blades. Indeed, in all my years of playing I've never had a blade that separated, but then again, I've never purchased a Fulya blade.

For the past year, we had been waiting for Eliel to have a breakout tournament so that we could approach a table tennis company and inquire about sponsorship. But it never happened. Eliel had several tournaments with great wins, but invariably he had at least one bad loss at each of those tournaments, preventing him from moving up significantly in the rankings.

At the 2018 Nationals, Eliel's best friend from the Maryland Table Tennis Center, where Eliel has spent many summers training, was exclusively wearing PongMobile shirts. Eliel asked him about it and it turned out he was sponsored by PongMobile. PongMobile is a website developed and maintained by a table tennis player named Mossa. Mossa is very bright, generous, enterprising, and probably a bit eccentric: a perfect fit for the US table tennis community. He is a computer programmer and was unhappy with how the USATT organized the ratings and club information on its website. He was not alone, but he was alone in offering an alternative. He built a website that contains the same information but is much cleaner and operates much better on cell phones.

In addition to clothing, his friend received rubber and blades of his choice from PongMobile, as well as entry fees to local tournaments. Maybe this was an opportunity. Eliel wrote to Mossa and, indeed, Mossa welcomed Eliel as a PongMobile ambassador. Finally, a sponsorship, and a good one at that. Mossa not only pays for whatever equipment Eliel needs, but he has provided Eliel with an entirely new table tennis wardrobe, including, with seeming appreciation for our New England residence, two new winter coats.

Despite our disappointment with how the 2018 Nationals ended, we couldn't complain about the fruits of the trip. Things were looking up.

CHAPTER 13

Growing Pains

By the fall of 2018 it was clear that Eliel was at a critical crossroads in his development as a player. He had spent the summer training intensively at the Maryland Table Tennis Center and Lily Yip Table Tennis Center in New Jersey. He attended a National Team training camp and won the tournament at the camp. They also assessed physical fitness at the camp and not only was Eliel in better shape than all the other players, his fitness was rated higher than all the young coaches, who were professional athletes. Apparently, he had many opportunities to display his fitness, including a punishing midnight run resulting from the players' failure to clean up after dinner. I wonder, is this reprimand what the parenting advice books recommend? Maybe my kids should be thankful that I didn't read them after all.

Despite his success at the camp, I was concerned. Of the Junior boys in the 2200–2400 range, Eliel was probably the strongest player. However, his level of play was not quite where I would have anticipated after such an intensive period of training. His rating of low 2300s had not changed in more than a year. He appeared to be a much better player than he was a year earlier, but it had not led to better tournament results and the players at his level were improving as well. Indeed, a year ago I would have argued that Eliel was improving faster than any Junior in the country. Even my biased parental eyes could see that was no longer true. At the end of the summer we attended the monthly Westchester tournament. After a summer of training, we, or at least I, had big expectations. But the tournament ended as most tournaments had over the past year, defeating lower-rated players and losing to higher-rated players. More disconcerting, he lost to a younger player whom he had trained with at the Lily Yip Table Tennis Center the entire week prior to the tournament. He had never lost at a tournament to this player before, and it appeared that the tide had turned in their friendly rivalry.

Throughout the previous year we had been waiting for a breakthrough tournament: a tournament in which Eliel eclipsed 2450 or 2500 and moved himself into the conversation as one of the top Juniors in the country. It didn't happen, and for the first time I began to wonder if what once seemed inevitable would actually happen at all. School was beginning and he no longer had the opportunity to train intensively. On most days during the school year, assuming he was not overwhelmed with homework, he played on our robot for an hour or so and did some physical training before going to bed. On two days a week he played at the New England Table Tennis Club, but he rarely hit with anyone over 2200 at the club. The camaraderie at the club was better than the training. Indeed, in most matches Eliel spotted points to other players or placed limits on how he could score points, such as playing games where he was only allowed to lob. This was adequate a year ago, but he was unable to improve with this training regimen. He was certainly not able to keep pace with the other Juniors, all of whom received regular private lessons.

As a parent I felt helpless. I offered significant solutions to the problem, including homeschooling, moving to the New York area for the remainder of high school, and hiring a live-in coach as many players have at his level. He was not interested in any of them. I was particularly surprised that he was uninterested in a live-in coach. His older siblings had all moved out, so we now had the space to accommodate such a coach. If nothing else, I assumed he would enjoy the company without his siblings around. But he was adamant that he did not want a private coach, outside of his father. Nor did he wish to be homeschooled. He liked his Jewish day school, especially his classmates, and wished to remain there.

During the 2018–2019 schoolyear, we attended many of the tournaments we had been frequenting over the past several years. These included Northeastern tournaments at the Westchester Table Tennis Center and Lily Yip Table Tennis Center, as well as national tournaments such as the US Open and the US Teams in Washington DC, the largest annual tournament in the country. Throughout this period Eliel never had a breakthrough tournament; good wins were always offset by inopportune losses. His playing had hit a plateau and we were essentially treading water, waiting for school to end so he could resume more intensive training.

SUMMER ARRIVED AND SCHOOL, finally, ended. Eliel arranged to train with an Iranian friend in California before the 2019 Nationals. When his friend generously invited him, it solved a problem for us: there was no one in New England at his level with whom he could intensively train for the Nationals. For the previous three years, after his last final exam we would drive down to my sister's home in Maryland and he would train at MDTTC. But by the previous year he was the top player at their pre-Nationals training camp. Nonetheless, we could have returned this year. However, he would have been not only the best player, but also the oldest, as the other kids his age had stopped training over the past year.

This early retirement from table tennis had been planned for years, so it was not a surprise when Eliel's friends stopped playing. The parents of these kids felt that eleventh grade required the full academic attention of their children, and it was hard to disagree with them. Eleventh grade is demanding. The parents of older players at this club had provided the model. These parents had ended their children's playing careers in eleventh grade and were able to celebrate their kids' entry into Ivy League schools following high school graduation. So dropping out of table tennis to study was the norm in this club. Even the previous summer two of his friends stopped attending the training camp to study for the SATs, one of them enrolled in an actual SAT camp. Who knew there was such a thing as an SAT camp? As I'm writing, it dawned on me that although I had never heard of such a camp, more parents probably know about SAT camps than table tennis camps. Humans remain mysterious to me.

It is not only at the Maryland Table Tennis Center where high schoolers drop out of the sport; the hemorrhaging of high school players is a genuine problem for table tennis in the US, one that USATT needs to address. Eliel and I recently tried to count how many of the cohort of players he was competing against four years ago were still playing, and sadly, we estimated that at least half of his cohort no longer competed, or even played at all. I think there are three relevant factors.

First, many kids play table tennis because their parents pushed them into it, rather than because of their own interest in the sport. While parents born in the US often instinctively sign their children up for little league, gymnastics, dance lessons, and so forth as a normal part of childhood, many Asian immigrant parents, especially in the Chinese community, likewise naturally register their young children for table tennis lessons. Most of these kids begin playing long before they can effectively voice their opinions about whether they wish to play. When they do find their voices as teenagers, they speak with their feet and walk away from the game. Having been pushed by their parents, often quite hard, these kids never fall in love with the game the way that Eliel and I did. Indeed, I am regularly asked by parents how I keep Eliel motivated to continue playing and my answer is simple: I don't. I tell them that if you want your kid to remain in the sport, they need to discover the joy of table tennis on their own. I never pushed Eliel to train or compete, and if I had, I suspect he would be among the many kids who no longer play.

Second, and relatedly, those kids who discover a passion for table tennis almost invariably do so too late to compete at a high level, which is profoundly discouraging. Eleven-, twelve-, and thirteen-year-old kids who fall in love with the sport often fall out of love with it when they realize they will never be able to catch up to those players who started playing when they were five, six, and seven years old. Eliel is a rarity among the late starters and the truth is, yes, he trained hard, but he was also lucky. His athleticism, natural coordination, and being the son of a competitive player all worked in his favor. Not everyone has these advantages.

Third, unlike many other sports, success in table tennis does not help with college admissions. There are no college table tennis coaches advocating for players to be admitted to their university, as in other sports. As mentioned earlier, collegiate table tennis is not supported by universities or the NCAA. Thus, when high schoolers begin to turn their attention toward college, they see that table tennis is a dead end. Only those who wholeheartedly love the sport continue to compete for the simple reason that there is no other reason to compete.

In any event, back to our situation. California solved the problem of where to train for the upcoming Nationals. But it created another problem. I was that problem. Specifically, what is a ping pong pop supposed to do without his charge?

After his last exam of eleventh grade, I drove Eliel to the airport with a heavy heart. It was his first flight alone and I was feeling more nervous than he was. I helped him check his bag and I would have gladly gone through security to spend some extra time with him, but I didn't want to be overbearing. I kissed him goodbye, forced a smile from myself and waved, and then he was gone.

I turned around and walked slowly, not really looking at where I was going, just letting my feet carry me. I knew I was supposed to be walking, but that is about all I confidently knew at that moment. I felt a deep emptiness, as though part of my insides had been ripped out. And my head was spinning, trying in vain to answer the obvious question: What am I supposed to do now? After meandering around the airport aimlessly for a while, I eventually realized that the existential side of that question could wait; the mundane side needed immediate attention. I had to find the airport exit and remember where I had parked my car.

Focused on these simple goals, I managed to locate the exit that led to the parking lot. Without Eliel to remember where I had parked, I methodically walked up and down the aisles until I found my blue Prius hiding between two oversized SUVs. I opened the car door and sat down, temporarily relieved that one problem was solved. And then I cried, uncontrollably.

This was not a good start to the two weeks we would be apart. I got annoyed at myself, knowing fully that the time away would be good for him and for me as well. I pulled myself together and exited the airport parking lot, thinking about our eventual reunion in two weeks when we would meet up in Las Vegas. Despite his training in California, the Nationals would be unremarkable, similar to his other tournaments over the past year: some good wins and some difficult losses. The other kids seemed to be getting better, but we weren't seeing progress. On my drive home though, this was two weeks away, and optimism mercifully captured my thoughts and helped me regain my composure, at least for a moment.

As it turned out, Eliel was bored waiting for his plane, and to pass the time he called while I was driving home. I nearly burst into tears again when I heard his voice, but thankfully I was able to hold back. I was partially able to keep my emotions in check because I had another pressing issue at hand. I had taken a random exit off the highway, as I often do in traffic, and I was terribly lost. Eliel chastised me and reminded me that he always advises against such impulsiveness. In the countless hours we spend together driving to clubs and tournaments, he serves as my navigator, using his smartphone to guide us through the relentless Boston, New York, New Jersey, and Maryland traffic.

After we got off the phone, I recalled a recent dinner table conversation in which Eliel and the rest of my family were pestering me, as is their wont, about not having a smartphone (I have a cool *Star Trek* flip phone).

"Why do I need a smartphone?" I retorted. "I have Eliel and Eliel has a smartphone."

Eliel calmly replied, "You know, someday you are going to have to learn how to live on your own."

I cracked up, but that statement was more prescient than I realized. Driving home without the guidance of my trusty navigator, I was at the mercy of the East Coast traffic, feeling rudderless, in more ways than one.

CHAPTER 14

Olympic Dreams

If there is one universal in a sport as diverse as American table tennis, it is that all high-level players dream—unrealistically for most—of Olympic glory. But the imagined purity of Olympic glory is just that: imagined. Competitive sports are often clouded by economic, institutional, and political realities, and the Olympics, unfortunately, are no different than other competitions. To put it bluntly, for the 2020 Olympics in Tokyo, the path to glory for American table tennis players was hardly a yellow brick road. It was muddy. Quite muddy, in fact, including lawsuits, resignations, and no shortage of drama. The behind-the-scene details of this episode could undoubtedly fill a book, but those details are someone else's story to tell.

In the end, after the dust had settled, selection tournaments for the US Men's and Women's Olympic teams were scheduled for late February, 2020, in Santa Monica, California. Eliel was an extreme longshot for making the team, but the Olympics do not come around often, so we decided to attend the trials.

Although school prevented him from training as much as he would have liked, Eliel's training intensified and became more focused. Also, in preparation for the trials, we attended several tournaments outside of the Northeast, which we rarely do unless it is a national tournament. For one tournament, in Chicago, we arrived a few hours before a blizzard. We were amazed at Chicagoans' perseverance and willingness to endure the blizzard conditions and snowy roads, presumably for the love of the sport. As New Englanders we thought we were weather warriors, but we were humbled on that trip. Had we not been at a nearby hotel before the storm hit, we would have never made it to the playing hall.

During the stretch of preparatory tournaments, Eliel finally had his breakthrough tournament. We could not have asked for better timing: a week before the US Olympic Trials. Not surprisingly, it was at the monthly Westchester Table Tennis Center tournament, the tournament that Eliel has attended more than any other. Because of the generous—for table tennis—prize money, the tournament is among the most competitive in the US, and it regularly attracts foreign players. At this tournament Eliel defeated several 2400 players and avoided the upset losses that had in the past accompanied such wins. But his most significant victory came against a former US National Champion. A decade earlier, at age fifteen, Michael Landers became the youngest male to ever win the national title. He was also the first player rated over 2600 that Eliel had ever seen compete, during our first tournament at Westchester years earlier. Michael's play is absolutely beautiful to see live, and Eliel was mesmerized while watching his matches. In recent years Michael had not been a regular tournament player so this would be the first time he and Eliel would cross paths at the table. Like us, he was at Westchester to prepare for the Olympic Trials the following week. His initial, unsuccessful, attempt to make the US Olympic Team, in 2012, was documented in the movie *Top Spin*.

Eliel won the first game and Michael looked rusty. But rusty or not, he was a stronger player than Eliel, so even after winning the first game I had little expectation that Eliel could pull off the upset. But by the second game, I realized that Eliel was locked in and playing brilliantly. At 9-9, Eliel served and Michael misread it and popped the ball off the table. But a ball from a neighboring match had rolled into the court and, even though Michael hadn't noticed it, Eliel, honest to a fault, called a let. Michael laughed; he knew it was a gift. Good players capitalize on such opportunities, and Michael won the replayed point, going on to win the game 14–12. After letting a chance to go up 2–0 slip through his hands, I expected Eliel to collapse under the pressure and power of Michael's game. But Eliel continued to play well and the match went to a fifth game. Over the past year, Eliel had come close to beating other 2500 and 2600-level players, but closing out such matches had proved elusive. On this day, however, Eliel finished off the match in strong form.

Michael lost the match, but he won two fans on that day. He was, hands down, the most gracious opponent Eliel or I have faced in many years of competition. We spoke for a long time after the match and I couldn't have been more impressed. Instead of making excuses—as, incidentally, Eliel's next opponent did—he endlessly praised Eliel's high-quality play. I had always felt badly for Michael—the *Top Spin* documentary is heartbreaking—but after speaking to him I realized that being a thoughtful and considerate human being is a much greater accomplishment than making the Olympic team. As a parent, I knew that his parents, who had been featured in the documentary, must be enormously proud of him. He's a mensch. The following week, on the flight out to California, I playfully asked Eliel who he would like to join him on the Olympic team. Without hesitation he responded "Michael Landers." We were in full agreement.

AFTER ELIEL'S SUCCESSFUL TOURNAMENT at Westchester, our expectations for the Olympic Trials were a little different. Making the team was not realistic, but he could advance and have the opportunity to play some of the best players in the country. We knew he would have to win two single elimination matches before reaching a three-player round robin. He would be the lowest seed in the round robin, but if he was able to win the round robin he would make it to the final sixteen, which would be quite an accomplishment.

If he did happen to win his round robin, we would have an issue that the two of us hadn't discussed: competition for the final sixteen was scheduled to begin on Saturday. Whether or not to compete on Shabbat had always been Eliel's decision, and his decision had always been clear. No competitions—table tennis, bowling, or otherwise—on Shabbat. Throughout his playing career we had avoided tournaments in which the main events were played on Saturday, so it was rarely a decision that he needed to make during a tournament. In this case, I wasn't sure what he would do, but I avoided raising the issue because I did not want him to be distracted by such "what if" scenarios.

Despite my avoidance, the topic raised itself, unexpectedly, on the day before the Westchester tournament. We were eating Shabbat lunch at a friend's home and two people at the table had seen articles about an observant American woman, currently studying in Israel, who would not be attending the Olympic Trials because the USATT refused to accommodate her Shabbat observance, that is, they would not reschedule any of her matches that fell on Saturday. We hadn't seen the articles, but the situation had received attention in the Israeli press and the story had been picked up by the *New York Post*. I eventually looked up the articles and found, as we had guessed, that they were about a friend of ours from New York. Unfortunately, the articles were filled with misinformation that made for a better story (not our friend's fault, of course), including implications that she was a viable contender for a spot on the Olympic Team, which she was not. But at the Shabbat table we were fielding questions without knowledge of the articles. We were being asked questions out of genuine curiosity—table tennis was a foreign world to everyone there, as it is to most people—but underlying these questions was an implicit contradiction that they were trying to reconcile: if this woman could not compete in the trials, how could Eliel? I answered evasively and steered the conversation toward safer waters.

OUR FLIGHT LEFT BOSTON at six thirty a.m., getting us to Santa Monica around noon on the day before the trials began. The prospectus indicated that the venue would be set up by three p.m., but when we arrived at one-thirty they were still laying down the rubber floor and not a single table was set up. Tahl Leibovitz, six-time Paralympian, was already at the playing hall, but otherwise only workers were present. Tahl is the most decorated Para player in US history and, although his playing career is far from over, he has already been inducted into the USATT Hall of Fame. Born in Israel and homeless in New York for part of his childhood, Tahl is one of the most intense players on the tournament circuit. His tenacity astonished me the first time I saw him compete, which was at the Westchester Table Tennis Center. During the match I watched, he kept a running dialogue with himself after every lost point, launched his racket into a ball barrier several times, and in the middle of one game he screamed at his opponent: "How does it feel to win a point against a cripple?!!!" His autobiography is appropriately titled *Ping Pong for Fighters*, and I insisted that Eliel read it. I don't necessarily want Eliel shouting at his opponents, but Tahl's single-minded focus on every shot of every point holds a much-needed lesson for Eliel. Tahl also presents one of the strongest examples of Mozart's wisdom shared years earlier: separate the player on the table from the human being off the table. Despite his John McEnroe routines, Tahl has been incredibly generous and kind to Eliel every time we cross paths, continually encouraging him throughout his development as a player. Inspirational words from champions mean a lot to youth players; unfortunately, not all our champions are as accessible as Tahl.

Tahl also plays a vital role in a story that has become a family favorite, told and retold at nearly all family gatherings. It all began one summer when Eliel flew to Israel to visit some friends. Regrettably, his checked luggage did not join him on this two-week jaunt. When he landed in Israel he was told that his bag was still in Munich, and there it would remain, for reasons we still do not understand, during his entire stay in Israel. All Eliel had with him was a small carry-on backpack. No clothes, no toiletries, and no phone charger. But no one has ever questioned Eliel's priorities: he had his ping pong paddle with him. You can't wear a ping pong paddle—I speak with some authority on this matter as I spent a year wearing nothing but a loincloth during fieldwork in Micronesia, and that is surely the lower limit of what can be worn in decent society—so Eliel borrowed clothes from his friends.

On his third day in Israel, Eliel boarded a train to visit a friend in Tel Aviv. He had been staying with another friend, Shimon, and he was wearing Shimon's clothes, including a pair of pocketless shorts. While on the train Eliel promptly fell asleep, with his wallet in his hand. Yes, a foolish place to store a wallet, but as Eliel always facetiously points out at this juncture in the story, this was all Shimon's fault: Who buys shorts without pockets? As you can probably guess, when Eliel woke up, his hand was empty. He looked around, hoping he had just dropped his wallet, but he couldn't find it anywhere. He continued to search until the train arrived at his stop. Despite Eliel's exceedingly charitable view of humanity, he had to admit that his wallet had been stolen and there was nothing he could do but exit the train.

His wallet, on that fateful day, contained an unusual amount of cash. Lots of cash. Way too much cash. At that point in life Eliel did not have a bank card, so lacking good sense I gave him a big wad of cash before his trip. Admittedly foolish, but in my defense, I have never lost my wallet and I certainly didn't foresee Eliel traveling in pocketless attire. As has been pointed out to me many times, though, Eliel has much more common sense than I do, and in this situation, he appropriately tried to refuse all the money I was foisting on him. But sometimes foolishness and stubbornness go hand in hand, and this was one of those times. I insisted that it was better to be safe than sorry: hence, Eliel had way too much cash in his wallet.

If I was traveling in a foreign country and I had lost my luggage, and my wallet, and I had a phone I couldn't keep charged because my phone charger was in my lost checked luggage, it is a safe bet that these inconveniences would put a severe damper on my travels, even if I still had my ping pong paddle with me. But Eliel is cool, calm, and collected … always … not just at the ping pong table. There was no damper for Eliel; without missing a beat, he had the time of his life. For two weeks he traveled around Israel, having a blast visiting his friends and borrowing their money and pocketless clothing.

Tahl Leibowitz? Don't worry, I haven't forgotten about our accessible champion. On the day Eliel left Israel he received a text from Tahl. Tahl had heard that Eliel was in Israel—the world of table tennis is small and Israel is a small country. Tahl was in Israel for the Maccabiah Games (the Jewish Olympics) and he wanted to know if Eliel was free to warm him up. Eliel said he would have loved to, he even had his paddle with him, but he had just left Israel that morning. Tahl was disappointed, but a few hours later, he texted Eliel again with a phone number he should call immediately. Had Eliel lost his wallet? Israel and the world of table tennis might be small, but how on earth did Tahl know that? Eliel called the number and learned that his wallet had not been stolen: it had fallen between two seats on the train. The *tzaddik* who found his wallet looked inside, where he learned Eliel's name, but there was no information on how to reach Eliel. So, he Googled Eliel and justifiably concluded that Eliel must be in Israel to represent the US in table tennis at the Maccabiah Games! In short, this *tzaddik* called a friend, who called a friend, and so on until he found an Israeli table tennis player (as I said, it's a small country). This player knew Tahl, which is how Tahl learned about the missing wallet. One of Eliel's friends would be returning to the US two weeks later, so this friend arranged a meeting to pick up the lost wallet. Not a dime was missing. And the day after Eliel received his wallet from his friend, his suitcase—phone charger, pocketed clothing, and all—was also returned, unexpectedly delivered by the airline to our front door. Maybe there is a reason nothing seems to faze this child of mine.

Back at the hall, and speaking of accessible and supportive champions, Danny Seemiller was the next player to arrive, and once a few tables were set up, he and Eliel warmed up together. Danny had taken a hiatus from his coaching position in South Bend to train for the Olympic Trials. It was a longshot, but he wanted to make one more run at making the Olympic team. We were happy to see him as we had crossed paths at the tournament in Chicago, but he had left that tournament early because of injury, and we were unsure if he would be able to compete in the trials.

The level of disorganization and lack of professionalism was disheartening on that first day. The reality of the scene was hard to reconcile with the fact that the trials, and the sport in general, meant so much to us and the other competitors. But it was clearly an amateur affair for a marginal sport. The players themselves wound up setting up many of the tables because the organizers were so far behind schedule. Nonetheless, Eliel got in a good afternoon of practice and in the evening the draws were eventually revealed. Eliel would face a player we did not know in the first round, but if he reached the second round he would likely encounter a friend from California, a full-time professional coach, who would certainly provide a competitive match.

When we entered the playing hall the next morning, the transformation from the previous day was remarkable, and my concerns about incompetence were quickly forgotten. The hall was beautifully arranged with eight professional-sized courts. Video cameras on tripods were set up in the corners of each of the courts and the walls were decorated with Olympic emblems and American flags. When we entered the hall, music was blaring through the loudspeakers and the song couldn't have been more apt: Pat Benatar's "Hit Me with Your Best Shot." It definitely set the mood.

Although COVID-19 cases were still isolated incidents in the US, because of the large numbers of Chinese-American players and spectators, there were heightened concerns about the virus at the trials. On the first day there were signs on the doors of the playing hall that anyone who had been in China during the previous fourteen days would not be permitted entry. This sign was eventually removed—I assume such a restriction was illegal—but over the next few days there would be many discussions about recent experiences in China since some of the players had been training there prior to the trials.

Every morning during the trials, right before the matches began, the hall was silenced and "The Star-Spangled Banner" was played over the loudspeakers. I was surprised by the power of these moments, especially that first morning. The majority of players were either immigrants or the children of immigrants, but this ritual briefly erased our undeniable cultural, ethnic, and religious differences. It clarified, albeit fleetingly, our shared dreams. Not just Olympic glory, but dreams of happiness, health, and freedom, devoid of oppression and discrimination, and flourishing lives in which we could live up to our potential as human beings. As anthropologists have long appreciated, rituals don't transform such hopes into reality, but they do symbolically express ideals and aspirations that are otherwise difficult to articulate.

Eliel's first match was against a lower-rated player, and I was not nervous. But Eliel looked nervous and he was not sharp, although he took care of business easily enough. Eliel faced an unexpected opponent in the second round: a 2200-level college student from Texas had upset our friend from California. He was better than his rating, but Eliel was at a different level, and he won the best-of-seven match four games to zero. As often happens, Eliel secured the victory as well as a new friend. They would spend much of the next few days hitting together when matches were not being played.

Eliel was through to the round robin stage, one of thirty-two remaining players whose Olympic dreams were still intact. But not all our friends were so fortunate. One of Eliel's training partners from MDTTC lost a heartbreaker, deuce in the seventh game, in his second-round match. That match was running simultaneously with arguably the best match of the tournament: Danny Seemiller was playing Chi-Sun Chui, the son of one of Danny's former competitors and national standout Lim Ming Chui. Danny's Olympic quest had been nationally covered by various media outlets so everyone was aware of the stakes, and it was among the last matches of the second round, so most of the tables were empty and nearly everyone was watching. Danny was down three games to one and faced three match points in the fifth game. Miraculously, amid much cheering and encouragement from the crowd, he won the next five points, winning the game 12-10. He took the sixth game and was up 10-8 in the seventh game. But he could not convert either match point. At deuce they went back and forth in a series of jaw-dropping, tension-filled points. The level of play, especially given the situation, was stunning, but ultimately Danny lost the game and match at 14-12. This dream was over, but no match, however disappointing, could detract from his remarkable career and accomplishments.

Eliel would be competing against two 2550 players in his round robin. Neither of them was unbeatable, although they were certainly favored over Eliel. His first match was against another Junior, one who was quickly rising and had passed Eliel over the last year. Eliel had lost to him a few months earlier in Washington, DC, but that match was tight and we felt that Eliel had not played his best. Eliel had good reason to be confident, and his confidence was evident early in the match.

In the first game Eliel took a commanding 8-1 lead. Somehow, however, he managed to let the lead slip away and he lost the first game at 16-14. It was painful to watch. But Eliel is consistently resilient, and in the second game he was up 8-3 and in complete control. Yet again, he lost the lead and ultimately the game at 14-12, on an unreturnable net ball. In the third game, Eliel again took a lead, this time 8-6, but of course that was not a large enough lead to prevent the third straight deuce game. This time, however, Eliel won the game 13-11. After finally winning a game, Eliel lost his focus in the fourth game. At 4-0 I called a timeout, but it proved to be unhelpful as I was unable to get him back on track. He lost the game at 11-4. In the fifth, Eliel regained his intensity and was up 8-6 toward the end of the game. But he dropped five of the next six points, losing the game 11-9, again on a net ball.

This was a hard defeat to swallow. I ran into his opponent's coach, former World Champion Stellan Bengtsson, later in the day. He shook his head in disbelief at the match and praised Eliel's play. He acknowledged that they were very lucky—they should have been down 3-0 in the match. Indeed. He was rightfully proud of his student's resolve during every point, regardless of the score. It was something we surely needed to work on.

But Eliel was not eliminated. If he could win his next match there was still hope of advancing. Unfortunately, there was no time to recover from the loss. After a quick break he was scheduled to play three-time men's national champion and two-time Olympian Timothy Wang. Eliel had never played Timothy, but we had seen him play many times, and we thought stylistically it would be a good match for Eliel. And others we spoke to, who had played Timothy before, felt similarly. But Eliel had no chance against him. Timothy was simply too steady and Eliel did not have the power to hit through him. Timothy easily controlled the first three games, but in the fourth game, shades of Eliel's previous match surfaced, and Eliel went up 8–2. Incredibly, he lost the last nine points of the game to end his tournament. His Olympic dream was over.

Afterward we were describing the matches to Eliel's friend Shoushan, with whom he often practiced in New York. We noted that for whatever reason, the turning point in nearly every game occurred when Eliel reached eight points. Shoushan commented that eight is a lucky number in China.

"It didn't feel so lucky," I remarked, still chafed by the losses.

"But it was for his opponents, and they are both from China."

Oy. Our entanglement with this lucky or unlucky number—depending on your perspective—didn't end there. The license plate of *every* Uber we took throughout our four-day stay in California began with the number eight. We had no idea what to make of that. If the table tennis gods or some other cosmic force in the universe was trying to send us a message—God seems partial to the number seven, so we discounted that possibility—we were having trouble with the translation.

WITH OUR EXIT FROM the trials we avoided any potential conflict that would arise from competing on Shabbat. On Saturday afternoon we did walk over to the playing hall to watch matches. The matches were exciting—I'm a player and coach, but equally a fan—although it was bittersweet once the reality of Eliel's elimination fully sank in. But we came, we tried, and it was a good experience. Those who were still competing deserved to be where they were and they were better players than Eliel, even if such truths didn't lessen my disappointment.

As we sat in the stands, watching the matches and cheering for our favorite players, I noticed two young boys in the row ahead of us. One had come with his mother, whom I had spoken to earlier. She had seen table tennis televised during the Rio de Janeiro Olympic games and was intrigued. When she saw an advertisement for the trials in a local newspaper she was thrilled that she would be able to see the sport played live. She was not disappointed. But my attention was on her son, who never removed his eyes from the video game he was playing on his cell phone. Close by was another boy, maybe about eight years old, who was solving problems in a Chinese math workbook, with his back facing the courts. The sport that had captured my heart, and my life, clearly had a long way to go to even capture the attention of the next generation, let alone their hearts.

CHAPTER 15

On Timeouts and Empty Nests

And then it was all over. Just like that. Within days of our return from California, concerns about an emerging pandemic filled the daily headlines. Within a few weeks, tournaments were canceled, table tennis clubs were closed, and of course so were the schools and non-health related workplaces.

Like everyone, we waited for the world to return to normal. And we waited. Eliel and I played at home, but he trained with his robot more than he trained with me. For a few weeks one of the NETTC coaches opened the club to hit with Eliel, until the owner found out and completely shut NETTC down. We continued to train at home, but at some point it became unclear what Eliel was training for. By May the 2020 US Nationals were canceled, which was a bitter disappointment for Eliel. It was his last year in the Juniors and for the first time he had a legitimate shot at finishing among the top players. I would have loved for the 2020 Nationals to provide a fairytale ending to this book, with Eliel capturing a national title. In the midst of a pandemic, however, maybe the sober and contemplative ending that follows is more fitting.

THE PANDEMIC GAVE US a new appreciation for the sport we both loved. In Judaism, the highest form of devotion is known as *torah lishma*, which means the study of Torah for its own sake, without incentives.

Without the possibility of tournament competition, we were playing table tennis *lishma*: in other words, playing purely for its own sake. Not for whatever limited glory there is in table tennis or the ephemeral thrill of victory. We played because we still sought to improve, seeking to refine our respective games, knowing we could only assess our progress against each other. We experienced table tennis as philosopher Leon Kass insightfully perceives sport in general:

> Sport is a species of play, but not a frivolous activity. It is true that our games serve no utilitarian purpose; they do not feed the hungry, or cure the sick, or shelter the cold. But sport, like all play, is valuable as an end in itself, not just for the sake of victory or profit or some other result. It belongs to the domain of human activities that are done for their own sake—not the realm of necessity, but that of leisure, of freedom, of cultivation.

It may seem surprising, but philosophers have been thinking about sports since humans began playing them. And the philosophizing has generally been positive. Michael Novak, for instance, asserts that "Sports are not merely entertainment, but are rooted in the necessities and aspirations of the human spirit." And Plato spends considerable time discussing athletics in the *Republic*, repeatedly emphasizing the importance of athletics in childrearing. Aside from the benefits of physical exercise, Plato recognizes the contribution of athletics to learning moral rules, coping with challenges, and experiencing the value of commitment and diligence. French philosopher Albert Camus evidently concurs, relating "All I know most surely about morality and obligations, I owe to football." Indeed, Plato's nearly 2,400-year-old observations are all benefits that still populate the academic literature on sport, and, incidentally, are all merits of table tennis that I've experienced firsthand with Eliel. Alfred North Whitehead's comment that the European philosophical tradition "consists of a series of footnotes to

Plato," may have actually shortchanged Plato, failing to give him credit for his continuing relevance outside of philosophy.

WHAT IS IT ABOUT this strange, marginal sport known as table tennis? How does it continually pull me back within its orbit? Is there something special or even unique about it? I've grappled with these questions for years, but I've come to realize they are the wrong questions to be asking. It is easy enough for me to point to all the things I like about table tennis. It is both cerebral and physical; it offers endless opportunities for creativity; its enthusiasts are diverse in every way humanly imaginable; it attracts quirky eccentrics who are comfortable outside the mainstream, which is my comfort zone as well. And so forth. But these characteristics, and the many others that I could list—such as it doesn't involve getting tackled, kicked, or punched—are probably exhibited by numerous other activities that people pursue with similar zeal and commitment. Table tennis is special to me, but it is not necessarily special. Trying to explain why it grabbed me, then grabbed my son, is like trying to explain why two particular people fall in love. People just fall in love, and while they can offer rationalizations and reasonings, such explanations always fall short.

There is nothing like a pandemic to force life's important matters to the surface, and conveniently, there is nothing like a stay-at-home lockdown to provide endless hours to ponder these matters. As is true for many middle-aged folks, life's meaning has been on my mind, and more so with each passing month of the pandemic. Now that my children have all left for college and beyond, the issue of meaning is even more salient: their absence clearly revealed that I derived much meaning from the more than two decades that my wife and I spent raising them in our home. So maybe a better question than any of those

I posed above concerns whether sports can provide sustained meaning for people. A few years ago I would have scoffed at the idea that I, or anyone, could derive meaning from table tennis. It's just a game, after all. But maybe the biases of my training in anthropology—a field that unlike philosophy, hasn't taken sport seriously (see notes to the Preface)—blinded me to the possibility. As I suggested earlier, I now suspect that deriving meaning from a game may be essential for many people in our anomic contemporary world. Indeed, there are two reasons why I would disagree with my former, pre-pandemic, self.

First, I've become convinced that growth is the key to understanding how humans derive meaning. For whatever reason, people find meaning by transcending themselves. I don't think this has to be religious transcendence, although religions have surely been a source of deep meaning for many throughout human history, and they continue to serve this function. Judaism has certainly provided meaning in my own life. But I suspect humans can derive meaning from nearly any type of life-affirming growth. Sports provide opportunities for such growth, or as Kass puts it, opportunities for "cultivation." As philosopher Michael Novak observes in his classic *The Joy of Sports*:

> ... the ultimate competition in sports is not with others but with oneself ... The presence of other good athletes forces one to "outdo" oneself, to push oneself to new accomplishments. Still, one does not quite so much defeat one's rivals as defeat one's old self. Both in training and in the meet, one's attention is ultimately on one's own performance ... One keeps trying to extend one's achievements further ... the essence of that struggle is to exceed one's own previous limits.

Among athletic endeavors, table tennis seems particularly, possibly uniquely, well positioned for creating meaningful experiences through growth and self-transcendence because it is a sport that can be pursued throughout one's life. Albeit extreme, some children begin as young as two, and I've had the privilege of hitting with ninety-five-year-old players. I can't think of another sport where competitions include both under-10 and over-90 age categories; it is indeed "The Lifetime Sport."

Second, playing table tennis is a community experience and people derive meaning within communities. As I mentioned earlier, I have spent much of my academic career studying utopian societies. I am endlessly fascinated by the communities people create and how people continually try to adjust and improve those communities with the aim of perfecting humanity. If we could only get society right, the thinking goes, human happiness and flourishing will fall into place. But these ambitious and noble ideals never succeed: like Churchill's renowned assessment of success, humans seem to go from one utopian failure to the next without loss of enthusiasm. Or as Oscar Wilde put it, most accurately I believe: "A map of the world that does not include Utopia is not even worth glancing at, for it leaves out the one country at which humanity is always landing." I certainly do not want to claim that humanity has finally found its utopia in table tennis. Far from it. Like every human endeavor, table tennis is filled with pettiness, dishonesty, fighting, and so forth. But there is also dignity, kindness, and grace. Local table tennis clubs, the heart and soul of American table tennis, are deeply human places. And in that way perhaps they are more promising than unattainable utopian dreams. They are places of caring and fellowship. Eliel is a living testament to the generosity of the players who frequent these clubs. It would be a gross understatement to claim that it took a village to fashion Eliel into the player he is; it took multiple villages. The two most prominent villages in his journey were Mozart's club and NETTC, but there have been many other clubs throughout the US where players and coaches worked tirelessly and selflessly with Eliel to improve his game, simply because they could see that he loved the game as much as they did. These clubs and others like them are places, albeit not utopian, where meaningful lives can flourish.

Although I am convinced that table tennis and other sports can add meaning to people's lives, sports are not inherently meaningful. Our meanings are constructed, that is, we create them. A meal can be a simple act of energy consumption or we can transform it into a meaningful experience, such as the weekly Friday night meal I celebrate with my family to welcome Shabbos. Hitting a hundred forehands in a row can be drudgery or a powerfully moving experience. As anthropologists correctly note, ritualizing an activity, such as a meal or an athletic contest, doesn't necessarily make it meaningful. Meaning requires an act of interpretation; it is a matter of perspective. And it demands effort. Not strained effort, simply care and attention, which come naturally when an activity is passionately pursued. Such affections afford us an opportunity to appreciate even sports, including table tennis, as meaningful.

Importantly, when we interpret the world around us, we create stories. That is, we apprehend meaning in our lives in narrative form. This is why I continue to insist that anthropology is vital for understanding the human condition and experience. Anthropologists study people's stories to provide a window into their lives. They interpret interpretation, and when anthropologists do their job well, other people's meanings become meaningful to us. I hope the glimpse of the hidden world of table tennis I've provided has opened that window, at least a little bit.

Our contemporary world is likely too complex, too varied, for any one idea or activity to fully support the meaningful goals that we as humans evidently require to lead thriving lives and keep nihilism at bay. This is true even for those who are religious. Religions today rarely have the exclusive attention of their adherents, and thus even religiously committed individuals must navigate multiple meaning systems in their lives. Sports, and the communities of individuals who pursue them, provide one avenue that can complement other meaning-making pursuits, such as literature, art, or music, and also religion.

While many scholars, including anthropologists, have commented on the similarities between sport and religion, some have argued that their overlapping domains place sport and religion in competition with each other. For example, historian Jeffrey Gurock observes:

> For sports, in many ways, is a competing, secular religion complete with its own book of rules and holy in its own right. It possesses traditions to be followed, a lifestyle to be adhered to, central historical figures and personalities worthy of emulation, holidays—think of that American civic observance called Super Bowl Sunday—and even a belief system that speaks reverently about personal salvation at the end of days, the quest for immortality through victory at the finish line.

Religious studies scholars Bain-Selbo and Sapp further argue that "the human drives and needs that compel some to be part of a particular religion are the same drives and needs that compel some to be part of sport ... Sport can function like a religion in that it meets the same needs and desires ... promised by formal religions." For many people, these scholars claim, sport has ostensibly replaced religion because it can provide meaning and purpose.

Unlike these scholars, I would not characterize sport as a religion (rather, it has shared features), and I see complementarity rather than conflict as the more common relationship between sport and religion. But their sociological assessments concerning the replacement of religion by sport might be accurate, and it is undoubtedly true that sport and religion can be directly incongruous, as Eliel has experienced on more than one occasion. But tension is often productive, driving humans forward. Indeed, this seems to be one of the most valuable lessons that sport offers: competition, which is filled with conflict and tension, can create excellence. Countless autobiographies by athletes, whether professional or amateurs, convey the important interplay of their religious convictions and athletic passions. These athletes often credit both their religious and athletic commitments for their triumphs on and off the field.

PARENTS ARE OFTEN ACCUSED of living out their dreams through their children. Perhaps, but I think such criticisms are a bit lazy and too easily endorsed. I'm as susceptible to self-deception as anyone—probably more so as an academic—but I don't believe my extensive time, financial, and emotional investments in Eliel's table tennis activities were aimed at fulfilling my own unfulfilled table tennis fantasies and dreams. Did I dream of becoming an Olympian and national champion? Sure. Have I imagined such accomplishments for Eliel? Absolutely. But expectations for myself, as well as for Eliel, were always tempered by a heavy dose of realism. I'm fairly certain I've been motivated as a parent by a desire to enable Eliel to pursue a passion to the best of his ability. I feel pain when he loses because I know the pain of losing. He's my child and I don't want him to suffer, even when I know that he learns more from his losses than from his wins. My feelings when he loses, or experiences any of the other small injustices he's endured as a player, do not differ from how I experience his illnesses, broken bones and teeth, or setbacks in other domains of his life. As a parent I can't help but feel his pain. And I share Eliel's pride and happiness in his achievements, whether in math, art, school, or his other interests, in the same way I experience his joy after he wins a tough match.

There is no doubt that some of my commitment to Eliel's table tennis pursuits has been in reaction to my parents' investment in my own table tennis activities when I was growing up, which I believed fell short. I was admittedly unappreciative. But then I experienced what surely every parent who has ever lived experiences: the humble realization that parenting is so much harder than it looks! Who knew? Hindsight has helped me appreciate, belatedly, that my parents did an amazing, selfless job after all.

Although the luck of Chinese eights was not on our side at the Olympic Trials, my life has been one steady stream of (mostly undeserved) good fortune. My kids have turned out to be thoughtful, mature, grounded, and remarkably accomplished adults, despite countless parenting mistakes—mistakes, incidentally, that my parents did not make. Each of my children has helped me learn about myself, and I have loved sharing their interests, whether literature, poetry, history, music, art, computer-programming, swimming, hiking, camping, or good food. Maybe especially good food. I feel particularly blessed that one of my kids, unexpectedly, reacquainted me with a sport that was such an integral part of my childhood.

But my children, including Eliel, have all left home. They are of course exploring different worlds, beyond the horizons that our comfortably chaotic home provided. And while they are exploring, hopefully they are preparing for the day when they will turn me into a grandfather. Yes, I'm ready. Is this too much to ask for? In the meantime, like many parents with an empty nest, I feel a void that was once filled with the tumultuous, but incomparable and precious roller coaster ride of raising children. What now is left?

My empty nest reminds me of a Yiddish song, "Hob Ich Mir a Mantl" (I Had a Little Overcoat), which has been turned into a story, one that I used to tell my kids when they were younger.

> A man had an overcoat, but it got old and worn. So, he made a jacket out of it, but it got old and worn. So, he made a vest out of it, but it got old and worn. So, he made a scarf out of it, but it got old and worn. So, he made a tie out of it, but it got old and worn. So, he made a handkerchief out of it, but it got old and worn. So, he made a button out of it, but one day he lost the button. The man thought he had nothing left, but then he realized, he had a story he could tell.

Epilogue

I turned to my partner, Dave, and unnecessarily reminded him about the importance of the next point.

"I didn't come all the way out here to lose to Fred." Dave nodded and I saw that he completely understood: we'd never hear the end of it if we lost.

Thankfully, we managed to win the point and the match, which was competitive, but not too competitive. We spent much of the time laughing, making fun of each other's misses and inability to move toward the ball. In my early fifties, I was the junior player of this foursome.

At one point during the match Fred picked up the ball and looked at us seriously: "Here is what I don't understand," he said, pausing for effect. "Why doesn't everyone play table tennis? It's so much freakin' fun!"

Good question.

MY REUNION WITH FRED began a week earlier. When Eliel left for college, I had no script. Not that I had a script for his childhood years, but I had grown accustomed to my role as a ping pong pop and I knew what was expected of me. In addition to playing with him at home, I drove him everywhere, so even though I often worked while he trained, I generally played at least part of the time as well. But without Eliel, I was unsure if I would continue to play.

Months after Eliel left for college I went to visit friends in Allentown, Pennsylvania, where I was raised. I was there for an extended stay, and one evening my friends were busy, so on a whim I Googled "Allentown table tennis." It always starts with Google, doesn't it?

The Allentown/Lehigh Valley Area Table Tennis Club popped up and I checked out the website. Aside from one of the most awkward looking acronyms I had ever encountered (ALVaTTc), I was amazed to see that Fred was still running the club. As a teenager in the early 1980s I had played at the club often, albeit at a different location. At that time, it was one of several clubs in the Lehigh Valley Area, including the club in the community college dance studio where I learned how to play. ALVaTTc is the last one standing, undoubtedly testament to its charismatic founder.

Charismatic indeed, but not without controversy. Even as a teenager who was left out of most adult conversations, I was aware that Fred was a provocative and polarizing figure. Rumors about the legality of his paddles were abundant. More problematic was his forthright demeanor; it would be fair to say that his candor lacked delicacy. But I loved Fred's larger-than-life personality and I found his quirky sense of humor to be colorful. Who else paid for two USTTA memberships, one for his right hand and one for his left? When the monthly *Table Tennis Topics* would arrive in the mail, I always checked to see how Fred LH Kistler was faring in comparison to the other Kistler. The left-handed Kistler never quite reached the level of the right-handed Kistler, but not for lack of effort. More importantly, as a teen all I wanted to do was play, and Fred was always a willing and competitive opponent.

Fred founded the ALVaTTc in 1972. When I caught up with him he had been running the club nonstop for nearly fifty years. I'm not sure how many times the club has changed locations—in the early eighties we played in a church basement—but it is now comfortably situated at the YMCA in downtown Allentown. Club members meet on Tuesday and Friday evenings, with strict setup and cleanup times because the YMCA closes at nine p.m. The playing conditions are respectable: six tables, ample barriers, sufficient space, bright lighting, and I never slipped on the tile floor. Admittedly, it is not suitable for the World Championships, but neither were any of us who played at the club.

EPILOGUE

When I arrived at ALVaTTc I was immediately welcomed by a woman who informed me of the cost (six dollars) and the rules of the club. The most important rule—I could tell by her seriousness—concerned not walking into a neighboring court. I was informed that if my ball rolled into another court, I was not under any circumstances to enter that court; the closest player would return the ball to me. Given the sanctity of this rule, I wondered if someone had been unwittingly decapitated by a powerful forehand while retrieving a stray ball. Maybe this sport was more dangerous than I thought.

I was paired with another man who had also just arrived and we hit together casually—no powerful forehands. About ten minutes later Fred walked in. He was unmistakable. His red hair and mustache were now grey, but otherwise he looked like he did in the 1980s. I, on the other hand, with a grey beard, little hair, and more than a few extra pounds, looked nothing like the teenager I once was, so I had the advantage.

Fred sat down on a chair by our table and looked at us in disgust. "Are you guys going to hit the ball? You call that table tennis? You're wasting space." Same looks, same acerbic attitude.

I smiled, walked over to him, and stuck out my hand. "Rich Sosis. Good to see you, Fred." He shook my hand but looked at me uncomprehendingly. I just smiled and waited for it to sink in.

"Rich F***ing Sosis??!!!"

I knew I was a real adult now. When I used to show up at Fred's club as a fourteen-year-old he would announce, "No more cursing, the kid is here." And to his credit, he successfully shielded my ostensibly wholesome ears, as I never heard a foul word there. This is not to say that Fred wouldn't get upset after missing a shot. But he replaced the usual expletives I heard at other table tennis clubs with "Fudge!" and "Sugar!" It is a noble tradition, one that I adopted when Eliel started playing.

For the rest of the evening, whoever walked through the door, Fred would announce: "Rich Sosis is here!" thankfully leaving out my new middle name. And when players stopped arriving he would simply shout it out at roughly ten-minute intervals. He even shared the news with the YMCA staff, all of whom Fred had clearly befriended. Fred still commands the center of attention, but for this evening, in his own way, he was sharing the stage with me. In truth though, not only did the YMCA staff have no idea who I was, but most of the players didn't either. Only two players at the club that evening had played at the club in the early eighties. It was a treat to see both of them, even if the other club members were bewildered by my presence and Fred's pronouncements.

Although I was understandably unknown at the club, ALVaTTc is the home club of at least one famous player: Fred's wife. Noga Nir-Kistler was born in Israel, and while I was visiting ALVaTTc she was visiting her family there, so regrettably I did not get to meet her. Fred said that she's treated like a rock star when in Israel, as she should be. She is not only a table tennis Paralympian, competing for the US in the 2008 Beijing Paralympic Games, but she also competed in the 2012 and 2016 Paralympic Games as a swimmer. Impressively, at the 2012 London Paralympic Games she took home the bronze medal in the 100-meter breaststroke.

AN EVENING AT ALVaTTc is remarkable for a number of reasons; I'll just mention three. First, when visiting a new club, one of the first questions invariably asked is "What is your rating?" Yet, not only was I never asked this at ALVaTTc, I never heard any mention of ratings either time I visited the club. How refreshing to be a person rather than a number. Second, the club has the strongest egalitarian ethic I have ever witnessed at a table tennis club, which might be why nobody is concerned about ratings. Everyone plays with everyone. This is particularly amazing since the club only meets for roughly two hours, twice a week. The temptation for the better players to play with each other must be strong, but there was abundant evidence that they did not succumb to such temptations, if they experienced them at all. Third, an evening at ALVaTTc promises plenty of irrepressible Fred humor.

Here is a sample. In our doubles match Fred's partner missed an easy shot. His partner exclaimed, in his Eastern European accent, "How could I miss that shot? I'm rushing!" Fred looked at him earnestly. "No you're not. You're still Ukrainian."

One other nice feature of the club: there is always at least one doubles match going on. Doubles is a mainstay at the club and Fred, ever imaginative, told me about a doubles tournament they held in which players served not only from the right side of the table, but also from the left. It was apparently a huge success. Doubles creates camaraderie, or maybe it is the other way around. Regardless, there is clearly a great camaraderie among the fifteen-to-twenty players who show up at ALVaTTc on Tuesday and Friday nights. After the club closes, many of the players, including Fred, head to a local diner for more laughs and food.

AS MY SECOND VISIT to the club was winding down we were sitting around, taking off our table tennis shoes, and talking. Fred looked haggard. He admitted that he was exhausted, having done three hours of yardwork before arriving at the club.

So I asked, quite reasonably I thought, "Fred, you are over eighty. Don't you think someone else could do your yardwork for you?"

He shot back, "Where's the workout in that? My neighbor has a sit-down lawn mower and he has offered to let me use it. Who needs it? I have a push mower. And look at his ass and look at my ass. That tells you all you need to know."

Dave, who was sitting nearby, chastised Fred: "Did you have to say that? Now when you stand up I won't be able to resist; I'll have to look." We all smiled.

It is indeed a mystery why more people don't play table tennis.

APPENDIX A

What an Anxious Ping Pong Pop Keeps in His Table Tennis Bag

"Are you moving out?" Aviva, my youngest daughter, asks. I look at her quizzically but silently, pretending not to know what she is talking about. My kids like to pick on me—evidently, I'm an easy target—and I know from experience that responding verbally will only encourage her.

"What do you have in that thing? Aren't you just going to the table tennis club?" she continues.

A verbal riposte is clearly required.

"Yes, but I have to bring stuff for Eliel as well," I say, which reveals shades of truth. I do bring some things for Eliel, but he does not request that I bring these things and he brings a bag of his own to the club. I could fit three of his bags, even if they were overflowing, into my bag.

"And I'm over six feet tall so my clothes take up a lot of space." Also, shades of truth. Over twenty years of fatherhood has helped me master this art. My clothes do take up more space than, say, Eliel's clothes, especially my size-thirteen sneakers, but this hardly requires a bag three times the size of Eliel's bag.

She is not satisfied, so I try a different tack. I rely on wisdom from her Girl Scout days for the rescue.

"Isn't your motto 'always be prepared'? I just want to be prepared in case we need anything at the club." I think my argument is unassailable. Aviva is undeterred, although I think she is surprised to learn I was paying attention to the Girl Scout activities of her youth.

"So why is your bag ten times the size of Eliel's bag?" We've entered the world of exaggeration and I know this is not an argument that can be won or lost. It's simply the way my kids remind me that I'm a nut and they know it. I consider a parting shot to Aviva about how she reads fiction, but for the moment I play the role of the adult and wisely refrain.

I pick up my bag, realizing that under the circumstances I can't, without risking further insult, ask Eliel to carry it to the car as I usually would. "See you later!" I exclaim through a forced smile. "We'll be home after dinner."

AVIVA AND MY OTHER CHILDREN, as usual, are not wrong. We often joke that I could fit a Chinese coach inside my table tennis bag, which of course would be more useful than anything actually in the bag. In my defense, I'm open to the possibility that I'm a nut, as my children insist, but lugging around my large bag feels rational to me. And since my goal is to make the obscure world of table tennis seem normal and natural to readers, I think it is worth defending myself and justifying the size of my bag.

The bag, as hinted at in Chapter 9, was purchased at the US Nationals in Las Vegas. To evaluate my purchasing decision, one must fully appreciate the size of the playing hall at the Nationals. The yearly tournament is held, at least in recent years, at the Las Vegas Convention Center. I don't know the square footage of the playing hall, but I can report without exaggeration that it takes about five minutes to walk from one end to the other. The place is massive. Moreover, the walk from the hotel to

WHAT AN ANXIOUS PING PONG POP KEEPS IN HIS TABLE TENNIS BAG

the playing hall, even though the hotel is connected to the convention center, is considerable. On our first day at our first Nationals, in 2016, I schlepped my medium-sized table tennis bag over one shoulder, a cooler bag with snacks and lunch food over the other shoulder, and a backpack across my back, which held my computer that I was reluctant to leave in our hotel room. After a few hours it was clear that this was unworkable. Most of the major table tennis companies have booths at the US Nationals, so I poked around the booths and stumbled across my solution: a bag that could fit into it all three of my current bags, and most importantly, it had wheels. I didn't hesitate. I made the purchase, stuffed in my other bags, and rolled my behemoth away. This was a literal weight off my shoulders, and I felt like I was flying at that moment. Afterward, on many occasions, I would remark that this bag was one of the best purchases of my life and I still stand by that sentiment.

I'm aware that my defense has holes. As Eliel likes to point out, yes, the behemoth bag makes sense for Las Vegas, but we are only there once or twice a year: Why carry it around for the rest of the year? Here I am on shakier ground, but my rationale is a combination of Girl Scout principles noted earlier, an insatiable tendency to hoard, and an inherent laziness that rarely goes unpunished. The bag is not only useful for Las Vegas, but it is useful for all tournaments because it carries everything we could need at a tournament, which I'll describe in a moment. Eliel attends a tournament about once a month, so the bag has been put to good use. Eliel agrees, yet admittedly, this still does not explain why I schlepp the bag to various clubs two or three times a week. Why not take out what I need for the club and put it into a smaller bag? In fact, this is precisely what Eliel does. He has a bag he brings to the clubs and a slightly larger bag he uses for tournaments. Eliel is right, of course, but you can't underestimate the power of slothfulness. I just can't be bothered to continually transfer my table tennis equipment in and out

215

of bags. Instead, I'd rather risk another hernia operation every time I take Eliel to a table tennis club.

Susan Cain, author of the introverts' manifesto, *Quiet*, suggests that we all have baggage—literally, a suitcase—filled with prized and personal possessions that we schlepp through life. While acknowledging that it might be difficult, she encourages introverts to share the contents of their suitcases. And while my kids' repeated queries about the contents of my bag only receive "stuff" as a response, Susan Cain is right. It is worth sharing what is inside my bag. There is no doubt that examining the items we regularly interact with can inform us about how we live. Indeed, my archaeological colleagues reconstruct entire lives out of the material culture they unearth.

More importantly, our material culture can inform us about how we experience the world. The objects that populate our environment provide what ecological psychologist James Gibson described as affordances. That is, there is a relation between humans and their physical environment that is crucial for their socialization (actually, the concept applies to all organisms). Some anthropologists, who have adopted Gibson's ideas, understand affordances as the possibilities of action that we perceive as we navigate our physical environments. The spoon in my silverware drawer, for example, provides the possibility of eating yoghurt. Of course there are other ways I could consume my yoghurt, but I experience spoons as offering the possibility of yoghurt consumption and I engage with them accordingly. There are cultural patterns to how we interact with things in our environments, but this should not blind us to individual variation. My parents, for example, experience their dining room table as a formal place to serve meals when they have guests; thanks to my babysitter, I will forever see it as a potential ping pong table. The environments in which we live, and the objects through which we construct these environments, thus offer us insights into how we experience the world we inhabit. Table tennis players, of course, experience the world of table tennis through the objects that enable them to play.

So, what are those objects? Or, as Aviva has asked, what's in my bag?

Actually, just stuff. Each item on its own is not exciting, and in fact, even together they are not terribly exciting. But it is this bag of stuff that accompanies us every time we cross the threshold into the table tennis world to train or compete. And that is exciting.

Clothing. Minimally I carry two extra t-shirts in my bag, two pairs of socks and underwear, and an extra pair of shorts. I do not change my clothes frequently while at the club—at most, once—but many players do. One of Eliel's practice partners, a Russian Jew whose table tennis ambitions were constrained in Russia by his heritage, changes his shirt after each match, often going through five shirts an evening. Eliel changes his clothes one to three times during each club visit, depending on the kind of workout he is getting.

Table tennis clothes are not significantly different from other athletic attire, but they do have some distinctive characteristics. Most notably, and distinguishing table tennis from tennis attire, table tennis shirts and shorts cannot be white. White clothing can camouflage the ball and it is thus banned in tournament play. Shirts and shorts tend to be made out of a light, fast-drying synthetic material, although some players, myself included, play in cotton t-shirts. Because of the speed and quick movements of the sport, lightweight clothing is generally preferred. In addition to the shirts manufactured by table tennis companies, players often wear shirts purchased or provided at tournaments that commemorate the event. It is always impressive to see shirts from the seventies and eighties that have withstood the test of time; there is a bit of status in sporting such a shirt, at least in my eyes. And of course most clubs have shirts with club logos. Some entrepreneurial types have marketed shirts with aphorisms like "Ping Pong is My Religion" or "Ping Pong Master," and others I won't mention since they would turn this into an R-rated book. There is also the ill-informed shirt I've seen sported by several Russians—"Table tennis is hard. It's not baseball."—which absurdly imagines that hitting a swerving baseball at over 90 mph with a wooden stick is somehow easy. They don't play baseball in Russia so they can be forgiven for this misperception. At tournaments, the most frequently donned shirts are imitations of the US National Team uniforms, with the wearer's personal name imprinted on the back.

Shoes. The most important table tennis attire—in terms of play rather than fashion—is footwear. Table tennis shoes are not dissimilar to volleyball shoes: they tend to be much lighter than other sneakers, have additional side support for quick lateral movements, and have rubber soles that provide good traction. Table tennis does not have the same clientele as volleyball or basketball, so in terms of height, or more relevantly, shoe size, I'm an outlier. It is no easy task finding size-thirteen table tennis shoes—most Asian companies max out at 11.5—but thankfully some German companies make shoes I can squeeze into. At times I've tried to play with non-table tennis sneakers, including those made for volleyball (which are a bit too heavy), and I've never found a pair that works. None of them have all three characteristics that are essential for a suitable table tennis shoe.

You may, rightfully, ask what shoes are doing in table tennis bags: Why not just wear your table tennis shoes to the club? The short answer is because that would be sacrilegious. Table tennis shoes are not worn outside, unless of course you are trying to invite ridicule and shame. Rookies might make the mistake, but once they've been appropriately enculturated into the table tennis world, they too will follow the unwritten law that table tennis shoes must be removed before returning to the secular world. Why are table tennis shoes treated with such reverence? One plausible reason is fear of unnecessarily wearing down the soles, which are vital to securely grip the floor. Another might be discomfort. Table tennis shoes are light, and although they provide excellent lateral support, they don't provide much support overall. Moreover, they tend to be worn tightly so that your feet do not slip within the shoe. Or it may just be a cultural norm that began for a sensible reason—early table tennis shoes were more like grippy slippers than sneakers—but eventually took on a life of its own, even after table tennis shoes evolved to provide more support than they once did. I suspect all these factors are relevant.

Paddles. Eliel and I always carry one extra paddle in our bags. I used to carry around more, but even I came to realize *that* was crazy. However, having a backup paddle is essential for tournaments. At larger tournaments, such as the US Nationals and US Open, paddles are checked by officials prior to matches. A paddle can be disqualified if the rubber has a bubble, which I'll explain in Appendix B, or if there is a tear in the rubber. These officials will also check that the rubber and blade are ITTF (International Table Tennis Federation) approved. At a recent US Nationals, prior to an important match, the paddle of a former US champion and one of my table tennis heroes, Danny Seemiller (see Chapter 6), was disqualified because his rubber was not on the ITTF approved list. Despite his justified protests, he had to use someone else's paddle for the match, which he lost. I say "justified" because it turns out that the officials were using the wrong list and Danny's rubber was legal after all.

Some players carry around multiple paddles because they will use a different paddle depending on the style of their opponent. If they are worried about the power of the opponent, they might use a slower paddle with more control, or if they are playing a lower quality opponent, they might use an extremely fast blade to end the points quickly. Professional players would never do this, but those who play table tennis as a hobby rather than a living are always experimenting with new rubbers and blades, and many of them walk around with their experiments in their bags.

Balls. This used to be easy. Club and tournament players would always carry at least a few Nittaku 3-Star balls in their bags. The only variation was whether the balls were white or yellow; preference usually depended on the background walls of the club where the player played. These were the official balls at every US tournament, so there was no reason to explore other balls on the market. It is not clear to me how other balls even survived on the market. But those simple days are long gone and I am not alone when I wax romantic about those simpler times. A little history is necessary.

For all of the twentieth century, table tennis balls were made of celluloid. In 1900, celluloid balls were introduced in England, the birthplace of table tennis, and quickly replaced cork and other materials that were used at the time. The ball was thirty-eight millimeters in diameter and remained that size until 2000, when the size of the ball was increased to forty millimeters in an attempt to slow down the game and make it more watchable for viewing audiences. Celluloid balls remained the standard until 2014, when the ITTF introduced plastic balls into international play. Manufacturers had experimented with plastic balls in the 1980s, but players rejected them en masse as unplayable. By the 2010s, however, it was widely recognized that the death of celluloid was imminent. By the second millennium there were only two products in the world that relied on celluloid: guitar picks and table tennis balls. Mr. McGuire's prophetic advice to Benjamin was being realized: plastics was the future. Efforts to create a playable plastic ball began in earnest and every major table tennis company entered the race. The Nittaku monopoly on the ball market could finally be challenged.

There were several consequences to this state of affairs. The most frustrating for tournament players was that there was no longer one standard tournament ball. It was possible to play in six consecutive tournaments and compete with six different balls, such as Nittaku, Xushaofa, Joola, Butterfly, Gewo, and DHS balls. Moreover, companies often put more than one ball on the market at a time to see which were most preferred, so it was not enough to know the company that was sponsoring the tournament balls, you also needed to know the specific type of ball being used. And throughout this experimental phase, as new brands emerged, other brands became obsolete. If the balls had been similar, all this would have been manageable and endured, mostly, without complaint. But in fact, the balls differed considerably in how they bounced and how receptive they were to spin. Thankfully, over the last few years there has been greater convergence on how the different brands of balls play, although different brands are still used at different tournaments. So it is not unusual for players to carry about three or four different balls in their bags, depending on the tournament season.

The move to plastic balls has impacted the game in a much more significant way than increasing the number of brands of balls toted around in table tennis bags. Although the balls vary in how they play, it was much easier to impart spin on celluloid balls than on any of the plastic balls on the market. Consequently, players whose playing style relied on heavy spins were suddenly at a disadvantage. Players, however, who take the ball right off the bounce, relying on speed rather than spin to control the point, now had a considerable advantage. Notably, this is the style of younger players before they develop the leg and upper-body strength to generate heavy spins. In the 2017 World Championships, a fourteen-year-old Japanese player, Tomokazu Harimoto, rode this advantage to the quarterfinals, an unprecedented accomplishment for someone his age. Admittedly, other factors were relevant such as the fact that he began playing when he was two years old and launched his tournament career by the time he was three. At fifteen, he was ranked fourth in the world, and he remains one of the world's top players.

Other Stuff. There are various other items in my bag that I use regularly and would be found in most table tennis bags. First, I keep two hand towels in my bag. Most players bring a hand towel to the table when they play since paddles are difficult to grip with sweaty palms. To speed up the pace of play, during tournaments players are allowed to use their towels only every six points. Most players follow this rule during league play as well, although during league play a player would never lose a point if they used their towel at an inappropriate juncture, which can happen during a tournament (usually though, a player is just given a warning). Second, like all players, I keep a sponge in my bag. Table tennis rubber is effective only if it can grip the ball, and for the rubber to do that it must be clean. Therefore, players regularly wash the rubber on their paddles with a moist sponge. To Eliel's annoyance, I am constantly reminding him to wash his paddle before each match when we are at a tournament. Often, I just wash it for him while he's not looking, to avoid an argument. Third, I keep a full complement of silverware in my bag, to the annoyance of everyone in my family. This annoyance is justified (so is Eliel's for that matter) as I don't keep track of whether I have put my dirty utensils in the dishwasher or not so I have a bad habit of accumulating cutlery. I denied this at first, but then my daughter Rivka went through my bag and found more spoons—at least seven—in my bag than were in the silverware drawer. There were forks and knives too. Ever since, I accept with humility and silence the verbal thrashing my silverware pilfering evokes.

My bag also contains an assortment of unnecessary but useful equipment. For example, I have a net measure in my bag. It is essentially a long, rectangular-shaped plastic U that is put over the net to see if it is the correct height. The width of most paddles will also serve this purpose, but since a millimeter might be the difference in winning and losing a point, it is better for the neurotic player to be sure about such things. My bag also contains glue since the rubber around a paddle's edge often becomes unattached and needs to be reaffixed. I have a notebook in my bag that I use for notetaking when I am coaching Eliel. I don't trust my memory anymore, especially when I am anxious. And

I carry around an extra pair of shoelaces. Believe it or not, these have come in handy more than once when Eliel has broken a shoelace at a tournament. God bless the Girl Scouts: I'm prepared. Although I regularly use a sponge with water to clean my racket, I also have a manufactured rubber cleaner that I use when my rubber or Eliel's rubber needs a deeper clean. Lastly, I have about a dozen plastic grocery bags—the kind now outlawed in many states—that serve as dirty laundry bags.

Miscellaneous Bag Filler for the Neurotic Table Tennis Player. Here is where being advised by the Girl Scouts is particularly evident. I live life with a useful dose of pessimism, so injury is always just around the corner. For players over forty, such a prognostication is not unreasonable. Nearly every older player plays with an injury, and those who are injury-free at the moment have likely just recovered from an injury—or their turn will come soon. Players spend much of their time at the clubs talking about their injuries, and a quick glance at the tables provides ample evidence of persistent injuries and the measures players are taking to prevent them. Many players wear supportive straps on their knees, straps on their forearms for tendinitis, or ankle supports; if they lift up their shirts, many expose the back braces they are wearing. And I've endured the overpowering smell of Bengay at every of the several dozen clubs I've played at across the country. Unfortunately, it is not just the elderly who suffer injuries. Many of the top players also suffer injuries. Sometimes these injuries are career-ending. Ma Long, winner of three consecutive Men's World Championships and the only player to win two Olympic gold medals in Men's Singles (he is arguably the G.O.A.T.), says his greatest threat to winning is injury. Eliel and I have seen injuries derail the development of many youth players, some having to quit the game because of recurring tennis elbow or shoulder issues. I see an increasing number of Juniors who use athletic tape on their shoulders. I also had to use athletic tape on my shoulder to get through a tournament, and Eliel had to use it on his torso to get through one of the US Nationals.

But I'm prepared. If the table tennis gods decide it is my turn, or God-forbid Eliel's turn, to be stricken with injury, I'll be ready. Athletic tape now has a permanent place in my bag. I also carry two knee, ankle, and wrist braces—one for each half of by body, of course. In case of an ankle injury my bag contains an ace bandage, which has been shared with others on more than one occasion. Another permanent treatment in my bag is the strap I wear on my forearm every time I play because of tendinitis. Other injuries are just lurking around the corner. Feet are at particularly high risk, so I carry various bandages and padding to deal with blisters and foot sores that are almost inevitable after a long day of playing. A cold is only one germ away, so a bottle of vitamin C can always be found in my bag. Ibuprofen is also in ample supply, which helps with my arthritis and other assorted pains. It is also not bad for headaches resulting from my family ganging up on me, about my bag of course. And if recourse to modern medicine fails, I'm prepared to turn to the spiritual world for protection and help. I always have a mini prayer book in my table tennis bag. You never know when a *minyan*, a Jewish prayer quorum, will break out at a club or tournament. It has never happened yet, but when it does, I'll be ready.

I guess for the sake of full disclosure I should mention one last item, one that admittedly not only reveals my neuroticism but also supports my friend's contention, noted earlier, that I might be a little absent-minded: I carry a pair of Eliel's shorts. I added his shorts to my bag when I added a pair of my own. Or more specifically, I put them both in my bag after I took off my sweatpants at the club only to discover that I was standing in my underwear—I had forgotten to put on shorts. No, Eliel has never done this, and he assures me he never will. But as a ping pong pop I feel it is my responsibility to be ready for anything. And I am.

WHAT AN ANXIOUS PING PONG POP KEEPS IN HIS TABLE TENNIS BAG

I'VE PROVIDED A GLIMPSE of what is inside my bag, and as I've mentioned, most players have similar things in their bags, minus the specialty items for neurotics. And yes, all table tennis players carry bags with their equipment to their clubs and when competing at tournaments. Indeed, if you mistook a tournament hall for an airport terminal you could be forgiven, although hopefully the ping pong tables would help you accurately identify your location.

As I was finishing this appendix I decided to go through my bag in case I had forgotten to mention an item. Aviva noticed what I was doing and she suggested I return any stolen silverware. There were three spoons and two forks; I returned one of each. She also asked if I was finally emptying out whatever crap (her word choice, not mine) I had in there. I said no, but I was comforted to know that someday, after reading this appendix, my daughter will realize that I'm not a nut. She will fully appreciate why I needed such a large table tennis bag, and maybe she'll apologize for the harassment—with, of course, some Girl Scout Cookies.

APPENDIX B

How an Anxious Ping Pong Pop Affixes Table Tennis Rubber

Among my many roles as a ping pong pop—chauffeur, coach, financial backer, warm-up partner, eye-roll recipient, and so forth—my least favorite, with the exception of being a live target for smashing practice, is "gluer." When you purchase a ping pong paddle at a sporting goods store, you are buying a complete paddle that is already assembled. Once it is removed from its plastic casing it is ready to be used. But such pre-made paddles are never used by tournament players. In fact, they are not ITTF approved, so they could not be used even if a tournament player went momentarily insane and considered using one. These paddles simply do not hit the ball fast enough, and their rubber is not tacky enough to generate the spin needed to compete in the modern game. Club and tournament players make their own paddles by purchasing two sheets of rubber, a blade, glue, and applicator for the glue.

Glue might seem to be the least important of these items. It is true that players do not agonize over which type of glue to use, nor do they change the type of glue they use with the frequency that they change the types of rubber and blades they use. Yet, glue is hardly inconsequential. Indeed, gluing is watched closely by the ITTF.

When I was playing as a teenager, top players used what was known as "speed glue" to increase the power of their paddles. The problem with speed glue was that its effects only lasted for a few hours, so players had to reglue their paddles before every match. And they did. Indeed, it would have been impossible to compete among the top players without using speed glue; that would be akin to using a wooden tennis racket while everyone else is using graphite rackets. The ITTF ultimately banned this practice, either for health concerns (inhaling glue fumes several times a day cannot be healthy) or to make table tennis more viewer friendly by slowing down the game. In the club we regularly attend there is still an old-school player who speed-glues before each match, but for the most part the practice has died. Frank Rossitano (aka Judah Friedlander) commemorated the practice with a "Speed Glue" hat in the fifth season of *30 Rock*.

Most non-professional players who were not speed-gluing simply used rubber cement to affix rubber to their blade. Table tennis companies had always marketed different types of glue, but most players found it easier and cheaper to pick up some rubber cement at the local hardware store. When Eliel became interested in playing and I returned to the table tennis scene, people were still using rubber cement.

Mozart, however, did not. And Mozart was constantly changing his rubber, always exploring new rubbers. One day I asked him about the glue he used, which was white. I specifically asked him why he did not use rubber cement. He responded, "Because it's illegal."

"What do you mean?" I protested.

"ITTF banned all non-water-based glues over a year ago," he responded, without looking up from the glue he was spreading.

I was incredulous. "What are you talking about? Everyone uses rubber cement." Eliel had been playing in tournaments for over a year and Mozart was no longer a tournament player, so I incorrectly assumed I was more knowledgeable about what was happening in the table tennis world outside of our backwater New England bubble.

"It's illegal," he calmly repeated. "Go to the ITTF website and see for yourself."

When I returned home I went straight for my computer, and to my surprise he was entirely correct. On one hand, I was shocked that I had not heard about this before. On the other hand, I was relieved that we had not learned of it by having Eliel's racket disqualified. As it turns out, one of the reasons I saw so many players still using rubber cement was because after a day or so, officials are unable to detect the difference between rubber cement and water-based glues. Rubber cement is cheaper, easier to acquire, and provides a different feel of the ball than water-based glues, so most players were reluctant to switch. I did not want to risk it, however, so we immediately switched.

CHANGING RUBBER IS TERRIFYING. Call me a namby-pamby milksop coward or what you wish, and I would not disagree, but it would not alter the fact that I replace Eliel's rubber with pronounced trepidation. The terror lies in messing it up. You may rightfully ask, so what if you do a poor job? What is the worst thing that could happen if you affix his rubber improperly? Well, Eliel could miss a shot because of how I glued the rubber and consequently lose a critical point in a critical match, forever crushing his table tennis dreams. In my warped and imaginative mental universe, the difference between elimination in the first round and a national championship rides on how I change his rubber. Admittedly, "anal" and "delusional" may be more apt than "namby-pamby milksop coward," but these distressing thoughts weigh heavily on my mind every time I change his rubber.

It is worth pointing out that while I may be obsessive, I am far from the most obsessed table tennis player or parent, which once again proves that my mother was right. While I was growing up, her most oft-repeated kernel of wisdom, invariably offered when I had failed at something, was "There will always be someone who is better than you at [fill in whatever I had just failed at] and there will always be someone who is worse than you at [fill in same thing]. That's the way the world works." Such good sense was not comforting at all. After all, I knew that someone must be the worst and someone must be the best, and she never made it clear why either of those, especially the former, couldn't be me. Also, what if there was only one person worse than me? That wasn't very comforting either. With such advice she was plainly not aiming to nurture a champion. Nonetheless, I have yet to prove her wrong, although I am pretty sure that among bald, grey-bearded, bespectacled Jewish anthropologists with size-thirteen feet, I'm the best table tennis player in the world. Not sure if that counts. Anyway, one person who is more obsessive than I am is our famed German server, Dimitrij Ovtcharov. He is famous for, among other things, assiduously searching balls for cracks before he serves, and he finds them more than any other player on the professional tour. Admittedly, I'm probably one of the few who respects him for displaying such an extreme compulsion openly, but this is just the tip of the iceberg. I know he is more obsessive than I am because I'm happy for Eliel to use any rubber that his sponsor sends to us. Ovtcharov, on the other hand, reputedly will only use rubber that was produced early in the rubber-making machine's cycle, since he believes that rubber made later in the machine's cycle has a less consistent quality than the first sheets produced. He apparently visits the factory to specifically choose the sheets he'll use. I secretly respect him for this obsession, too, but mostly because he makes me feel comparatively sane.

I change Eliel's rubber a week before a tournament, which gives him enough time to adjust to the speed and tackiness of the new rubber. Thus, for most of the year I change his rubber about once a month. Professionals change their rubber more frequently; some use new rubber for each tournament match. Club players, on the other hand, will wear out their rubber in four to eight months, depending on the type of rubber they use and how frequently they play. A sheet of rubber costs between sixty to one hundred dollars, and two sheets, of course, are required for each paddle. You can do the math and understand why I was so thankful once Eliel received a sponsorship.

Table tennis rubber comes in a square sheet, slightly smaller than a piece of Manischewitz matzah. Rubbers consist of two layers. The top layer is made of rubber; the flat side contacts the ball and the other side consists of pips that attach to the bottom layer, which is made of sponge. Sponges vary in hardness (soft, medium, and hard) and thickness (1.9–2.2 millimeters). The thicker the sponge, the faster the rubber plays. Usually beginners start out with thin sponge to help them control the ball, whereas higher-level players use the thickest sponge available in order to maximize their power. Overall, rubbers vary in their durability, ability to impart spin, power (or how fast they play), feeling of control, and trajectory in which they launch the ball, which is known as the throw angle.

As I mentioned in Chapter 6, each side of the paddle must have a different color rubber, one red and one black, although new colors are beginning to emerge on the market. Players often use different rubbers on their forehand and backhand sides, adopting the rubber which they feel best accommodates the particularities of their backhand and forehand strokes. Eliel uses the same rubber on both sides; I use a slower rubber on my backhand than my forehand. The slower backhand rubber improves my control when I am backhand blocking, which as Eliel always points out, is a shot that I rely on far too often. He is correct, but I have the right rubber for this style of play; it's a vicious circle.

In addition to the standard materials needed to put a racket together—rubber, blade, glue, applicator, and scissors—a flat space is also required. Most players probably take this for granted, but I have the typical professor's desk that will require an excavation by one of my archaeological colleagues when I retire. But I do have one sacred item that remains unburied: *The Compact Edition of the Oxford English Dictionary*. So, my flat space is the cover of the dictionary, specifically the P-Z volume, which lies on top of the A-O volume. I place two sheets of blank paper on top of the horizontal dictionary to prevent glue from dripping onto my beloved word bank.

To replace Eliel's rubber, the first thing I do is remove the old rubber. Although it is nearly impossible to pull the rubber off store-bought paddles used by basement players, competitive players regularly change their rubber, and if rubber is properly affixed to the blade, it easily peels off. I set the used rubbers aside for Mozart so that he can bring them to the kids in Haiti. The rubbers are used, but they still have plenty of life, especially for beginners. I then scrub both sides of the blade with a dry paper towel or tissue to remove any remaining dried glue. My goal is for the surface of the blade to be as smooth as possible. Once this task is completed I lay the blade on the left half (just habit, possibly superstition) of the dictionary, with the side that I intend to affix the black rubber to facing upward.

Next, I open the package of black rubber. Black is always first, which is undeniably a necessary superstition. Changing rubber is treacherous business, and I am willing to elicit any force in the universe that may potentially increase my chance of success. Incidentally, as I tell my students when I teach theories of magic, magical practices and superstitions are normal, natural, and extremely common. Polish-born anthropologist Bronislaw Malinowski argued that they tend to emerge under conditions of uncertainty and uncontrollability. Under such conditions, magical and superstitious practices provide a sense of control for performers, arguably reducing their anxiety and helping them perform whatever tasks are at hand. There is a library full of studies supporting Malinowski's claims, and nearly everyone is aware of anecdotal evidence that is consistent with the theory. I perform magic in front of students prior to each lecture—consuming at least one banana—that eases my terror of public speaking. It is a habit I picked up in graduate school after depositing my lunch on the sidewalk—already consumed, if that was not clear—on the way to my first lecture ever in front of students. For my second lecture, I avoided the Indian buffet I had previously enjoyed and consumed a banana instead, without incident. Changing rubber, like lecturing, is not entirely uncertain or uncontrollable, but the outcome—success or failure—feels enough out of my control that I'll take all the help I can get.

Back to changing rubber. I next lay the black rubber flat, sponge facing upward, on the right-hand side of the dictionary. The subsequent step is the most unpleasant in the process. I open the bottle of glue, which emits an odor that resembles rotting fish. Even writing about this experience makes me cringe. I always expect Jumpy, our cat, to be clawing at my office door, seeking the fish I must be hiding from him. But I think even he is repulsed by the smell. Once I recover from the initial shock of the stench, and after finding a paper clip to unclog the glue spout, I squeeze glue onto the sheet of rubber in random squiggly patterns. Too much glue and I'll have a mess on my dictionary; too little glue and I won't be able to adequately cover the surface of the rubber. With practice, I generally now manage to get it just about right. I then use a rectangular piece of foam, which comes with the purchase of the glue, to spread the glue across the rubber. Once the glue is spread evenly across the entire sheet, I make more squiggles on the blade and again spread the glue around the blade as evenly as possible. I then wait a few minutes for the glue to dry and I repeat the process, sometimes twice.

When I am satisfied that the glue is evenly spread and relatively dry—I don't like to wait until it is completely dry, but some do—my anxiety levels rise dramatically. Now is the moment when it can all go awry. I take the rubber and turn it over, carefully placing it on the blade. I smooth it out with my hands, whereas in the past I would use a rolling pin, but I was told that a rolling pin should not be used with the new rubbers because it would damage their springiness. I then grab one of my largest books—a book of Jewish history—and while standing on a chair, I put the book on the paddle and place my full weight on the book to make sure the rubber is flat on the blade. After a minute I remove the book, step off the chair, and the moment of truth arrives: I check to see if the rubber is smoothly attached to the blade. If not, I get online to search for a therapist. However, if it is okay, I cut off the excess rubber (recall, sheets of rubber are square and blades are oval-shaped). I don't cut right to the edge of the blade, but rather, I leave about a millimeter of rubber extended over the edge to protect the blade from damage. Then I repeat the entire ritual precisely, this time with the red rubber.

When both sides are completed I stick the racket, handle facing out, between both volumes of my *Oxford English Dictionary*. I then place four hand weights on top of the dictionary and leave the paddle overnight. This last phase is unnecessary—many players use their paddles right after they are made—but I got in the habit of letting the paddles learn some English through osmosis and I've stuck with the habit. Yes, another superstition.

So what can go wrong? There are three main possibilities, all resulting in the ball not hitting off the racket in the way it is expected to. And yes, I have firsthand experience with all these failures. First, an air pocket could form, thus creating a bubble or raised area on the racket. If a bubble forms, when the ball contacts that spot it dies off the racket. Not that a player would want to play with one anyway, but rackets with bubbles are illegal. The rubber must be removed and it is usually thrown out, although I've heard that some players are able to successfully reglue bubbled rubber. I'm not one of them. Second, if there is an area that does not receive glue, the ball will also die off the racket if it hits in that spot. This is not officially illegal, but it would be a disadvantage to play competitively with such a paddle. We actually just encountered this mishap at a national tournament last week, and Eliel had to use his backup paddle throughout the tournament. Third, glue could be spread unevenly. Thicker amounts of glue tend to produce more powerful shots, which is why players often apply more than one layer of glue when they are attaching rubber (also to avoid the previous problem). Players, however, do not want unevenness in how the ball bounces off their rubber because in the heat of a point players can rarely control exactly where they hit the ball on their paddle.

I fear all these failures every time I change Eliel's rubber, and Eliel has to endure my neuroses when he plays with new rubber: "Is the rubber okay? Are you sure?" Yes, I'm well aware that I'm being annoying, and if I forget, Eliel reminds me. I'm comforted by the fact that, at least according to my mother, I'm not the best or the worst parent on the planet. And of course I'm not the only parent who changes their kid's rubber. Parents with common sense, though, let their children's coaches take care of their paddles. But parents without common sense are the truly fortunate ones: they become their children's coaches.

ACKNOWLEDGMENTS

In the Foreword to the second edition of *The Lord of the Rings*, JRR Tolkien explains why he wrote his classic trilogy: "The prime motive was the desire of a tale-teller to try his hand at a really long story that would hold the attention of readers, amuse them, delight them, and at times maybe excite them or deeply move them." My children know me as a tale-teller, especially a teller of Hasidic tales, and although I am less imaginative than Tolkien, and much less talented, my own motivations for writing this book were similar. Also, like Tolkien's experience, "This tale grew in the telling..." And I should add, Anaïs Nin's observation that "We write to taste life twice, in the moment and in the retrospect," most certainly captures my experience and motivation in writing this book.

But I didn't write this book alone. In Chapter 15, I wrote: "It would be a gross understatement to claim that it took a village to fashion Eliel into the player he is: it took multiple villages." The same is true for this book. Indeed, the players who populate the multiple villages that fashioned Eliel into the player he is are the same people who appear within the pages of this book, although most of them have been anonymized. I nonetheless thank them for their friendship and continual support of Eliel. But other villages were also involved. Notably, I turned to my academic village for feedback as I was genuinely unsure about the quality of what I had written. I had simply never written anything like it before and I felt unqualified to judge it. Professors Jesse Bering, Joseph Bulbulia, Agustin Fuentes, Jeffrey Schloss, and Sarah Willen provided invaluable feedback. More importantly, these highly respected and accomplished scholars assured me that what I had written was interesting, engaging, and worth publishing. I'm incredibly grateful for their enthusiastic endorsements of this project, as well as the generous endorsements of Candace Alcorta, Ariel Burger, Dominic Johnson, Gene Rogers, Adam Seligman, Ed Wehrle, and Charlotte Witvliet. My intended audience for this book, however, was never academics. So another village I turned to for assessment was my friends and family: those who know table tennis—Cory Johnson, Ken Kaminsky, Flint Lane, Phil Poresky, Sangita Santhanam, Dan Seemiller, and Will Shortz—and those who do not—Ellen Sosis, Elior Waskow, Elisha Ziskind, Rachel Ziskind, and my partner in crime (although I never read the advice books, we didn't do too badly, did we?). I thank all of them for their time and for providing insightful comments on all or parts of this book. For publishing advice I turned to another village, and I thank Liz Dubelman, Sue Sonnier, and David Sloan Wilson for sharing their expertise with me. Chris Donelan, Dave Rohr, Molly Silverstein, Melody Stanford Martin, and Wesley Wildman of Wildhouse Publishing provided welcome feedback, guidance, and assistance; I deeply appreciate their belief in this book. I also gratefully acknowledge the generous support (financial and otherwise) of the James Barnett Endowment, Issachar Fund, Templeton Religion Trust, my department's endlessly tolerant and dependable administrative assistants, Andrea Booth and Rebecca Laquitara, and the world's greatest department head, Natalie Munro. A massive collective "thank you" to all these residents in my villages.

My deepest gratitude, however, is reserved for the village that is closest to home: my children, my *tzaddikim*. They are my severest critics—in life and in writing—and I am a better person and writer because of them. Which reminds me of a Talmudic story (*Bava Metzia 84a*):

After Reish Lakish's passing, Rabbi Yochanan was lecturing and the comments afterward were all supportive, reassuring Rabbi Yochanan that his halachic argument was correct. But Rabbi Yochanan despaired, dismissing such praise and exclaiming that he does not need confirmation of his position. He lamented the loss of his brother-in-law and study partner, Reish Lakish: "When I would make a halachic pronouncement he would challenge it with twenty-four questions, and I would answer each of them, and by that dialogue, true understanding would become clear." Rabbi Yochanan grieved, "Where are you, son of Lakish? Where are you, son of Lakish?"

So, yes, my *tzaddikim*, you are all my Reish Lakishes and I miss your presence around the house. I even miss your teasing of me. Sometimes. Thank you all for reading, commenting, and encouraging me to publish this book. I have always believed in each of you; thank you for believing in me too. This book is ultimately a love letter to the four of you, so I will sign off accordingly.

Love,

Daddy

NOTES

Preface

...if someone else could perform the required movements without impacting the competition ... As one chess commentator quipped regarding attempts to get chess introduced as an Olympic sport, "If Stephen Hawking can do it, it's not a sport." Evans, L. (2007). *This Crazy World of Chess*. Cardoza Publishing, p. 75.

...one of the most popular sports in the world ... https://www.worldatlas.com/articles/what-are-the-most-popular-sports-in-the-world.html

The Talmud relates ... The Talmud, or more specifically the Babylonian Talmud (*Talmud Bavli*), is the central text of Jewish ritual study, even superseding the Torah in hours of commitment, if not sanctity and authority. Its breadth, covering the gamut of human activities, and length, consisting of over 2,700 double-sided folios in sixty-three volumes, are massive. The Talmud's meandrous arguments, use of multiple archaic languages, lack of punctuation, and inclusion of the opinions of more than a thousand rabbis, often in disagreement, yield a text that demands a lifetime of study to master. The passage referred to in the main text is from *Bava Batra* 9b.

In the US, anthropology embraces a holistic four-field approach ... For an introduction to anthropology, see Engelke, M. (2019). *How to Think Like an Anthropologist.* Princeton University Press; Ingold, T. (2018). *Anthropology: Why it Matters.* Polity; Metcalf, P. (2005). *Anthropology: The Basics.* Routledge; Peacock, J. L. (1986). *The Anthropological Lens.* Cambridge University Press.

... perhaps the last of the great nineteenth-century conglomerate disciplines ... Segal, D. A. & Yanagisako, S. J., eds. (2005). *Unwrapping the Sacred Bundle.* Duke University Press, p. Back Cover.

Apprenticeship as a mode of ethnography ... Apprenticeship would seem to be an ideal way to approach my topic, table tennis. The problem is, as I describe in Chapter 1, I can hardly be considered an apprentice. Although it is fair to say that we are all always learning, in the table tennis world I am not learning a new culture; it is a culture that I have been embedded in, on and off, for much of my life. What is new for me is being a father in this community, and I will have much to say about that experience. You could say I'm apprenticing as a ping pong pop, although if so, I'm an apprentice without a formal guide.

... for studying embodied activities ... For example, ritual (Luhrmann, T. M. (1991). *Persuasions of the Witch's Craft: Ritual Magic in Contemporary England.* Harvard University Press), musical performance (Downey, G. (2002). Listening to capoeira: phenomenology, embodiment, and the materiality of music. *Ethnomusicology,* 46(3), 487–509.), pilgrimage (Myerhoff, B. G. (1974). *Peyote Hunt: The Sacred Journey of the Huichol Indians.* Cornell University Press.), healing (Stoller, P. & Olkes, C. (1987). *In Sorcery's Shadow: A Memoir of Apprenticeship among the Songhay of Niger.* University of Chicago Press.), game playing (Desjarlais, R. (2011). *Counterplay: An Anthropologist at the Chessboard.* University of California Press.), craftwork (Marchand, T. H. (2008). Muscles, morals and mind: Craft apprenticeship and the formation of person. *British Journal of Educational Studies*, 56(3), 245–271.), and dance (Dalidowicz, M. (2015). Crafting fidelity: pedagogical creativity in kathak dance. *Journal of the Royal Anthropological Institute*, 21(4), 838–854; Mason, P. H. (2009). Brain, dance and culture: The choreographer, the dancing scientist and interdisciplinary collaboration. *Brolga: An Australian Journal about Dance*, (30), 27.).

… **including sport.** Downey, G. (2005). *Learning Capoeira: Lessons in Cunning from an Afro-Brazilian Art*. Oxford University Press; Wacquant, L. (2004). *Body & Soul: Notebooks of an Apprentice Boxer*. Oxford University Press.

Anthropology has historically ignored the study of sport or considered it secondary to more vital areas of human activity such as kin relations, mating, political maneuvering, religion, resource acquisition, and identity construction. There are undoubtedly various factors involved in this neglect, including elitism and concerns about being taken seriously within the academy. Archetti has suggested that anthropological neglect of sport was partially a function of conceptions of sport as a modern phenomenon, thus it was perceived to have little relevance to the traditional cultures of ethnographic interest to anthropologists. Archetti, E. P. (1998). The meaning of sport in anthropology: a view from Latin America. *Revista Europea de Estudios Latinoamericanos y del Caribe/European Review of Latin American and Caribbean Studies*, 65, 91–103.

However, as anthropologists have increasingly explored contemporary transnational cultures, interest in the study of sport has also gained traction, particularly concerning issues of globalization, embodiment, gender, and power. See Besnier, N., & Brownell, S. (2012). Sport, modernity, and the body. *Annual Review of Anthropology*, 41, 443–459; Besnier, N., Brownell, S. & Carter, T. (2018). *The Anthropology of Sport: Bodies, Borders, Biopolitics*. University of California Press;

Carter, T. (2002). On the need for an anthropological approach to sport. *Identities: Global Studies in Culture and Power*, 9(3), 405–422; McGarry, K. (2010). Sport in transition: emerging trends on culture change in the anthropology of sport. *Reviews in Anthropology*, 39(3), 151–172.

If interested in sport ethnographies, in addition to those cited at the beginning of this note, see Azoy, G. W. (2003). *Buzkashi: Game and Power in Afghanistan*. Waveland Press; Brownell, S. (1995). *Training the Body for China: Sports in the Moral Order of the People's Republic*. University of Chicago Press; Gonzalez Abrisketa, O. (2012). *Basque Pelota: A Ritual, An Aesthetic*. University of Nevada Press; Kelly, W. W. (2018). *The Sportsworld of the Hashin Tigers*. University of California Press.

Apprenticeship allows the ethnographer ... Downey, G., Dalidowicz, M., & Mason, P. H. (2015). Apprenticeship as method: embodied learning in ethnographic practice. *Qualitative Research*, 15(2), 183–200; Wacquant, L. (2005). Carnal connections: On embodiment, apprenticeship, and membership. *Qualitative Sociology*, 28(4), 445–474.

... anthropologists have become increasingly skeptical ... Clifford, J., & Marcus, G. E. (eds.) (1986). *Writing Culture: The Poetics and Politics of Ethnography*. University of California Press; Fernandez, J. & Herzfeld, M. (1998). In search of meaningful methods. In Bernard, H. R. (ed.) *Handbook of Methods in Cultural Anthropology*. Sage, pp. 89–129.

... if the locals engage in peyote rituals ... For example, see Myerhoff, B. G. (1974). *Peyote Hunt: The Sacred Journey of the Huichol Indians*. Cornell University Press. Yes, before studying Jewish grandmothers, Myerhoff took a peyote ride with the Huichol Indians.

... earlier generations of anthropologists ... For histories of anthropology and ethnography see Barnard, A. (2000). *History and Theory in Anthropology*. Cambridge University Press; Evans-Pritchard, E. (1981). *A History of Anthropological Thought*. Basic Books; Kuper, A.

(2014). *Anthropology and Anthropologists: The Modern British School*. Routledge; Moore, J. D. (2012). *Visions of Culture: An Introduction to Anthropological Theories and Theorists*. Rowman Altamira.

Ethnographers recognized ... See Geertz, C. (1974). From the native's point of view: On the nature of anthropological understanding. *Bulletin of the American Academy of Arts and Sciences*, 28(1), 26–45.

Since that time anthropology has largely been divided ... Anthropologist Roy Rappaport describes the situation well.

> Two traditions have proceeded in anthropology since its inception. One, objective in its aspirations and inspired by the biological sciences, seeks explanation and is concerned to discover causes, or even, in the view of the ambitious, laws. The other, influenced by philosophy, linguistics, and the humanities and open to more subjectively derived knowledge, attempts interpretation and seeks to elucidate meanings ...

But Rappaport ultimately argues that "any radical separation of the two is misguided." I agree. We are biological organisms who are born into, and cannot exist, without swimming in a cultural sea. Rappaport, R. (1994). Humanity's evolution and anthropology's future. *Assessing Cultural Anthropology*, 153–167, p. 154.

... Barbara Myerhoff explains ... Myerhoff, B. (1980). *Number Our Days*. Simon and Schuster.

Or Loic Wacquant ... Wacquant, L. (2004). *Body & Soul: Notebooks of an Apprentice Boxer*. Oxford University Press.

... as anthropologist Ruth Behar has put it ... Behar, R. (1996). *The Vulnerable Observer: Anthropology that Breaks Your Heart*. Beacon Press, p. 18.

The insufferable, excruciating, hair-pulling, exhaustive descriptions ... Feeling like you need some help with that middle-aged insomnia? Try keeping your eyes open through Bronislaw Malinowski's treatise on Trobriand gardening, collectively more than eight hundred pages of uninterrupted excitement. Malinkowski, B. (1978). *Coral Gardens and their Magic: A Study of the Methods of Tilling the Soil and the Agricultural Rites in the Trobriand Islands*. Dover Publications.

... **or "thick description" as Geertz put it** ... Geertz, C. (1973). Thick description: toward an interpretive theory of culture, In C. Geertz (ed.) *The Interpretation of Cultures*. Basic Books.

... **my family is Jewish** ... For an introduction to Judaism, see Sacks, J. (2007). *To Heal a Fractured World: The Ethics of Responsibility*. Schocken.

... **the Wandering Jew** ... For a comprehensive history of this nearly 2000-year-old legend, see Anderson, G. K. (1970). *The Legend of the Wandering Jew*. Brown University Press.

... **Chinese food, complaining and arguing** ... Complaining and arguing have a long tradition among Jews. Even after being freed from several hundred years of Egyptian bondage, the Israelites incessantly complain of hunger and thirst, arguing with both God and Moses. In one of my favorite lines in the Torah, the Israelites ask with characteristic biting sarcasm: "Were there no graves in Egypt that you had to take us into the desert to die?" (*Shemot* 14:11).

... **anthropology** ... Much has been made of the fact that Jews played a significant role in the development of anthropology (see Klein, M. (2017). Anthropology. In Valman, N., & Roth, L. (eds.) *The Routledge Handbook of Contemporary Jewish Cultures*. Routledge.). Influential early theorists, such as Emile Durkheim and his cousin, Marcel Mauss, had many rabbinic kin, and the father of ethnographic fieldwork was the German-Jewish refugee Franz Boas, mentioned above. Other Jews—Paul Radin, Melville Herskovits, Edward Sapir, Hortense Powdermaker, Robert Lowie, and Meyer Fortes, just to name a few— all followed suit and became luminaries in the field. This influence continued into the latter half of the twentieth century with scholars such as Marshall Sahlins, Roy Rappaport, Sherry Ortner, and Claude Levi-Strauss, and there are of course many Jewish anthropologists who have not achieved the status of these academic superstars, most notably the one writing this book. My department is over a quarter Jewish and oddly enough, nearly another quarter are married to Jews. It has been claimed that, as outsiders, Jews possess a double-consciousness that makes them particularly open and sensitive to the anthropological perspective that seeks to understand different lives. While my Jewish upbringing undoubtedly played a role in my interest in anthropology, I think the anthropological seeds that blossomed into my career were primarily planted through my childhood experiences playing table tennis.

... Ellis Island to Ebbets Field ... Levine, P. (1993). *Ellis Island to Ebbets Field: Sport and the American Jewish Experience.* Oxford University Press.

Leah Thall-Neuberger, a nine-time US Singles Champion ... Gao Jun, the current US women's national coach, also won nine US women's national championships.

As Milton Himmelfarb memorably put it ... Himmelfarb, M. (1973). *The Jews of Modernity.* Basic Books, p. 359.

The Big Lebowski is currently ranked 23rd ... https://en.wikipedia.org/wiki/List_of_films_that_most_frequently_use_the_word_%-22fuck%22

Move over Rabbi Hillel ... The Talmud relates that when a convert approached Rabbi Hillel and asked him to explain the Torah while standing on one foot, he famously replied: "That which is hateful to you, do not do to another. That is the whole Law. The rest is commentary. Now go and learn" (*Shabbat* 31a).

If this book is not an anthropological ethnography ... Behar, R. (2007). Ethnography in a time of blurred genres. *Anthropology and Humanism,*

32(2), 145–155; Geertz, C. (1980). Blurred genres: The refiguration of social thought. *The American Scholar*, 165–179.

... Harry Burns, of *When Harry Met Sally* ... Harry Burns (Billy Crystal) is explaining to Sally Albright (Meg Ryan) his dark side in this 1989 classic film: "When I buy a new book, I read the last page first. That way, in case I die before I finish, I know how it ends. That, my friend, is a dark side."

My anthropology colleagues tell me that everything is political ... For a useful introduction, see Gupta, A., & Ferguson, J. (eds.). (1997). *Culture, Power, Place: Explorations in Critical Anthropology*. Duke University Press.

Gregory Bateson's *Naven* ... Bateson, G. (1958). *Naven: A Survey of the Problems Suggested by a Composite Picture of the Culture of a New Guinea Tribe Drawn from Three Points of View*. Stanford University Press, p.1.

Chapter 1: Escape from the Basement

... my best friend Timmy's basement. That is not his real name. Anthropologists generally anonymize the populations they study. Sometimes, not only are people anonymized, but entire institutions, communities, and villages are given fictitious names. The extent to which ethnographers go to protect the identities of the people they have studied often depends on the sensitivity of the subject matter. That said, there are no strict rules about anonymization and there is considerable debate among ethnographers concerning the ethics of anonymization (e.g., Rhoads, R. A. (2020). "Whales tales" on the run: Anonymizing ethnographic data in an age of openness. *Cultural Studies ↔ Critical Methodologies*, 20(5), 402–413.). Outside of anthropology and sociology, others, particularly journalists, find anonymization simply fraudulent. They find it reprehensible that ethnographies are presented as research yet they are impossible to fact-check once anonymized. I've had countless debates with journalists and anthropologists about this issue, all inconclusive. Maybe the only thing that has been conclusive, for me, is that hard and fast rules on this issue would be a mistake; loose norms and decisions on a case-by-case basis seem like the best solution.

This book is most definitively not a research study—it is a story told through an anthropological and parental lens—so I don't feel bound by the same conventions I adhere to when presenting my academic research; I feel bound by common sense. Although I deferred to Walter Sobchack when seeking to explain Jewish observance, here I turn to the more conventional summary of Judaism offered by Rabbi Hillel to guide my thinking for this book: "That which is hateful to you, do not do to others" (Talmud, *Shabbat* 31a). I have no desire to appear in anyone else's book, so I have used pseudonyms for nearly everyone who appears in the following pages who is not a public figure. The few exceptions are people who I wanted to acknowledge because of their unrecognized importance to the table tennis community in the US, and friends and acquaintances who passed away whose memories I wanted to document. When using real names, I have sought permission when possible, even among some of the public figures. Similar to many ethnographies, I have also anonymized the primary club that Eliel trained at in order to protect the identities of club members. If journalists are bothered by this, they can read the book as though it were a novel. Or if they prefer, they can imagine that the subtitle of the book is "Based on a True Story."

In actuality, the gap between anthropological and journalistic positions seems, partially, to be one of attitude rather than assessment. Many anthropologists see ethnography in fictional terms, but they are not as disturbed by this as journalists tend to be. As anthropologist Clifford Geertz writes,

In short, anthropological writings are themselves interpretations, and second and third order ones to boot. (By definition, only a "native" makes first order ones: it's *his* culture.) They are, thus, fictions; fictions, in the sense that they are "something made," "something fashioned"—the original meaning of *fictio*—not that they are false, unfactual, or merely "as if" thought experiments.

Geertz, C. (1973). Thick description: toward an interpretive theory of culture. In C. Geertz (ed.) *The Interpretation of Cultures*. Basic Books, p. 15.

... are taught footwork movements long before they ever pick up a ball ... Playing without the ball is also used in elite tennis training, such as at the famed Spartak Tennis Club in Moscow. See Coyle, D. (2009). *The Talent Code: Unlocking the Secret of Skill in Maths, Art, Music, Sport, and Just About Everything Else.* Random House.

As Steve Brunskill ... Priestly, S. & Larcombe, B. (2015). *Expert in a Year: The Ultimate Table Tennis Challenge*, p. 30.

... wider than the Atlantic. Since it is *my* autobiographical disclosure I feel compelled to point out that my preferred simile would have referenced Belegaer, the ocean separating the Undying Lands from the western shores of Middle-earth, rather than the Atlantic. My children, however, insisted that referencing Belegaer would be losing readers before the book has even begun. As usual, they are probably right, but I cannot promise to restrain myself in subsequent pages. One family pastime—during everything from our camping trips to Passover Seders—is to drop allusions and quotes from *The Lord of the Rings* into our conversations. Since this book is essentially an invitation into a family conversation, Middle-earth references are inevitable.

Because of my affection for Tolkien's writings, on birthdays I am often the recipient of homemade Middle-earth gifts from my children—all my kids, including Eliel, are quite artistic. These include drawings of Smaug, Hobbiton, and the witch-king of Angmar, a clay model of Barad-dûr, and poetry play such as:

One Daddy to rule them all,
One Daddy to find them,
One Daddy to bring them all,
And in the darkness bind them.

Yes, as I note below, my kids sometimes mistake me for Sauron. One of my favorite gifts is an engraved rubber stamp, given with ink, that my children told me should be used when grading exams. They etched a picture in the rubber of Gandalf standing on the bridge of Khazad-dûm, holding his staff and sword. Underneath Gandalf's image they inscribed, for my struggling students: You cannot pass!

... and a member of the US Junior Team ... he reached the round of sixteen ... Those tales are not told here, but who knows, maybe they will be narrated in a sequel to this book.

Chapter 2: To Tennis or Not to Tennis ...

... Sauron ... If you do not know who Sauron is, I urge you to put this book down and immediately head to your local independent bookstore to purchase a trilogy known as *The Lord of the Rings*. You may return to this book only after completing the trilogy and acknowledging *The Lord of the Rings* as the greatest piece of literature ever written. If you need further convincing, see Shippey, T. (2014). JRR Tolkien: Author of the Century. Houghton Mifflin Harcourt.

By the time a fourth child ... Chabon, M. (2018). *Pops: Fatherhood in Pieces*. Harper, p. 24.

These included giving him a nine-point lead in an eleven-point game ... If you have never played or observed tournament-level table tennis, you are likely to think that games are played up to twenty-one points. You would have been correct in the last millennium, but in 2001 the ITTF (International Table Tennis Federation) shortened each game to eleven points and increased the number of games needed to win. Traditionally, matches were best of three games, or in high-level competitions, best of five games. Following the shortening of the games, matches increased to best of five and best of seven games respectively. Unlike in tennis, where there is a sex difference in the length of matches during elite competitions—during Grand Slam tournaments men's singles matches are best of five whereas women's matches are best of three—the length of table tennis matches are always the same in men's and women's draws.

The ITTF's logic in shortening the game was to make table tennis matches more exciting for viewers. By shortening the game, each point becomes more critical. This is the primary motivation behind most of the ITTF's rule changes (switching to plastic balls seems to be an exception; see Appendix A). All rule changes have consequences: some of them intended, others unintended. The experience of players under the two game lengths is different. As you would expect, shortening the game does indeed increase the importance, and stress, of each point for the players. There is simply less opportunity to dig oneself out of hole during a game. Coming back from a six-point deficit is not uncommon in a twenty-one-point game; it is much rarer in an eleven-point game. The increased importance of each point also means that some games can turn on good or bad fortune. A game where an opponent wins three or four points via a net or an edge can be insurmountable. This appears to be less common in elite-level play, possibly because top players are more likely to return net and edge balls, but also because points are often shorter at the elite levels.

The transition to eleven-point games also changed the service experience of players. In the twenty-one-point format, players alternated between serving five consecutive points each. In the eleven-point format, players alternate between serving two consecutive points each. The experience of the two formats differs radically because when players served five consecutive points considerable strategy was involved in setting up the order of serves. As discussed in Chapter 5, the key in table tennis serving is deception. Deception is achieved, primarily, by maintaining the same service stroke but either varying the point of contact on the paddle, the point of contact during the stroke, or both. When players had five consecutive serves they could, for example, lull opponents into believing that a certain serve was always an underspin serve (by giving the player two or three consecutive underspin serves) then contacting the ball on the upstroke rather than the downstroke, thus generating topspin. Returning a topspin serve as though it were underspin will result in the ball popping up, enabling an easy put-away. Serves vary not only in their spin, but also in their length, and this is another way that servers can set up and surprise their opponents. Serves at the higher levels of play are usually short and slow, but long and fast serves can catch opponents off guard. Long and slow serves, of course, are avoided since a slow ball off the end of the table will give an opponent an opportunity to get in position for a strong attack.

Anthropologists rarely take social conversations ... see Bauman, R. & Sherzer, J. (1974). *Explorations in the Ethnography of Speaking.* Cambridge University Press.

Multi-ball training ... In multi-ball training, the coach has a large container of balls that she rapidly hits at the trainee. The coach does not return the shots of the player; indeed, she is generally sending another ball over the net as the player makes contact. The advantages of multi-ball training are that shots can be experienced faster than they would be experienced if the coach and player were simply hitting back and forth, and the player can hit many more strokes in a short time span because the coach and player are not picking up the ball after each miss. For an example of how multi-ball training transformed a player, see Syed, M. (2010). *Bounce: Mozart, Federer, Picasso, Beckham, and the Science of Success*. Harper.

Clifford Geertz, used Balinese cockfights ... Geertz, C. (1973). Deep play: Notes on the Balinese cockfight. In C. Geertz (ed.) *The Interpretation of Cultures*. Basic Books.

... **"[t]he double entendre** ... Geertz, C. (1973). Deep play: Notes on the Balinese cockfight. In C. Geertz (ed.) *The Interpretation of Cultures*. Basic Books, p. 417.

... **conversations that compare tennis and table tennis** ... Table tennis players are not alone in making the comparison. Jerry Seinfeld, with his keen observational skills that would make any anthropologist jealous, remarks to his girlfriend following a tennis date: "Next time let's play ping pong. It is easier to jump over the net." From *The Switch*, season six of the sitcom *Seinfeld*.

Time magazine ... http://content.time.com/time/specials/packages/completelist/0,29569,1852747,00.html

Chapter 3: Almost a Brief History of Whiff-Waff

Table tennis began as a parlor game ... The main sources for the historical information throughout this chapter are Grant, S. (2012). *Ping Pong Fever: The Madness that Swept 1902 America*; Griffin, N. (2014). *Ping-pong Diplomacy: The Secret History Behind the Game that Changed the World*. Simon and Schuster.

Many Native American groups played such games ... Culin, S. (1975). *Games of North American Indians*. Dover.

The French were playing a tennis-like game ... Gillmeister, H. (1998). *Tennis: A Cultural History*. New York University Press.

The word tennis itself ... Fox, J. (2012). *The Ball: Discovering the Object of the Game*. Harper Perennial.

NOTES

Ivor Montagu ... See Griffin, N. (2014). *Ping-pong Diplomacy: The Secret History Behind the Game that Changed the World.* Simon and Schuster.

... third son of Lord Swaythling ... In his honor the World Champion Men's Team is awarded The Swaythling Cup. The World Champion Women's Team is awarded The Corbillon Cup, donated by the president of the French Table Tennis Association, Marcel Corbillon. The original Corbillon Cup, however, was a casualty of World War II.

... but 1902 is notable ... See Grant, S. (2012). *Ping Pong Fever: The Madness that Swept 1902 America.*

... limiting the length of the match. In the modern era, the "expedite rule," which itself has evolved over time, is rarely needed, but I have seen it used a few times when two choppers compete. If an umpire institutes the expedite rule, the server must win the point before the opponent returns thirteen shots or the opponent is awarded the point. Such matches can be intriguing because the rule forces choppers to use tactics that are otherwise uncommon for defensive players.

Technology is often a major source of innovation in sport ... See Kew, F. (1987). Contested rules: An explanation of how games change. *International Review for the Sociology of Sport,* 22(2), 125–135; Kew, F. (1990). The development of games: An endogenous explanation. *International Review for the Sociology of Sport,* 25(4), 251–267.

More than 30 percent of the competing table tennis players ... https://www.nytimes.com/2016/08/18/sports/olympics/at-least-44-table-tennis-players-in-rio-are-chinese-born-six-play-for-china.html?mwrsm=Email&_r=0#story-continues-1

... dubbed "ping pong diplomacy." Griffin, N. (2014) offers the most comprehensive, and entertaining, history of "ping pong diplomacy" available.

... if you go carrying pictures of Chairman Mao ... Lyrics from "Revolution 1" on the *White Album*, of course.

... "spiritual nuclear weapon," ... Griffin, p. 85.

... "a weapon for peace." Griffin, p. 273.

Chapter 4: For the Love of the Sport

... USA Friends of Association Haitienne de Tennis de Table ... If you would like to support this worthy effort, see https://friendsofahtt.org/

He is a tzaddik ... The Hebrew word *tzaddik* shares a root with *tzedek* (justice) and *tzedakah* (charity), suggesting an interconnection between these concepts in Jewish life. Among Jews, righteousness is expressed as the pursuit of justice. And charity is not an act of sacrifice or generosity; rather it is an act of justice.

... nothing holier than improving the world around you ... Repairing and improving the world is a central—likely *the* central—concept of Judaism (known as *tikkun olam*). I was recently chided by a Malaysian-born friend, a devout Christian who had been raised as a Buddhist, that Jews have not done enough to promote and publicize the concept of *tikkun olam*, which he saw as vital for human flourishing. He is probably right. See Sacks, J. (2007). *To Heal a Fractured World: The Ethics of Responsibility*. Schocken.

... anthropologist to be misled by informants ... For a classic example, see Chagnon, N. (1974). *Studying the Yanomamo*. Holt, Rinehart, and Winston, where Chagnon describes how his Yanomamo informants misled him about their kin relations, rendering a year's worth of genealogical data useless.

... The Metaphysics of Ping-Pong ... Mina di Sospiro, G. (2015). *The Metaphysics of Ping-Pong*. Quest Books, p. 57.

NOTES

One Levi Yitzchak story ... For uninspired versions of other Levi Yitzchak stories, see Buber, M. (1961). *Tales of the Hasidim: Early Masters*. Schocken Books. For inspired versions, see just about any other collection of Hasidic tales.

... similar to the way Jews read the Torah. Historically, the rabbis divided the Torah into *parshiot*, loosely translated as chapters, which are chanted on Saturday mornings in synagogue (portions are also chanted on Monday and Thursday mornings). The completion of the annual cycle is celebrated with the holiday Simchat Torah, in the fall. If you've ever seen people dancing in the streets with parchment scrolls, who appear to have just attended a ZZ Top look-alike convention, they were probably Jews celebrating Simchat Torah.

Chapter 5: A Guide for the Perplexed: Serves, Sounds, and Status

... one of the coaches asked ... For useful books on table tennis technique, I recommend Hodges, L. (2009). *Table Tennis Tales and Techniques*; Seemiller, D. & Holowchack, M. (1997). *Winning Table Tennis*. Human Kinetics.

... his windshield wiper serve ... The windshield wiper serve is back! In 2022, French teenage phenom Alexis Lebrun reintroduced the windshield wiper serve to the Men's World Tour, and remarkably, the serve challenged many top players. And phenom is not hyperbole. Prior to 2022 Lebrun was not ranked within the top one thousand players in world; by the end of 2022 he was ranked within the top thirty and had beaten three of the top ten players in the world. On the Women's World Tour, Adriana Diaz and Xiaoxin Yang have the windshield wiper serve in their repertoires, but they do not use it often and it is less effective than Lebrun's serve.

... known as the *banana flip*. It is also referred to as the *banana flick*, but flip seems a more accurate description of the stroke to me.

... our cultural surroundings influence our sensory perceptions ... Stoller, P. (1989). *The Taste of Ethnographic Things: The Senses in Anthropology*. University of Pennsylvania Press.

... to associations with certain tastes ... And different smells as well. On the cultural influences of perceived mushroom aromas, see Tsing, A. (2015). *The Mushroom at the End of the World*. Princeton University Press, pp. 45-52.

... such as that a jaguar passed this location about three hours ago ... I experienced this first hand while accompanying my graduate advisor on fieldwork with hunter-gatherers in Paraguay.

... anthropologist Nathaniel Roberts ... Roberts, N. (2016). *To be Cared For: The Power of Conversion and Foreignness of Belonging in an Indian Slum*. University of California Press.

Like tennis and badminton athletes ... See Hung, T. M., Spalding, T. W., Maria, D. L. S., & Hatfield, B. D. (2004). Assessment of reactive motor performance with event-related brain potentials: attention processes in elite table tennis players. *Journal of Sport and Exercise Psychology*, 26(2), 317-337; Starkes, J. L. & K. Anders Ericsson, eds. (2003). *Expert Performance in Sports: Advances in Research in Sports Expertise*. Human Kinetics.

... the Chinese expression "*Hao qiu!*" ... There is apparently some debate about the meaning of this expression. Eliel knows some Chinese (two years of study), but I don't, so I'll leave it to others to sort out. The translation I've offered, "Good ball!", is the most common one.

In a classic anthropological example ... See the documentary, *Trobriand Cricket: An Ingenious Response to Colonialism*, directed by Gary Kildea and Jerry Leach (1979), Ronin Films. Also see Blanchard, K. (1995). *The Anthropology of Sport*, revised edition. Bergin & Garvey.

NOTES

... until the score is tied. Playing until the score is tied is not limited to cricket. The Gahuku-Gama of Papua New Guinea, for example, used rugby as a substitute for intertribal warfare—replacing warfare with sport is not uncommon in traditional populations—and feuding groups would compete until the elders agreed that a tie had been reached. Besnier, N., Brownell, S. & Carter, T. (2018). *The Anthropology of Sport: Bodies, Borders, Biopolitics.* University of California Press, p. 4.

Quantification, as historian Allen Guttmann argues ... Guttmann, A. (2004). *From Ritual to Record: The Nature of Modern Sports.* Columbia University Press.

Don't get me started on how sabermetrics is ruining baseball ... You got me started. Game six of the 2020 World Series, Blake Snell vs. Kevin Cash is all I need to say.

... players gain rating points ... Exactly how ratings are calculated can be found at: https://www.teamusa.org/USA-Table-Tennis/Ratings/Rating-System

... Jack Howard ... See https://www.teamusa.org/USA-Table-Tennis/History/Hall-of-Fame/Profiles/Jack-Howard

... USTTA morphed into USATT for some opaque reason ... I suspect it was the US Olympic Committee that encouraged the name change.

Yet ratings are artificial ... Like any institutionalized system, some will manipulate the rating system to their own advantage. While some players avoid risking their inflated ratings, other players will dump matches to deflate their ratings so that they can win prize money in lower-rated events. One player, after winning the same rating event at a regularly-held tournament seven straight times, was banned from tournaments by USATT for six months. This player managed to keep his rating down, and thus stay eligible for the same event even after winning it, by selectively dropping matches (and lots of rating points) to low-rated players in his opening round robin. He would beat the other players in the round robin, and since the low-rated player would lose his other matches, the sandbagger, as many referred to him, would advance out of the round robin into the main draw, which he would win. Incidentally, chess, which also uses a ratings-based system for tournaments, has the same sandbagging problem. See Evans, L. (2007). *This Crazy World of Chess*. Cardoza Publishing, chapter 38.

Paraphrasing his assessment of democracy ... "Democracy is the worst form of government, except for all the others." Churchill is also credited with saying "The best argument against democracy is a five-minute conversation with the average voter."

... except for all the others. Yes, there are others. For example, an enterprising MIT graduate developed Ratings Central, which uses a sophisticated algorithm for calculating ratings, rather than simply adding or subtracting points depending on whether a player won or lost. The system, which is not sanctioned by USATT or ITTF, is used in various non-sanctioned tournaments around New England. Although the Ratings Central website (https://www.ratingscentral.com/WhatIs.php) claims that it is "the world's most accurate rating system," we have not found this to be so. I suspect that the system would be more accurate if it was used regularly among frequent tournament players. Since the time between tournaments is factored into the ratings calculations, the system is not accurate when used infrequently, which is always the case since it can only be used at non-sanctioned tournaments.

Chapter 6: The Letter

It just dawned on me that I am making Eliel sound like Dwight Schrute
... In the episode "The Deposition," during season four of *The Office*, Dwight confides: "All of my heroes are table tennis players. Zoran Primorac, Jan-Ove Waldner, Wang Tao, Jorg Rosskopf, and of course

Ashraf Helmy. I even have a life-size poster of Hugo Hoyama on my wall. And the first time I left Pennsylvania, was to go to the hall of fame induction ceremony of Andrzej Grubba." Eliel had the honor of playing Rosskopf at the 2018 US Teams in Washington DC. No upset, but we have a photograph, albeit not life-sized.

Danny acknowledged in his autobiography ... Seemiller, D. (2016). *Revelations of a Table Tennis Champion.*

... we survive and succeed on cultural information ... Boyd, R. (2018). *A Different Kind of Animal.* Princeton University Press; Henrich, J. (2016). *The Secret of our Success.* Princeton University Press.

"I always try the weirdest serves I can think of in practice." https://www.teamusa.org/usa-table-tennis/history/hall-of-fame/profiles/danny-seemiller

My brother Rick and I trained in our backyard barn to beat the Chinese someday, and we did. At the 1977 World Championships in England, Danny and Ricky shocked Guo Yuehua (then World #1) and Liao Fu, 3-0, in the round of sixteen. They unfortunately lost to a Yugoslavian duo, Surbek and Stipancic, in the quarterfinals.

Chapter 7: All That Is Gold Does Not Glitter

... played at Lawrence's in Midtown Manhattan ... Reisman, M. (1974). *The Money Player.* Morrow, p. 30; Flegenheimer, M. (March 8, 2012). A throwback player, with a wardrobe to match. *New York Times.*

Journalist Nicholas Griffin ... Griffin, N. (2014). *Ping-pong Diplomacy: The Secret History Behind the Game that Changed the World.* Simon and Schuster, p. 179.

One of my areas of academic expertise ... If interested, see Sosis, R. (2000). Religion and intra-group cooperation: Preliminary results of a comparative analysis of utopian communities. *Cross-Cultural*

Research, 34, 70-87; Sosis, R. & Bressler, E. (2003). Cooperation and commune longevity: a test of the costly signaling theory of religion. *Cross-Cultural Research*, 37, 211-239; Sosis, R. & Ruffle, B. (2003). Religious ritual and cooperation: Testing for a relationship on Israeli religious and secular kibbutzim. *Current Anthropology*, 44, 713-722. For popular accounts of this work see Sosis, R. (2003). The adaptive value of religious ritual. *American Scientist*, 92, 166-172; Sosis, R. (2019). Do religions promote cooperation? Testing signaling theories of religion. In Jason Slone and William McCorkle (eds.) *The Cognitive Science of Religion: A Methodological Introduction to Key Empirical Studies*, 155-162. Bloomsbury Academic Press.

Chapter 8: Where Everybody Knows Your Name

Achieving such expertise at table tennis, or any sport, late in life is rare ... See Colvin, G. (2010). *Talent is Overrated*. Portfolio.

Tim Boggan ... https://www.teamusa.org/USA-Table-Tennis/History/Hall-of-Fame/Profiles/Joseph-R-Tim-Boggan

... an unwieldy multivolume compendium on the history of table tennis in the US ... *The History of U.S. Table Tennis* is currently more than twenty volumes.

A trickster is a cultural figure ... Hyde, L. (2010). *Trickster Makes this World: Mischief, Myth, and Art*. Farrar, Straus, Giroux.

... Hershele of Ostropol ... Kimmel, E. A. (1995). *The Adventures of Hershel of Ostropol*. Holiday House.

According to anthropological wisdom ... For good anthropological books on tricksters, see Evans-Pritchard, E. (1967). *The Zande Trickster*. University of Oxford Press; and my favorite, Pelton, R.D. (1980). *The Trickster in West Africa: A Study of Mythic Irony and Sacred Delight*. University of California Press.

...table tennis is chess on steroids... There have been various media stories suggesting that because of its cognitive demands—specifically the high speed of play and tactical complexities—table tennis is "good for your brain." For example, see this ABC News report titled *This is Your Brain on Ping Pong*: https://abcnews.go.com/Technology/brain-ping-pong/story?id=12721610. These articles and videos are largely based on the research of NYU neuroscientist Wendy Suzuki. See Suzuki, W. (2015). *Healthy Brain, Happy Heart*. Dey Street Books. I don't doubt her findings, but I'm a little skeptical that there is anything unique about table tennis on this front. There are likely other sports with similar benefits and I've heard the "chess on steroids" claim also applied to squash (the sport, to be clear).

As his article, entitled "Odd-Boiled Eggs," ... Kaminsky, K. & Scheman, N. (2010). Odd-boiled eggs. *MathAMATYC Educator*, 1(3), pp. 62–64.

... *All Things Shining*, philosophers Hubert Dreyfus and Sean Dorrance Kelly ... Dreyfus, H., & Kelly, S. D. (2011). *All Things Shining: Reading the Western Classics to Find Meaning in a Secular Age*. Free Press, p. 192.

... the work of sociologist Ray Oldenburg ... Oldenburg, R. (1999). *The Great Good Place: Cafés, Coffee Shops, Bookstores, Bars, Hair Salons, and other Hangouts at the Heart of a Community*. Da Capo Press.

... "people do not get uncomfortably entangled in one another's lives" ... Oldenburg, p. 22.

... "easily join and depart one another's company" ... Oldenburg, p. 22.

As author Kurt Vonnegut observes ... Vonnegut, K. (2014). *If This Isn't Nice, What Is?* Seven Stories Press.

In Middle-earth, what distinguishes ... See Dickerson, M. (2012). *A Hobbit Journey: Discovering the Enchantment of JRR Tolkien's Middle-earth*. Baker Books.

Chapter 9: The Pilgrimage

... a cantankerous wizard and a befuddled hobbit ... As Gandalf asked Bilbo in *The Hobbit*: "Do you wish me a good morning, or mean that it is a good morning whether I want it or not; or that you feel good this morning; or that it is a morning to be good on?"

This turns out to also be common ... For an introduction to the anthropology of pilgrimage, see Eade, J., & Sallnow, M. J. (eds.). (2000). *Contesting the Sacred: The Anthropology of Pilgrimage*. University of Illinois Press.

The difference between the Nationals ... Unlike in many other US sports, players do not have to qualify for the US Table Tennis Nationals; anyone can register and compete. The USATT has recently instituted state-level qualifying tournaments where winners are placed directly into the main draw, avoiding the round robin stage. But these qualifying tournaments are optional and the cause of much grumbling by those who compete in them, as well as those who do not: they invariably mess up the draws at the Nationals.

Comedian Frank Caliendo ... See his interview on *The Rich Eisen Show*: https://www.youtube.com/watch?v=iRYZHivmGcQ

... Errol Resek ... https://www.teamusa.org/USA-Table-Tennis/History/ Hall-of-Fame/Profiles/Errol-Resek

... no lawyers, guns, or money ... Yes, an appreciative nod to the late Warren Zevon.

The cultural and ethnic boundaries ... Commenting on psychologist Susan Fiske's research showing that it is possible to overcome prejudice when people have an opportunity to work together and cooperate, Isabel Wilkerson singles out sports as one of the few arenas in American society that provide such opportunities for cooperation. Wilkerson, I. (2020). *Caste: The Origins of our Discontents*. Random House, p. 305.

Many have come to teach... *Kol Chevra* (2012), volume 18, p. 21.

Chapter 10: Identity

... he has played for over 3500 consecutive days ... https://www.theexaminernews.com/shortzs-table-tennis-iron-man-streak-reaches-10-years/ In October 2022, Will celebrated 10 years of consecutive play, and as this book goes to press his streak is still alive.

... at a 2019 exhibition at UCLA ... https://www.teamusa.org/USA-Table-Tennis/Features/2019/August/25/China-Prevails-in-Spectator-Thriller-Against-USA-at-UCLA

Henry Miller was ... Gershwin's violin case ... Mina di Sospiro, G. (2015). *The Metaphysics of Ping-Pong*. Quest Books, p. 10. For tales of other celebrity table tennis enthusiasts see Charyn, J. (2001). *Sizzling Chops & Devilish Spins*. Four Walls and Eight Windows. I stumbled across this book at a used book store as this book was going to press.

... who owns a table tennis robot ... Jacobs, A. J. (2017). *It's All Relative: Adventures Up and Down the World's Family Tree.* Simon and Schuster, p. 131.

... Victor Turner ... Victor Turner is most famous for his work on rites of passage, rituals that transform an individual from one social status to another, such as ceremonies that turn boys into men and girls into women. See Turner, V. (1995). *The Ritual Process: Structure and Anti-structure*. Aldine de Gruyter. Turner is also renowned for his study of "social dramas," pivotal events of tension that highlight social roles within a community. The table tennis world would provide fertile ground for such an analysis. See Turner, V. (1974). *Dramas, Fields, and Metaphors: Symbolic Action in Human Society*. Cornell University Press.

... physical activities—often rituals—are required ... Turner, V. (1995). *The Ritual Process: Structure and Anti-structure*. Aldine de Gruyter.

Chapter 11: Ping Pong Popping

... not supported by the NCAA and other university institutional structures ... Collegiate table tennis competitions are run by the National Collegiate Table Tennis Association, a dedicated but underfunded and understaffed non-profit organization.

Thus, I contacted Tomas hoping ... One lesson I've learned repeatedly as an anthropologist is that context matters, and it is a lesson I've taken to heart. If I were reading a text that presented a partial email chain I'd be rather suspicious about what the author was leaving out. So, for those who are similarly obsessed with detail, here in full are the initial emails described in the text.

Nov 6, 2017

Dear Tomas,

I wanted to ask you about invitations to the Supercamp at the end of December. I don't know if invitations have already been sent, but I wanted to put forward my son's name, as he does not play at any of the major clubs (we live in Massachusetts) so he is likely to be under the radar, so to speak. My son, Eliel Sosis, would be thrilled to play at the Supercamp. He is currently 15 years old and he finished 13th in the Juniors at the Nationals this past summer (ahead of some very strong players). He is a solid 2300 player but we live in an area with only a few players at his level, hence he would benefit greatly from the Supercamp. He is extremely committed to the sport—he simply loves it—and he trains hard every day. His hard work shows as he continues to improve despite the limited opportunities we have in the area. He does not have a coach but if you needed a recommendation from a coach you could ask Yinghua Cheng, Jack Huang, or Quingliang Wang of the Maryland Table Tennis Center about Eliel. He has spent several summers training at MDTTC and they are aware of how committed he is and how quickly he has developed into a strong player. Thanks so much for considering this and I look forward to hearing from you.

Best wishes,

Rich Sosis

Nov 7, 2017

Dear Richard,

First of all, thanks for your email!

I have very good news for your son: Because of the cancelation of another player, Eliel, as being the first substitute, has the opportunity to play in the Youth Olympic Qualification on 12/17. The prospectus is attached. Please confirm (or cancel) by email to myself and Gordon Kaye by 11/13.

In regard to the SuperCamp we didn't send invitations out yet, but in general this training camp is planned mainly for current National Team members, though not for all of them. This week we will plan the details, number of players, financial framework etc. because we would need to send out the invitations asap.

We will probably offer interested players like your son the opportunity to attend the camp, but if this would be possible, under the condition of self-financing.

It would be good if you could send me more information and details about Eliel's training environment, goals, etc..

Best,

Tomas

Nov 7, 2017

Dear Tomas,

Thank so much for your quick response! I really appreciate it. And thanks so much for the invitation to play in the Youth Olympic Qualification. That is very exciting. I will let you and Gordon know by the end of the week if Eliel is able to participate. And thank you for the information regarding the Supercamp. If invitations are extended to non-team members such as Eliel, he would love to attend. Thanks again for your response!

Best wishes,

Rich

Nov 7, 2017

Hello Richard,

please make just sure that you are in time with the response.

Furthermore I asked you to send me more information and details about Eliel's training environment, goals etc..

Not exactly tactful, but having lived in Israel for several years I'm actually a fan of bluntness and forthright communication, even if I am personally a little more circumspect in my engagements with fellow humans. I've tried to convince my children, often frustrated by my recurring noncommittal and ambiguous comments, that such circumspection is a survival skill in academia. They don't buy it.

Chapter 12: Invisible Things

There are eleven divisions in para competitions, and each division or class defines a particular set of disabilities ... Classes 1–5 are known as sitting classes, in which players compete in wheelchairs, and classes 6–11 are known as standing classes.

Because the seedings were based on Junior world rankings ... This requires a bit of explanation. All the main events—Juniors, Men's and Women's Open, Men's and Women's Doubles—were seeded based on world rankings, which was a change that had been instituted by Tomas. He saw it as a way to encourage US players to compete abroad in ITTF tournaments, which is the only way to secure an international ranking. This was problematic, however, because the world ranking system itself had undergone significant changes recently in which attending tournaments, or more specifically, making it into the main draw, was disproportionally rewarded. The alleged motivation behind these changes was to encourage the Chinese to frequent tournaments. With the increasing gap between their skills and those on the rest of the planet, Chinese players had been attending tournaments less and less, primarily just focusing on the major tournaments. Under the new ranking system, their world rankings would suffer from repeated absences at international tournaments. Tennis had already made a similar switch in computing their world rankings to keep their top players—those the fans were paying to see—active on tour. The consequence for both sports has been that world rankings often do not accurately represent the strength of players. There have been top ten tennis players, for example, who never beat anyone in the top ten. It is a bit like professors rewarding attendance; students can receive a better final grade than classmates with higher test scores when the classmates miss a few weeks of lectures. The inaccuracy of the table tennis world-ranking system is particularly evident among lower-ranked players because they generally attend international tournaments less frequently, so each tournament they attend has a huge impact on their ranking. Moreover, under the new system rankings are unaffected by whom a player loses to or defeats; rather, points are awarded based on what round they reach in the tournament. But the most significant problem with using world rankings to seed US tournaments had little to do with the accuracy of the world rankings; the problem was that most US players did not have world rankings.

The biggest casualty of using world rankings for seeding at the US Nationals was in the Women's Open draw. Our four-time (now six-time) national champion and two-time (now three-time) Olympian, Lily Zhang, played one match in Vegas. Her world ranking placed her as the top seed in the tournament, but a Chinese coach who recently became a US citizen had the highest USATT rating in the draw by more than one hundred points. This player, Liu Juan, was a former star in the Chinese Superleague, the strongest table tennis league on Earth. However, she had not played internationally over the past year so she did not have a world ranking. Lily, who had been given a bye to the round of sixteen, played the coach in her first (and only) match. As the top two women players in the US, by a wide margin, they should have been on opposite sides of the draw; that is, it was a match that should have been the finals. Liu Juan was victorious, 4–2, and it turned out to be the only competitive match Liu Juan played in the tournament. She dominated every other match 4–0.

... **being investigated by the Southern Nevada Health District** ... https://www.reviewjournal.com/life/health/illness-outbreak-at-the-westgate-hits-guests-workers/

Chapter 13: Growing Pains

… were able to celebrate their kids' entry … The path toward admission to elite colleges, of course, does not begin in eleventh grade for these kids. During lunchbreaks at the MDTTC summer camps, most of the children, even the youngest ones, were busy completing math and other homework that their parents had assigned them.

… table tennis does not help with college admissions … University of California, Berkeley, might be the one exception, or so I've been told.

Chapter 14: Olympic Dreams

…those details are someone else's story to tell. But who can resist a brief story? Here is the main thrust of what became public knowledge:

For context, the 2016 US Olympic Table Tennis Team was selected by six tournaments run on three consecutive days, three tournaments for the Women's Team, three for the Men's Team. The winners of each of these tournaments punched their ticket to Rio de Janeiro. The same format had been used in 2012. For the 2020 Olympic Team, however, it was decided that only one spot on the Men's and Women's teams respectively would be awarded through competition. The other two spots were to be chosen by a committee.

The argument for this change was logical and simple: anything can happen at a tournament. Why should the US send a player to the Olympics who simply has a good tournament, over, say, a player who has demonstrated stronger play more consistently? The top programs in the world, including the Chinese, do not have open competitions for their Olympic teams; rather, Olympic team members are chosen by national team coaches, those who have been watching the players train and compete every day. Who could argue with Chinese success? Well, as it turns out, nearly everyone. Bias on the selection committee was the obvious concern. Competition, most believed, was the fairest way to determine the Olympic Team, as had always been done in the US.

Ultimately, seventeen former US Table Tennis Olympians—essentially every former Olympian who would not be competing for a spot on the 2020 team—crafted and signed a two-page public letter demanding a return to a competition-based selection procedure. In the end, a compromise was reached. One woman, Lily Zhang, and one man, Kanak Jha, were automatically elected to the team. But as both players were in the top forty in the world at that point and were so much more accomplished than any other US player, this was generally believed to be fair. If the US was to have any success at the 2020 Olympics, everyone recognized that these players represented our best hope. The remaining four players (two women and two men), would be determined through tournament competition.

His autobiography is appropriately ... Leibovitz, T. (2017). *Ping Pong for Fighters*, ed. Kenneth Lim.

As anthropologists have long appreciated ... See Rappaport, R. A. (1999). *Ritual and Religion in the Making of Humanity*. Cambridge University Press; Seligman, A. B., Weller, R. P., Simon, B., & Puett, M. J. (2008). *Ritual and its Consequences: An Essay on the Limits of Sincerity*. Oxford University Press.

Those who were still competing deserved to be... The Men's Trial was ultimately won by the top Junior in the country, Nikhil Kumar, and Zhou Xin, who is the live-in coach of another Junior player. On the women's side, Liu Juan, US National Champion and a former player in the Chinese Superleague, went undefeated as had been expected. She was joined on the team by another Chinese immigrant, Wang Huijing, who lives and coaches in Houston. Many competitors had been training all year for the trials, so there was no shortage of disappointment, but these players rose above everyone else, and for the rest of their lives they will be known and honored as Olympians.

NOTES

Chapter 15: On Timeouts and Empty Nests

We experienced table tennis as philosopher Leon Kass ... Kass, L. R. (2017). *Leading A Worthy Life: Finding Meaning in Modern Times.* Encounter Books, p. 197.

Sports are not merely entertainment ... Novak, M. (1994). *The Joy of Sports, second edition.* Madison Books, p. 346.

Plato spends considerable time discussing athletics in the *Republic* ... For a book on Plato's continued relevance, despite missteps, see Goldstein, R. N. (2014). *Plato at the Googleplex: Why Philosophy Won't Go Away.* Vintage.

"All I know most surely about morality ... Quoted in Gonzalez Abrisketa, O. (2012). *Basque Pelota: A Ritual, An Aesthetic.* University of Nevada Press, p. 272.

... philosopher Michael Novak observes ... Novak, M. (1994). *The Joy of Sports, second edition.* Madison Books, p. 161.

... like Churchill's renowned assessment of success ... "Success consists of going from failure to failure without loss of enthusiasm."

"A map of the world that does not include Utopia ... Wilde, O. (1910). *The Soul of Man Under Socialism.* Castrovilli Giuseppe.

Our meanings are constructed ... See Basso, K.H., & Selby, H.A. (eds.). (1976). *Meaning in Anthropology.* University of New Mexico Press.

... we apprehend meaning in our lives in narrative form. See Ricoeur, P. (1988). *Time and Narrative, Volume 3.* University of Chicago Press; Mattingly, C., & Garro, L. C. (eds.). (2000). *Narrative and the Cultural Construction of Illness and Healing.* University of California Press.

I hope the glimpse of the hidden world of table tennis that I've provided has ... I'm fully aware that no matter how vivid the descriptions of an anthropologist, an unknown world is still distant and the lives of those who inhabit that world are still difficult to understand. At best, as Clifford Geertz writes, the understanding of 'others' that the anthropologist can provide is more like "grasping a proverb, catching an illusion, seeing a joke, ... or reading a poem." Geertz, C. (1974). From the native's point of view: On the nature of anthropological understanding. *Bulletin of the American Academy of Arts and Sciences*, 26–45, p. 45.

Our contemporary world is likely too complex, too varied ... See Taylor, C. (2009). *A Secular Age*. Harvard University Press.

While many scholars, including anthropologists ... Guttmann, A. (2004). *From Ritual to Record: The Nature of Modern Sports*. Columbia University Press; Rappaport, R. A. (1999). *Ritual and Religion in the Making of Humanity*. Cambridge University Press.

For example, historian Jeffrey Gurock ... Gurock, J. S. (2005). *Judaism's Encounter with American Sports*. Indiana University Press, p. 8.

Religious studies scholars Bain-Selbo and Sapp ... Bain-Selbo, E., & Sapp, D. G. (2016). *Understanding Sport as a Religious Phenomenon: An Introduction*. Bloomsbury Publishing, p. 2.

Unlike these scholars, I would not characterize sport as a religion ... If interested, see Sosis, R. (2016). Religions as complex adaptive systems. *Macmillan Interdisciplinary Handbooks on Religion. Mental Religion: The Brain, Cognition, and Culture*, pp. 219–236; Sosis, R. (2019). The building blocks of religious systems: Approaching religion as a complex adaptive system. In G. Y. Georgiev, J. M. Smart, C. L. Flores Martinez, and M. Price (eds.) *Evolution, Development & Complexity: Multiscale Models of Complex Adaptive Systems*, pp. 421–449. Springer; Sosis, R. (2020). Four advantages of a systemic approach to the study of religion. *Archive for the Psychology of Religion*, 42(1), 142–157.

Countless autobiographies by athletes, whether professional or amateurs ... For a table tennis example, see Johnson, D. (2017). *How the Years Passed By*. Xulon Press.

... math ... Eliel has won several math competitions and as team captain he led his high school math team to the state championships for the first time in decades (which, alas, was canceled because of the pandemic). Despite his youth, he already has two publications in academic math journals and he has delivered some of his research findings at an academic conference.

... art ... Eliel is a talented and award-winning artist. And he is generous with his art—soapstone carving and pencil drawing are his favorite mediums—especially on birthdays. The walls of my office (between the books) are a testament to such generosity.

... which has been turned into a story ... Taback, S. (1999). *Joseph Had a Little Overcoat*. Viking.

Epilogue

... he successfully shielded my ostensibly wholesome ears ... Such shielding, unexpectedly, has continued throughout adulthood in other clubs. At NETTC, for example, a few Russians are notorious for their uninhibited stream of expletives (in Russian) after losing a point. Indeed, many have noted how quiet the club is when these vocal Russians are not there (in most circumstances, I prefer quiet, but not at a table tennis club—the energy of the Russians is preferred). Whenever I ask the other Russian speakers to translate a tirade of a frustrated player I receive the same response: "Believe me, you don't want to know. Russian curses don't translate well into English."

It is a noble tradition ... In addition to "Fudge!" and "Sugar!", I also have an array of meaningless babble that I shout when I miss a shot I should have made. One day, Mozart commented that he likes the sound of Yiddish and he asked me if I could teach him some words and phrases. I was confused by his request, unsure why he thought

I was fluent in Yiddish. Beyond a smattering of expressions, I don't speak Yiddish, and I told him so. He responded, "Aren't you talking to yourself in Yiddish during your matches?" Oy vey.

Noga Nir-Kistler was born in Israel ... https://www.teamusa.org/para-swimming/athletes/Noga-NirKistler

... players served not only from the right side of the table, but also from the left ... In doubles, officially, players serve from their right-hand side and the second bounce must occur in the diagonal box on the opposite side of the table.

Appendix A: What an Anxious Ping Pong Pop Keeps in his Bag

... the introverts' manifesto, Quiet ... Cain, S. (2013). *Quiet: The Power of Introverts in a World that Can't Stop Talking*. Broadway Books.

... ecological psychologist James Gibson ... Gibson, J. J. (1966). *The Senses Considered as Perceptual Systems*. Houghton Mifflin.

Some anthropologists, who have adopted Gibson's ideas ... Ingold, T. (2011). *The Perception of the Environment: Essays on Livelihood, Dwelling and Skill*. Routledge.

Mr. McGuire's prophetic advice ... My children have convinced me that the memorable line from the classic film *The Graduate* is no longer a cultural reference that everyone will get; hence this note. Mr. McGuire's "Plastics." is ranked #42 on the American Film Institute's top 100 quotations from American cinema.

Appendix B: How an Anxious Ping Pong Pop Affixes Rubber

"Go to the ITTF website and see for yourself." https://www.ittf.com/handbook/

Polish-born anthropologist Bronislaw Malinowski ... Malinowski, B. (1954). *Magic, Science and Religion, and Other Essays*. Doubleday. The best-known anthropological studies that test Malinowski's theory were conducted by a former professional baseball player turned anthropologist, George Gmelch. See his ethnography of the minor leagues, Gmelch, G. (2006). *Inside Pitch: Life in Professional Baseball*. Bison Books. For a review of my own studies on this topic, see Sosis, R. (2019). Can rituals reduce stress during war? The magic of Psalms. In J. Slone and W. McCorkle (eds.) *The Cognitive Science of Religion: A Methodological Introduction to Key Empirical Studies*, pp. 193–202. Bloomsbury Academic Press.

... let their children's coaches take care of their paddles. After all, coaches are professionals and parenting is stressful enough without rubber-changing responsibilities. Moreover, coaches are also more likely than parents to boost their students' paddles, which is illegal, but it is illegal like driving fifty-eight miles per hour in a fifty-five-miles-per-hour zone is illegal: nearly everyone does it and no one gets penalized. Boosting consists of applying an oil to the rubber before affixing it to the blade. The benefits of boosting are that it increases the speed, spin, and control of the rubber. Not surprisingly, since it is tough for officials to detect, the top players in the world all boost their rackets (or more likely, their rackets are boosted by someone else). At least one US National Championships was won by a player who learned how to boost in Europe and then was among the first to boost in this country, riding this advantage all the way to the top. Now all the top players, youth and adults, boost. Coaches have informed me and Eliel that he is at a disadvantage because he does not boost. I can live with that, and gratefully, so can Eliel. Self-righteous back-patting for this stance, however, would be misplaced: I rarely hesitate to exceed the speed limit and speeding cars can have more significant consequences, and are thus more morally egregious, than speeding forehands. Nonetheless, I'm grateful that Eliel doesn't do either.

Richard Sosis is the James Barnett Professor of Humanistic Anthropology at the University of Connecticut. He is the coauthor of *Religion Evolving: Cultural, Cognitive, and Ecological Dynamics* and *Evolutionary Perspectives on Religion and Violence,* and cofounder and coeditor of the journal *Religion, Brain & Behavior.* He lives in Massachusetts, which he is still learning how to spell.

www.ingramcontent.com/pod-product-compliance
Lightning Source LLC
Chambersburg PA
CBHW031058080526
44587CB00011B/729